Beyond Amazement

NEW ESSAYS ON JOHN ASHBERY

edited by
DAVID LEHMAN

Cornell University Press

ITHACA AND LONDON

First published 1980 by Cornell University Press.
Published in the United Kingdom by Cornell University Press Ltd.,
2–4 Brook Street, London W1Y 1AA.

First printing, Cornell Paperbacks, 1980

Excerpts from the following works are reprinted by permission of John Ashbery: *Some Trees,* copyright © 1956 by John Ashbery; *Rivers and Mountains,* copyright © 1962, 1963, 1964, 1966 by John Ashbery; *The Double Dream of Spring,* copyright © 1966, 1967, 1968, 1969, 1970 by John Ashbery. All rights reserved.

"Dream Song #89 (Op. Posth. no. 12)" from *His Toy, His Dream, His Rest* by John Berryman, copyright © 1964, 1965, 1966, 1967, 1968 by John Berryman, is reprinted by permission of Farrar, Straus & Giroux, Inc.

International Standard Book Number (cloth) 0-8014-1235-8
International Standard Book Number (paper) 0-8014-9183-5
Library of Congress Catalog Card Number 79-6850
Printed in the United States of America
*Librarians: Library of Congress cataloging information appears
on the last page of the book.*

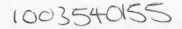

These are amazing: each
Joining a neighbor, as though speech
Were a still performance.

"Some Trees"

            beyond amazement, astonished,
Apparently not tampered with. As the rain gathers and protects
Its own darkness, the place in the slipcover is noticed
For the first and last time. . . .

"Houseboat Days"

Contents

CONTENTS

Acknowledgments

Upon the editor falls the pleasant task of acknowledging the debts this book owes to its friends. In particular I must thank Stefanie Lehman, Joel Black, Harry Mathews, and John Koethe for their unstinting support; David Kalstone, Harold Bloom, and David Kermani for their encouragement and sound advice; and my students for their uncanny ability to ask the necessary questions. To Marjorie Perloff, who was involved in every stage of this book's development, go my special thanks. In December 1977, at the annual convention of the Modern Language Association, I chaired a panel discussion devoted to John Ashbery's poetry; that all four of the other panelists, along with two interested members of the audience, joined me in contributing essays to this volume attests to the signal value of that Chicago gathering. In 1979, a summer grant from the National Endowment for the Humanities enabled me to work on the manuscript and to attend to the various exigencies inherent in making a book. Lastly, I must express my gratitude to the essayists—each of whom contributed more than an article—and to the object of our critical attention, whose poetry has so fascinated us as to make the present venture an inevitability.

Grateful acknowledgment is made to the following for permission to reprint copyright material:

Viking Penguin Inc. for material from *Three Poems* by John Ashbery, copyright © 1970, 1971, 1972 by John Ashbery; for material from *Self-Portrait in a Convex Mirror* by John Ashbery, copyright © 1972, 1973, 1974, 1975 by John Ashbery; for material from *Houseboat Days* by John

ACKNOWLEDGMENTS

Ashbery, copyright © 1975, 1976, 1977 by John Ashbery; and for material from *As We Know* by John Ashbery, copyright © 1979 by John Ashbery; all rights reserved; all reprinted by permission of Viking Penguin Inc.

Wesleyan University Press for material from *The Tennis Court Oath* by John Ashbery, copyright © 1957, 1959, 1961, 1962 by John Ashbery; reprinted by permission of Wesleyan University Press.

Z Press, Inc., for material from *Three Plays* by John Ashbery, copyright © 1960, 1961, 1964, 1978 by John Ashbery.

Harcourt Brace Jovanovich, Inc., for permission to quote from "East Coker" from *Four Quartets* by T. S. Eliot.

Faber and Faber Ltd for permission to reprint "Dream Song 89" from *His Toy, His Dream, His Rest* by John Berryman; and for permission to quote from "East Coker" from *Four Quartets* by T. S. Eliot.

Little, Brown and Company for material from *The Testing Tree* by Stanley Kunitz, published by Little, Brown and Company in association with the Atlantic Monthly Press, 1971.

W. W. Norton & Company, Inc., for material from *Sonnets to Orpheus* by Rainer Maria Rilke, translated by M. D. Herter Norton; copyright © 1942 by W. W. Norton & Company, Inc.; copyright renewed 1970 by M. D. Herter Norton; reprinted by permission of W. W. Norton & Company, Inc.

The Hogarth Press Ltd for material from *Sonnets to Orpheus* by Rainer Maria Rilke, translated by M. D. Herter Norton.

Trevor Winkfield for permission to quote from his translation of *How I Wrote Certain of My Books* by Raymond Roussel (Sun Press, 1977); copyright © 1975, 1977 by Trevor Winkfield.

Alfred A. Knopf, Inc., for material from *The Collected Poems of Frank O'Hara*, ed. Donald Allen, copyright © 1971 by Maureen Granville-Smith; and for material from *The Collected Poems of Wallace Stevens*, copyright © 1954 by Wallace Stevens; reprinted by permission of the publisher.

Random House, Inc., for material from *W. H. Auden: Collected Poems*, edited by Edward Mendelson; copyright © 1976 by Edward Mendelson, William Meredith, and Monroe K. Spears; reprinted by permission of the publisher.

Brief portions of "'Fragments of a Buried Life': John Ashbery's Dream Songs" by Marjorie Perloff appeared in somewhat different form in *American Poetry Review* 7, no. 5 (September–October 1978), 5–11, and in *Bucknell Review*, Fall 1979.

DAVID LEHMAN

Clinton, New York

Abbreviations

In citations of Ashbery's poetry, the following abbreviations are used.

AW   *As We Know*
DD   *The Double Dream of Spring*
HD   *Houseboat Days*
RM   *Rivers and Mountains*
SP   *Self-Portrait in a Convex Mirror*
ST   *Some Trees*
TC   *The Tennis Court Oath*
TP   *Three Poems*

Beyond Amazement

Introduction

DAVID LEHMAN

Admirers of John Ashbery have championed him as our most significant contemporary poet; in their differing vocabularies, his poetry is the "strongest" and the "most radically innovative" being written today. Long associated with the advance guard— in music and art no less than in experimental literary circles— Ashbery has exerted a singular and exemplary influence on poets distinguished by their commitment to the new and untried. While these poets could once justly consider themselves a small band of the elect, on an exploratory mission into the grand unknown, Ashbery's base of support has broadened considerably in the past decade. Having found impassioned advocates in familiar and in unlikely places, he is on everybody's reading list, and the most established of periodicals at home and in England greet each new volume of his poetry with extended commentary. When *Self-Portrait in a Convex Mirror* won all three of America's most prestigious literary awards in 1976, Ashbery attained a degree of fame that few would have thought possible a mere half-dozen years earlier; one now needs to be reminded of the long period when Ashbery's work elicited mere indifference from the literati.

If, however, the longitude and latitude of Ashbery's poetry are now thought to be known, the territory itself remains a dark continent. The public recognition Ashbery has lately received has hardly deterred a highly vocal set of critics from registering their displeasure, with arrows aimed at what might be called his poetic integrity; the poet continues to be censured, misunderstood, and in some quarters suspected of being a deliberate obscurantist or even a masterly charlatan. If a consensus may be found among these dissonant voices, it is probably that Ashbery is the single most controversial figure on the American poetry scene. No other poet of our time has managed so consistently to polarize his public, to arouse opposite reactions—as though there could be no middle road, as though it were impossible to respond to an Ashbery poem with a complacent nod or shake of the head. This phenomenon is itself cause for celebration at a time when poetry seems to have lost something of its power to move and incite, and it is in a spirit of celebration that we undertake the present effort to clarify Ashbery's poetic achievement.

There are critics who, while reluctant to acknowledge the limitations of their particular methodologies, throw their hands up in despair upon sight of Ashbery's poetry; as their attempts at extracting conventional meanings are frustrated, they are afraid of being "had." Even sympathetic readers will confess that on occasion they are somewhat perplexed by an Ashbery poem; it sometimes seems that what some most deplore comes close to defining what others find most winning in Ashbery's work. At any rate, for certain devotees, lack of complete comprehension is no obstacle to enthusiastic appreciation—far from it; their sincere adulation has taken the form of imitation, of grand and petty larcenies, and of reviews that tend to be long on praise and short on the kind of analysis that would elucidate the reasons for their admiration. In sum, what criticism of Ashbery we have is likely to tell us much about the taste and ingenuity of the critic, but precious little about Ashbery. There are, of course, important exceptions; one thinks of David Kalstone's insightful discussion of "Self-Portrait in a Convex Mirror" or Richard Howard's fine essay in *Alone with America,* which spoke of the convex mirror as a type of "imaginative schema or construct" by which Ashbery's work discloses itself to us—and this a good half-dozen years before the composition of the poem that would catapult its author to fame. By and large, however, the cross fire between eulogy and backlash has not allowed for the thoughtful appraisal the work merits. Everyone seems to want a go at Ashbery, but as often as not the resultant verbiage boils down to little more than a terse "no comment."

It would be difficult to imagine a more opportune moment for the critical investigations assembled here, and for many of the same reasons it would be equally difficult to conceive of a more formidable task than confronted us at the outset. We knew that as apologists we must perforce assume a didactic function, clearing the air of misconceptions and providing, if we could, persuasive readings of individual texts. After all, plaintiffs commonly cite their problems in presenting Ashbery in the classroom; the demand for serious practical criticism is all the more insistent because the poetry appears immune to close textual analysis and has therefore often met with disapprobation. One might well argue that the work deprives the critic of his conventional tools and resources, and that it does so by intention; granting such a premise, the level of audience bewilderment might be seen as furnishing a good index as to the success of the enterprise. Yet Ashbery's poetry is far from inaccessible; on the contrary, it could be said to open up a path of entry to whole areas of consciousness and feeling that could otherwise not be reached. In writing about Ashbery, then, we had to address ourselves not only to the poems but to a new and distinctive mode of utterance, one that challenges us to revise our assumptions about how poems come to be written, how they work, and what they wish to say or do. It was incumbent upon us to explain, without explaining away, this enigmatic figure whose power to astonish is legendary.

Samuel Johnson's remark about Milton conveys a sense of Ashbery's accustomed element: "He can please when pleasure is required; but it is his peculiar power to astonish." Reading Ashbery, we must indeed own up to our astonishment, and to the peculiar pleasure this affords; but we must also go further—beyond amazement, toward enlightenment—for Ashbery's true stature to be made plain. We are all too familiar with the species of critical lament sounded by Robert Boyers: "Some of us have tried, with small success, to explain Ashbery in the classroom, concluding that a great many complete poems, and large portions of others, resist any kind of explanation. Other more gifted interpreters have concluded that even where ordinary readings work, they discover nothing of genuine consequence in Ashbery's thought."[1] Both halves of Boyer's complaint need to be answered: extraordinary readings must be proposed to describe what is actually there, and in such a way that its "genuine consequence" is understood. We must, in short, aim at a level of critical discourse as advanced in its way as the poetry that occasions it.

In putting this book together, I particularly sought responses to questions such as these: Is there a method by which to extract the sense and flavor of an Ashbery poem? What ought the novice to keep in mind as he approaches the text? Does Ashbery's poetry yield meanings, or does it militate against the very possibility of articulating them? What is Ashbery up to with, for example, his robust use of clichés or his eccentric system of pronoun reference? How "private" a poet is he? Are his intricate ironies at the service of a larger aim? What mileage does he get out of his habit of rapidly shifting gears in a poem? Of what use is the label "the New York School of poetry" for understanding the very different writers (Ashbery, Kenneth Koch, Frank O'Hara, among others) frequently grouped under that heading? Has *The Tennis Court Oath* been too hastily dismissed? Did *The Double Dream of Spring* mark a complete rupture with the past and the birth of a "major" period—or does the early work merit equal praise with or without reference to what followed it? What is the nature of the affinity between Ashbery's writing and recent developments in music and painting? What is its relation to literary tradition? With a poet as reluctant to repeat himself as Ashbery, what unifying principles, tactics, figures, or concerns are there in his poetic output?

To understand the critical context in which these questions are raised, a synopsis of the historical record seems a necessary preliminary. Ashbery found his first critic in his first "official" sponsor, W. H. Auden, who awarded *Some Trees* the Yale Younger Poets Prize for 1956. In his introduction to the book, Auden offered a brief theoretical discussion of the mythological element in Ashbery's poetry, a subject Marjorie Perloff regards as central. According to Auden, a certain line of modern poets ("from Rimbaud down to Mr. Ashbery") pays homage to "the subjectively sacred," on the grounds that "the imaginative life of the human individual stubbornly continues to live by the old magical notions." While Auden registers his reservations with the "calculated oddities" of logic and imagery seemingly called for by this ideal, his comments on the perceived rupture "between reality and meaning" locate one of Ashbery's fundamental dilemmas, for which he has at different times tried different poetic solutions—now "the new realism" of time ("a succession of unique moments, each of which is novel and will never recur"), now "the new spirit" of the imagination ("a numinous landscape inhabited by demons and strange beasts"). As a rationale for Ashbery's deliberate departures from rhetorical conventions, Auden directs us to Rimbaud, to the conviction that a language of congruities could only falsify the imaginative experiences that matter most.[2]

A more purely ardent supporter was the late Frank O'Hara, who ended his review in *Poetry* with a bold proclamation: "Faultless music, originality of perception—Mr. Ashbery has written the most beautiful first book to appear in America since *Harmonium.*" (O'Hara's generosity of spirit is seen as all the more remarkable when it is recalled that an O'Hara manuscript had competed with *Some Trees* for the Yale award.) Celebrating his friend's combination of "honesty" and "tenderness," O'Hara singled out "the poems of elegiac content," "revealing a person other than the poet, whom we admire with the poet for his courageous otherness: Colin in *Eclogue,* the nun in *Illustra-*

tion, the poet as a child in *The Picture of Little J. A. in a Prospect of Flowers,* the solitary resident of the *Hotel Dauphin, The Young Son.* They are all people who meet experience on the most articulate lyrical terms and this gives their meetings an absolute value beyond their quietly tragic disappointment."[3] O'Hara also commended the humor in many of the poems, in particular their "amusing" manner of referring to poets of the past. From start to finish the review bubbles over with the excitement of discovery, the same excitement that informs O'Hara's spirited advocacy of the action painters.

Friends and associates such as O'Hara provided Ashbery with what little sustenance of readership he enjoyed in the decade he spent in Paris as art editor of the *International Herald Tribune.* It was during this period that John Bernard Myers, then with the Tibor de Nagy Gallery in New York City, coined the phrase "the New York School of poets" in promoting books by Ashbery, O'Hara, and Kenneth Koch that the gallery was publishing. Like the Holy Roman Empire, which was neither holy nor Roman nor an empire, the New York School of poets has always been an anomalous term—its individual components are less than accurate. The writers involved came from places like Rochester, Baltimore, Cincinnati, Chicago; met at Harvard; and, in the case of Ashbery and Harry Mathews, lived abroad when they were supposedly forming a "New York School." Nor were they poets exclusively—they have produced novels and plays of considerable merit. The term is not without its virtues, however, not least because, without thinking of themselves as parts of a collective, these writers demonstrated a unique capacity for sympathetic identification with one another. The fruits of such partnership went beyond the actual collaborations they produced, exhilarating though some of these are. Determined to make literary history, Ashbery, Koch, Mathews, and James Schuyler published an adventurous magazine called *Locus Solus,* which remains an inspiring model for small presses today and which incidentally provided a critical "on the other hand" to the more public criticism proffered by, for example, the irascible John Simon. In the autumn 1962 issue of the *Hudson Review*, Simon grouped Barbara Guest, Ashbery, and Koch as "abstract expressionists in words . . . every bit as undistinguished and indistinguishable as their confreres of the drip, dribble, and squirt." To Simon, *The Tennis Court Oath* (1962) seemed written in a code no cryptographer could hope or want to figure out; this second of Ashbery's volumes was, in a word, "garbage," Simon exclaimed, alliterating his disdain: "Mr. Ashbery has perfected his verse to the point where it almost never deviates into—nothing so square as sense!—sensibility, sensuality, or sentences."[4]

The Tennis Court Oath remains Ashbery's most curious volume, and a glance at the contents will show why: the words are severed not only from their familiar contexts, but from one another; the punctuation itself is eerie. Ashbery himself has deprecated *The Tennis Court Oath*, describing it as "the book of mine I feel least close to." An otherwise favorable critic, Harold Bloom, reports having been "outraged" by the "egregious disjunctiveness" and "calculated incoherence" in the poems. It has been argued that the book was a stepping-stone, "a necessary phase in the poet's development," to use Bloom's words (though he himself is unconvinced by this argument).[5] Charles Berger sees the book as a hurdle to be gotten over, a temptation that Ashbery rejected once and for all with *The Double Dream of Spring* in 1970. The book has always enjoyed a notable underground appeal, however, precisely because of its uncompromising opacity, its literary application of collage and cut-up techniques, its assumption of an autonomous life of words. As Fred Moramarco argues, the "word-play and linguistic invention" of poems such as "A Life Drama" and "Our Youth" link Ashbery's name and that of Raymond Roussel as connoisseurs of the abyss.

Perhaps surprisingly, given their surface ease relative to *The Tennis Court Oath*, succeeding volumes have provoked howls of disgust and ire as implacable as Simon's. Denis Donoghue discerned "a dangerous aesthetic" in *Rivers and Mountains* (1966). The same view is espoused, in a rather bizarre way, by J. W. Hughes in the *Saturday Review*, the occasion having been supplied by *The Double Dream of Spring:*

> The Doris Day of modernist poetry, [Ashbery] plays nasty Symbolist-Imagist tricks on his audience while maintaining a facade of earnest innocuousness.... [Some of his lines] have about as much poetic life as a refrigerated plastic flower ... [and some] are trite and silly.... [His failure] is the price he has paid for uncritically accepting the Symbolist-Imagist esthetic. The contrived image and the pseudo-profound symbol may enable a poet to continue his poem, despite the flaccid state of his emotion... but such a continuation may, in fact, embody a kind of poetic dishonesty. Ashbery is one of the inheritors of Eliot's Symbolist Waste Land. Eliot, at least, was honest about the agony and emotional barrenness he tried to describe. Ashbery, a professional mindblower, inhabits a Technicolor Waste Land where he seems to feel completely at home.[6]

Reviewers have also taken Ashbery to task for his alleged "refusal to sing"; to Roger Shattuck, for example, *Houseboat Days* (1977) represents a grave threat to "the auditory tradition."[7]

The more ambitious of Ashbery's recent thumbs-down critics have grudgingly conceded him a certain power. Yes, Robert Boyers says, "Self-Portrait in a Convex Mirror" "is a work of great majesty and inventive daring"; at the same time, we are told that Ashbery is merely trendy, that he is "literary America's favorite poet" for reasons Boyers regards as suspect.[8] And yes, Charles Molesworth avers, in his recent work Ashbery has overcome the need for irony as "a defensive reaction against this fear of the meaningless"; at the same time, "Ashbery's ascension" is attributed largely to "the triumph of a poetic mode" of little intrinsic interest.[9] Again and again, by Molesworth and Boyers and Shattuck, Ashbery is seen as part of a cultural movement, a force with wide and allegedly deleterious implications; by one and all, Ashbery's eminent place within "the tradition of the new" is taken for granted. In resisting Ashbery's poetry and poetics, hostile critics can thus have the pleasure of simultaneously resisting Pollock and de Kooning, or Webern and Cage, or "literary America," or semiology, or any of the proliferating ripples of cultural implication. Whatever else it does, such resistance implies, as it does in psychoanalysis, that the crucial nerve has been exposed. It is altogether in keeping with this phenomenon that one of the poet's staunchest advocates be the redoubtable Harold Bloom, for Bloom's philosophy of criticism has certainly aroused reactions every bit as indignant, and sometimes quite as hysterical, as those provoked by Ashbery's poetry.

In Bloom's critical vocabulary, Ashbery is seen as conscious of his "belatedness"; to establish himself solidly within the "central" Romantic tradition, "in the line of Emerson, Whitman, and Stevens," required that Ashbery master the various stages of a formative "influence anxiety." At first his poetic inheritance must have seemed as much a burden as a gift, and only by "misreading" his key precursors, the better to assimilate them into his autonomous self, could the poet reinvent his paternity and realize himself as "the most legitimate of the sons of Stevens," a supreme compliment in the Bloom lexicon. Although Ashbery has appeared to resist his destiny—by attempting "too massive a swerve away from the ruminative continuities of Stevens and Whitman" in *The Tennis Court Oath* and by wishing, on other occasions, "to be more of an anomaly than he is"— Ashbery's recent volumes have, we are told, amply justified the expectations of a triumphant centrality that Bloom reports to have felt tentatively upon the appearance of *Some Trees* and with confidence and renewed enthusiasm when *The Double Dream of Spring* was published.[10] This is not the place to debate the virtues and inadequacies of Bloom's critical thought, though a good case could be made on both sides and would be a valuable exercise. Let it simply be said that Bloom offers a remarkable synthesis of such eclectic sources as Freud, the Kabbalah, French structuralism, and the English critical heritage; that, in identifying rhetorical figures with psychological defense mechanisms, Bloom has contributed an incontestably original idea to our understanding of literature; and that his apparatus has enabled him to formulate a strong "misprision" of the poets he praises, such as Ashbery and A. R. Ammons.

Though the intent is never polemic, the essays collected here do much to rebut the various objections raised to Ashbery's work. Doublas Crase counters the cry of hermeticism with a celebration of Ashbery "not as our most private poet, but as our most public." Among contemporary poets, "Ashbery is most ruthlessly available to the present," Crase asserts, and as such his poetry may lay claim to the status of prophecy: here is a poet seemingly able to write with exactness about our reality before most of us have recognized it as our reality; here is "an attitude at last fitted to the actual country Americans live in now." For Crase, Ashbery is a Mannerist, in the best sense of that word—he is the stylist *par excellence,* drawn to "the elegance of combining many refined figures and of stretching each of those in a way that would shiver the woodlots in Concord." If Ashbery's poetry has proved so disconcerting an experience to some, Crase writes, it is partially because it communicates, in its disarmingly off-handed way, the anxiety of our current predicament: the inevitable consequences of a rampant narcissism, our grandiose sense of self pitted against the fragmented, inauthentic outside world. What disgruntled critics have dismissed as solipsism is arguably a form of negative capability, a quality of inner life capable of embodying the chaos of the culture around it.

In her delineation of Ashbery's methods, Marjorie Perloff sees vatic properties of a rather different sort. Ashbery's poetry is not an excursion into the merrily meaningless, she contends, but its meanings differ dramatically—both in their substance and in the way they are disclosed—from those to which the unwary reader is accustomed. For Perloff, Ashbery's poems are "hymns to possibility," "dream songs" in a more exact sense than is true for

Berryman's works under that title. Rather than filter dreams "through the rationalizing consciousness," such poems as "Pyrography" enact the dream process itself, modulating from an apparent "revealing" to an inevitable "re-veiling." In the process, familiar objects acquire an enigmatic glow; the American landscape is invested with a fairy-tale significance as the disparate phenomena momentarily cohere in strange and brilliant configurations, which Perloff likens to the Japanese flowers Proust describes, in the final sentence of the "Overture" to *Swann's Way*, as resulting from the act of dropping little crumbs of paper into a porcelain bowl of water.

Although Ashbery's corpus is not to be confused with a body of philosophical work, it may profitably be examined within the context of a philosophical inquiry, especially in light of the poet's unique conception of the self; it is this conception that John Koethe strives to elucidate in "The Metaphysical Subject of John Ashbery's Poetry." Koethe takes his title from Wittgenstein's *Tractatus*; Ashbery's poetry, he argues, issues from "the metaphysical subject" rather than from the self in any psychological sense. Where we might speak of Berryman's "voice" and mean it by a distinctive personality, bound in particular circumstances of history and feeling, in Ashbery's case it would be more nearly correct to speak of "an almost palpable presence" that exists *with* rather than *in* the world, acting as though it were independent of the succession of experience it monitors. To understand the shifting relations between psychological "ego" and transcendent "subject" is, in Koethe's view, to take a first step toward grasping the sense of freedom at the heart of Ashbery's enterprise.

Ashbery is sometimes "accused" of being an ironist, as though he were only that; certain critics appear to attach suspicion to irony, an inducement to shrug one's shoulders and label the poet defensive. In "The Shield of a Greeting," I argue the contrary position. Far from being a dead-end street, Ashbery's irony leads ineluctably to a boulevard of redemptive enchantment, "irony" here being a convenient term for the complexities of a modus operandi that embraces evasion, erasure, and eccentricity—eccentricity above all. In astronomy, *eccentricity* refers to the degree to which a planet is off center or nonconcentric, the extent of its deviation from circular form. While eccentricity was once seen as a departure from the norm, Einstein's gravitational theory suggests that the elliptical orbit is not an aberration at all, that for the stars there is no norm to speak of. From a reading of Ashbery we may infer a literary corollary, a poetics of eccentricity designed not as a means to escape from reality, but as a way to meet it on its own terms. With his ironies and cultivated eccentricities, the poet manages the most complex of apotropaic gestures, arriving finally at a state of "pure affirmation."

Is there any sense, Keith Cohen asks, in which Ashbery's poetry, without containing explicit political content, nevertheless gibes at reigning ideologies? Is there a political or philosophical rationale, unstated but real, behind the many examples of prefabricated discourse—colloquial banalities, clichés, media jargon, popular songs, greeting cards, comic books, and the Declaration of Independence—that one finds in Ashbery's work? According to Cohen, Ashbery appropriates such discourse so as to undermine it; the purification of tribal dialect is viewed as a radical critique of a corrupt "socio-economic system that relies crucially on language manipulation." We are fond of saying that "radical" change can come about only when our forms themselves are altered, when the very roots are shaken, but we lack examples of how this grand if familiar proposition works in practice; in "Ashbery's Dismantling of Bourgeois Discourse," Cohen argues that—notwithstanding the poet's disavowal of any political aim—poems as ostensibly beyond good and evil as "Daffy Duck in Hollywood" and "Decoy" launch "a frontal attack on such props of bourgeois discourse as continuity, utility, and closure."

Both Fred Moramarco and Charles Berger devote their critical energies to single volumes from the Ashbery oeuvre. Mora-marco's revaluation of *The Tennis Court Oath* is sparked by a perception of the poems as "evoking or constructing a reality generated solely by language itself." In addition to giving us fresh insights into a book it would be dangerous to neglect, Moramarco's essay is a useful introduction to the whole question of the poet's "French connection." For Charles Berger, *The Double Dream of Spring* is Ashbery's watershed volume, and as such makes a special claim on our attention. It was here, Berger writes, that Ashbery explicitly discarded an aesthetic of discontinuities in the interests of a sustained vision, "fierce beyond all dream of enduring" ("Parergon"). It was here that the poet's "urbane pitch" began to ascend "the chariot of poetic deity"—for which sake, Berger asserts, Ashbery was led to renounce, not without melancholy, the experimental instincts so evident in the earlier work.

Each of Ashbery's volumes to date is a book, not merely a collection, and the opening poem of a given book indicates a measure of its dimensions; thus Berger addresses himself to "The Task," and David Rigsbee to "These Lacustrine Cities," the keynote poem of *Rivers and Mountains*. "Against Monuments"—Rigsbee's title—conveys in miniature the thesis a-round which his study is organized. The cities the poem tells of are akin to works of art, and so their fate is doubly instructive: it warns us of "the impoverished status both of monuments and, by implication, of moments of illumination which we hasten to raise into monuments." By "flattening" the privileged moment, Ashbery is seen as emphasizing process rather than product, and Rigsbee's guided tour of "These Lacustrine Cities" allows us to examine the process by which the poem "evolves" into itself.

Critics invariably associate Ashbery with the abstract expressionists, yet the exact nature of the parallel is in need of clarification. To this end Leslie Wolf relates the poet's characteristic gestures to painterly models and establishes a context by which these models may be approached. Ashbery's involvement with the visual arts is deep and of long standing: he has made his living as an art critic; a number of his poems take their titles and nominal subject matter from paintings; the early sestina "The Painter" and the celebrated "Self-Portrait in a Convex Mirror" both propose statements of direct application to painting as well as to poetry. In evaluating Ashbery's career from this perspective, Wolf presents a strong case for the interdependence of art media, informed by the belief that access to the poetry is assured once it is read with the quality of "attentiveness" one gives to a painting.

To the charge that Ashbery's poetry fails to charm the ear, Lawrence Kramer replies with an extended analysis of Ashbery's "polyvocality," taking as his point of departure Elliott Carter's musical setting of the poet's "Syringa." The poem is about Orpheus, and by extension the Orphic tradition: poetry as song, the poet as one who, by casting a spell of enchantment over beasts and stones, praises and celebrates existence and can *almost* rescue the mortal beloved from the dead. As such, "Syringa"—in both its literary and its musical guises—provides Kramer with the occasion for meditating on the poet's attempt to "broaden the boundaries of temporality." In an Ashbery poem, Kramer observes, "time flows, but not in a straight line; it flows every which way." "Litany," the long poem in double columns which Ashbery has recently published, confirms the importance of this argument: what had been an implicit structure in "Syringa" has become an explicit formal principle in the new poem. Kramer's insights thus contribute not only to our awareness of Ashbery's elective musical affinities, but also to a more general understanding of his literary assumptions and accomplishments.

Some readers may be prompted to ask why, in editing this volume, I did not aim for greater "representation," which would mean including adversary points of view. I can only reply that editors will rightly feel no obligation to print articles of an objurgatory bent when putting together collections of essays on Stevens or Auden. In my estimation, Ashbery is their worthy successor.

1/

The Prophetic Ashbery

DOUGLAS CRASE

We are used to hearing of poets so private they speak for us all. We are not used to hearing, however, that John Ashbery is among them. Anyone who has ever been baffled by Ashbery's work will understand the temptation to conclude that here we have a poet so private he is truly private, so difficult he is truly inaccessible. But to arrive at that dead end is exasperating, if only because the reputation leads one to expect much more. Why shouldn't people expect access to a poetry so widely honored for what it is doing with their language? Why shouldn't they expect the poet, as Emerson promised, to apprise us "not of his wealth, but of the commonwealth"? These are not retrograde or feeble expectations, and because I think they are powerfully met in the work of John Ashbery I would champion him not as our most private poet, but as our most public one. The difficulty with Ashbery is that his poetry is *so* public, so accurately a picture of the world we live in, that it scarcely resembles anything we have ever known. Just so, the present is indeed a world none of us has ever known, because the words to describe it can be put together only after the fact. When the poet does put them together the combination comes as a shock. Understandably, one may at first regard that combination as hermetically private. Only gradually do we realize that it describes the public world we were living in just moments ago—that some prophet has arrived with news of the commonwealth.

I suppose "prophet" sounds as though I am claiming a generous role for the poet when anyone ought to know that the current audience for poetry is limited first in size and second in its willingness to suspend not disbelief, but irony. I would guess also that readers of poetry are even more disaffected than most when it comes to the commonwealth. They are not an audience to whom a poet as savvy as John Ashbery would innocently address Emersonian prophecies. True enough, but let me offer a proposition that should not be very surprising: the audience that reads his poetry is not always the one for which the poet writes. The events that produce a poet are many and various, but one of them is surely not his first contact with an English professor or his first reading at the local poetry project. The audience he would love to reach is more likely "the fair-sheaved many" who do not give a hoot for poetry. It will include the father he could never please, the mother bewildered by her strange offspring, the younger brother who died at the age of nine. It is made up, in other words, of all the unreachable people, the ones who appear in Ashbery's "Melodic Trains" as figures on the station platform while the poet watches them from the standing train. Though he identifies them as "my brothers," it is precisely their remoteness that accounts for the plaintive tone in which he continues.

If I were to get down now to stretch, take a few steps

In the wearying and world-weary clouds of steam like great
White apples, might I just through proximity and aping
Of postures and attitudes communicate this concern of mine
To them? That their jagged attitudes correspond to mine,

That their beefing strikes answering silver bells within
My own chest . . . ?

[*HD*, p. 25]

No, he could not communicate his concern, at least not in poetry. If they are reading at all, his brothers probably are occupied with the latest manual on how to get more out of life, and poetry will be far down the list of recommended exercises. One knows this, but it does not lessen the insistent wish to reach them. Instead, one dresses the wish in any number of disguises—ironic or even slapstick. In this way you can prophesy to your brothers all you want without fear of looking foolish before the worldly audience that comes to your readings. You release a little horse that "trots up with a letter in its mouth" (*TC*, p. 58), or in Hollywood fashion you direct a butler to enter "with a letter on a tray / Whose message is to change everything" (*SP*, p. 18), or you send some fool "shouting into the forest at nightfall... / News of some thing we know and care little of" (*SP*, p. 27). The poetry audience laughs at the joke, but the regularity with which Ashbery returns to the device makes me believe that, though he too is laughing, he is hopefully serious about the prophecy's having arrived.

Arrival is not the same as being understood, however, and we are told that the former Quiz Kid was at first hurt by the baffled response to his work. By now he may enjoy being a mystery, having confirmed his suspicion that it is the "mystery" part of truth that makes it marketable. But why does he remain so mysterious? There are two reasons, and the first is his style. By itself, his style is so beguiling or so outrageous, depending on your point of view, that the transfixed reader is powerless to get beyond it. The beguiled explain their condition by saying Ashbery does not "work" or "mean" like other poetry. The outraged assert that it is not poetry at all, or, if it is, then its essential ingredient must be obscurity. But no prophet sets out to be permanently obscure—where is the immortality in that? And no master stylist is after a result that fails to "work" its magic. With some effort, and some willingness too, I think we ought to be able to find his style out. The second reason Ashbery remains mysterious is his choice of subjects or, it would be better to say, his context. We are accustomed to pinched poetry, the kind whose context is one Incan rock, and we know how to deal with that. In Ashbery we encounter a poet who, as his friend Frank O'Hara wrote, "is always marrying the whole world." Readers who prefer their Incan rock may agree with the reviewer who complained of Ashbery that "you can't possibly quote anything 'out of context' since there is never a context." But every poet marks out his subject matter, and it is not possible for him to write independent of that context. It is simply that the Ashbery context is so wide open that it takes a great deal of reading before you can visit its boundaries. Until then, you may understandably feel that the signs along the way point in all directions and nowhere in particular.

Style and context do not occur separately in a poem, and the one is ultimately meaningful only as it is enfolded in the other. Much foolishness can be produced by trying to consider them as things apart. But this essay is not a poem, and so there is no alternative. I must try to untangle them, doing as little violence to their connections as possible, so that when they are reunited we may have some idea of how they came to make a coherent whole in the first place. I am going to begin with context—the context of a poet who married the world.

John Ashbery announced his engagement in the opening line of his first major book: "We see us as we truly behave." The strictness and the generosity are in that "truly." The strictness is that we will not see us as we might have behaved or as we ought to behave. The generosity is that we are going on a tour of the world as it might look on "a day of general honesty," knowing there is nothing larger or more extraordinary. It will be a vast excursion, and we can expect the itinerary to be recalcitrant even as we follow it: "As laughing cadets say, 'In the evening / Everything has a schedule, if you can find out what it is'" (*ST*, p. 9).

One way to learn the schedule is to go along with it; in retrospect it is easier to see what it was. If this sounds too spineless, think of it as a version of Keats's negative capability. It takes a strong constitution to live into the present so ruthlessly available to whatever is waiting there. And I do not think it exaggerates to say that, of the poets I know, Ashbery is most ruthlessly available to the present. In our time, that present is largely to be found in the curricula of the city and its sophisticated outposts. Arguably, the present has been there longer than this; yet we have grown up with a literature that would look energetically in almost any other direction—to the frontier, the sea, to Walden, or to a room in Amherst—in order, as it claims, to front the essential facts of life. Though he started life on a farm in upstate New York, Ashbery has done his "fronting" in the great metropolis—Boston, Paris, New York, and their suburbs—and a list of his cultural entanglements and cultured acquaintances would be staggering, many times longer than the lists of names he in fact included in the pages of *The Vermont Notebook*. Larry Rivers, Alex Katz, Willem de Kooning, Harold Rosenberg, Elaine de Kooning, James Schuyler, Jane Freilicher, Kenneth Koch—just a few names from these lists are enough to stand for the enormous and "timely" experiences that were there when Ashbery was. Nor are we star-struck if we insist on the importance of such a constellation. We are not star-struck to note that Mannerist painters Pontormo, Rosso, and Parmigianino, say, were all in Rome before the Sack of 1527 and that Rosso and Parmigianino worked side by side there for four years. It is important that, one with the other or one against the other, they worked toward a "timely" style that, unclear as it may have been to them, is now timelessly clearer to us. In making my case, I do not mean to suggest the Hamptons today equals Rome before the Sack. But I would not insist on the differences either. So much as John Ashbery has moved in a timely world, just so much is he able to make that world available to us.

Just so much, as long as we remember that negative capability was to be our guide. "The mind / Is so hospitable, taking in everything / Like boarders," says the title poem from *Houseboat Days* (p. 38). Wallace Stevens reports that his mind was similarly commodious; yet I think he was choosier than Ashbery when it came to which boarders to take in. Stevens, we remember, proposed to "live in the world, but outside of existing conceptions of it." Ashbery not only lives very much in the world, he seems to live by all existing conceptions of it simultaneously, regardless of how contradictory the lot may be. How else would it be possible to bring over accurately into language the ripe complexity of us as we truly behave in this almost "terminally sophisticated" society?[1] When you put his capacity for taking in boarders together with the timely milieus in which the man has moved, the result is a brilliant, and thus dense, mingling of attitudes and their languages. Just as all colors together equal no color, so what looked to the reviewer like no context is instead many contexts. Or, to use another illustration, it is many contexts tangled into one another like parts of a score—interesting in themselves, perhaps, but best all at once:

> The conductor, a glass of water, permits all kinds
> Of wacky analogies to glance off him, and, circling outward,
> To bring in the night. Nothing is too "unimportant"
> Or too important, for that matter. The newspaper and the
> garbage
> Wrapped in it, the over, the under.
>
> [*HD*, p. 14]

I hope I am not taken to mean that negative capability makes Ashbery timely, and headed for timelessness, because it prints out a rebus only for the painters, poets, and culturati who have been his friends. No, in the city one also sees a great many "real" people, most of them strangers. They come and go as types; one sees their faces and hears their news, and, as the poem I just quoted puts it: "Nothing is too 'unimportant' / Or too important, for that matter." The papers are on the stands, the radio is plugged in, films arrive at the movie theater, and all are filled with suggestive abstractions. To the extent that the city includes the past, it is alive with all the suggestions of our culture: "Rome where Francesco / Was at work during the Sack... / Vienna where the painting is today ... / New York / Where I am now, which is a logarithm / Of other cities" (*SP*, p. 75). With your Keatsian apparatus, you can be as big as the city you live in. But, unless we think this must be a painless way to gain an empire, you can also be as small, as passion-strewn, as constantly slapped up or yanked down—in other words, at civil war. "Is not a man better than a town?" asked Emerson, implying that the two were different. The question could hardly occur to Ashbery: "Whatever the villagers / Are celebrating with less conviction is / The less you" (*HD*, p. 27).

A good deal is said about the impenetrable solipsism of this poet who is so private he is truly private. It is said in exasperation and as an excuse to quit reading, and its best authority is the poet himself, who will tell us, as he does in *Three Poems*, that his "elaborate view" really comes from "looking inside." If he is so solipsistic, how can he mean anything? But grant that Keats was right, that there is such a thing as negative capability, and you have begun to answer the question yourself. For if Keats was right, then the elaborate landscape of the city and of the poet's timely entanglements in it may indeed be found, in their contrariness, by "looking inside." At one time or another, the mind will believe every squabbling part of itself, the poem mean everything it says. So the trick is turned: How can it be solipsism if he means everything?

> Everything is landscape:
> Perspectives of cliffs beaten by innumerable waves.
> More wheatfields than you can count, forests
> With disappearing paths, stone towers
> And finally and above all the great urban centers, with
> Their office buildings and populations, at the center of which
> We live our lives, made up of a great quantity of isolated
>   instants
> So as to be lost at the heart of a multitude of things.
>   [*DD*, p. 39]

It has become a cliché to note that the quantity of information in the world has exploded while space has collapsed, and the cliché does not make it less real. But to say we have turned into a global village is inaccurate. "Global" is a nod in the right direction, but "village" is a bow to nostalgia. Our culture is nothing so simple or settled as a village. It is more of a stellar explosion caught in an earthly jar, a revolving explosion of needs and demands and diversions, and in the midst of this tumult we take our chances on "daily life." *This* is the context of John Ashbery, because only in this reality can we see us as we "truly" behave. While he was living in Paris, Ashbery wrote in praise of Raymond Roussel a line that might have been written prospectively for himself: "it is no longer the imaginary world but the real one, and it is exploding all around us like a fireworks factory in one last dazzling orgy of light and sound." To be aware of this context is an immense help to knowing the poems. For example, if a fireworks of attitudes competes for the same pen (or typewriter in this case), won't they cross, won't they comment on one another? Yes, they will, sometimes in the poem itself and sometimes from offstage. So to have missed the context is also to miss this commentary—commentary that provides some of the best moments, playful and rueful, that Ashbery can offer.

There are good precedents for such serious play, though probably more in English poetry than our own. I am thinking especially of the "influence" who peeps out at us over two Ashbery titles ("The Picture of Little J. A. in a Prospect of Flowers," and "As One Put Drunk into the Packet-Boat")—and that is Andrew Marvell.[2] Like Ashbery, Marvell saw a lot of the "timely" world and, like Ashbery, seems to find a single point of view impossible, not even desirable. The masterly example is "The Garden," and a masterly reading of it is the one by Joseph Summers. The extravagant first stanza has begun, and what Summers says of it strikes me as exactly right: "The outrageous suavity and the calculated rationality . . . of the lines invite us to smile and warn us of extravagances to come. The poem is going to claim *everything* for a life of infinite leisure in the garden; but the ways in which it makes its claim reveal the urbanity of the poet who created this fictional voice, his recognition of values beyond those which he pretends to dismiss and those which he pretends exhaust all the pleasant and virtuous possibilities of human life."[3] I have quoted this remark because it goes directly to the point I am talking about. Consider the opening of John Ashbery's "Definition of Blue," which has caused its share of trouble.

> The rise of capitalism parallels the advance of romanticism
> And the individual is dominant until the close of the
>   nineteenth century.
> In our own time, mass practices have sought to submerge the
>   personality
> By ignoring it, which has caused it instead to branch out in all
>   directions
> Far from the permanent tug that used to be its notion of
>   "home."
>
> [DD, p. 53]

Robert Pinsky writes in his recent book that this opening is too funny for us "to take any subsequent idea quite seriously." If I read him right, he is disappointed because the poem therefore "fails to convince" us of the value advanced in its lovely last lines.[4] But we do not ask to be convinced of the argument in "The Garden." On the contrary, the "outrageous suavity and the calculated rationality of the lines invite us to smile and warn us of extravagances to come." Like Marvell, Ashbery is eating his cake and having it too, being serious and having fun. To know the wide context in which this is possible is to be let in on both seriousness and fun ourselves.

If we have decided, then, to give up our grumpiness and go along with the play, we will find it necessary to break out of the confines of the single poem. One attitude heckles another from poem to poem or forgives it from collection to collection. You can trace this in the recurrent appearance of the American garden suburb, whose boredom and beauty make for one of

Ashbery's dearest subjects, much as another kind of garden became one of Marvell's. *A Nest of Ninnies*, the novel written in collaboration with James Schuyler (which Auden called a minor classic), is about some nice people who live on Long Island, read Proust, go out for drinks at Howard Johnson's, and escort their European guests on a tour of the Walt Whitman Shopping Plaza. Then there is "Farm Implements and Rutabagas in a Landscape," where the very form—the troubador's sestina—becomes a deft satire because of its content. The envoy ends roughly: "Popeye chuckled and scratched / His balls: it sure was pleasant to spend a day in the country" (*DD*, p. 48). But the roughness is charmed in the same collection by the graceful "Evening in the Country," though we can hear Mr. Offstage Attitude still sniping away in the wings. One has to read twice the last phrase in these lines: "things eventually take care of themselves / With rest and fresh air and a good view of things" (*DD*, p. 33). In "Pyrography" (*HD*, p. 8) the theme hangs on: "At Bolinas / The houses doze and seem to wonder why... / Why be hanging on here?" But again it is both more fun and more poignant if we read this back against its echo in "The One Thing That Can Save America." That earlier poem begins fed up with the "overgrown suburbs, / Places of known civic pride, of civil obscurity"; yet it closes with an elegiac and mixed affirmation brought by another of those prophetic messages, this one telling of danger,

> and the mostly limited
> Steps that can be taken against danger
> Now and in the future, in cool yards,
> In quiet small houses in the country,
> Our country, in fenced areas, in cool shady streets.
>
> [*SP*, p. 45]

Realism, nostalgia, goofiness, and even a shred or two of the American Dream—in Ashbery's suburbia they all are available at once.

There are more complicated examples of serious play in Ashbery than this approach-avoidance bout with the suburbs. Yet this gentle contest can serve as a manageable illustration of how one mixes the wit and the sadness, the transport and the debunking, because the world is so contradictory that there is no single attitude clean enough to live life straight through. It is not always easy to keep many outlooks in the air at once, but it has been done. "I contain multitudes," said the Whitman who seems to have divided his time in Manhattan equally among going to the opera, drinking at Pfaff's, and stalking the trolleys. It is not one's first impression of him, but in the context of the real city he lived in his statement suggests a certain savoir faire. To repeat, the world is very much bigger now, in terms of all the information blazing into one man-size neocortex. To contain multitudes—the fireworks of experience, language, and belief—must now require an even greater, more elastic savoir faire.

> Something strange is creeping across me.
> La Celestina has only to warble the first few bars
> Of "I Thought about You" or something mellow from
> *Amadigi di Gaula* for everything—a mint-condition can
> Of Rumford's Baking Powder, a celluloid earring, Speedy
> Gonzales, the latest from Helen Topping Miller's fertile
> Escritoire, a sheaf of suggestive pix on greige, deckle-edged
> Stock—to come clattering through the rainbow trellis
> Where Pistachio Avenue rams the 2300 block of Highland
> Fling Terrace.

[*HD*, p. 31]

That is only the beginning of Ashbery's "Daffy Duck in Hollywood," which contains more multitudes to come: the Fudds' garage, the Gadsden Purchase, the Princesse de Clèves and the Wallets (including Skeezix); bocages, tanneries, and water meadows; London and St. Petersburg. We cannot reduce this to the still privilege we once expected from poetry. This is the exploded culture in which we truly behave, and it is no help to cry "No context!" because we cannot find one small enough to suit us. Here is no Incan rock but an avalanche—no still point in a turning world but the turning world itself, and it is exploding all around us like a fireworks factory in one last dazzling orgy of light and sound.

To fit the context of the turning world he lives in, Ashbery made the style we call "Ashbery." In fact, having named it "Ashbery" has apparently released some readers from the worry of whether it is also English. In one fundamental way, of course, it isn't English at all—it is American. But, whichever, it represents our language in the sense Wallace Stevens meant when he said a poet's dialect was analogous to common speech and yet not that speech. A poet's dialect is our language gone a little screwy, and it is the screwy part that gives us back the odd things we ordinarily say and do, only they come back a little odder. This is why screwiness may signify "Prophet Speaking." On the other hand, it may also signify a fake.

People in this country are notoriously leery of fakes, regardless of their being regularly taken in by them. And those of us who read poetry are no exception to this national virtue. One test many Americans use to identify fakery in a poet these days is the test of diction. If the suspect moves haltingly from word to word, if those words are tight little Anglo-Saxon islands, each one surfacing after obvious struggle in the depths, then the speaker is ipso facto cleared, his authenticity and our integrity proved. But if his words flow like the sea itself, if they alternately recede in demotic eddies and advance in Latin swells, then we turn away from him, secure in knowing we met temptation and were not weak. For poetry this makes a curious test.[5] Yet it was current long before its current proponents took it up. I haven't read Bronson Alcott's *Psyche* (not poems, though surely meant to be poetic). Still, I can sympathize with the abashed Alcott, who received from the hand of Emerson these shalts and shalt nots, via the United States mail: "To the prophetic tone belongs simplicity, not variety, not taste, not criticism. As a book of practical holiness, this seems to me not effective. This is fanciful, playful, ambitious, has a periphrastic style & masquerades in the language of scripture.... The prophet should speak a clear discourse straight home to the conscience in the language of earnest conversation." When it comes to virtuosity, we are a nation of prigs. Fanciful, playful, ambitious, periphrastic, a masquerade—what an indictment! And not one count on which we could acquit John Ashbery.

Even Ashbery's titles are playful, periphrastic, a masquerade—taking "As One Put Drunk into the Packet-Boat" from an index of first lines is hardly straight home to the conscience—and they deserve their fraction of credit for whatever confusion the Ashbery style stirs up. These titles are like the hand that looms forward in Francesco Mazzola's self-portrait, each one "thrust at the viewer / And swerving easily away, as though to protect / What it advertises" (*SP*, p. 68). In fact, "Self-Portrait in a Convex Mirror" is a good example because it is so frequently read as if Emerson's commandment held, as if this had been written straight home to the conscience. Why shouldn't it read as it seems to read? Here is the painter's self-portrait, here is the poet looking at the painter's self-portrait, and here, therefore, is the poet's self-portrait. The whole thing is commonly referred to now as "Self-Portrait," revealing our bias toward the private. Unquestionably, that is one way to read "Self-Portrait in a Convex Mirror." What troubles me is that we should fasten doggedly on the seeming straightforwardness of one title and one poem in the midst of a canon we know is everywhere else artful and foxy. What troubles me is that we should ignore the hint, there in the first four lines, that things are being simultaneously protected and advertised. What troubles me is that we have indeed swerved away with the hand thrust at us—"Self-Portrait"—and left the protected remainder of the title very much alone. What does it signify, "in a Convex Mirror"?

Since there is no answer that is not manifold and suspect, I may as well brave it and offer my own. On the poem's evidence I take the convex mirror to stand for at least three things beyond that physical object it actually is. One is the imagination, the convex brain, the thing called negative capability: "And the vase is always full / Because there's only just so much room / And it accommodates everything" (*SP*, p. 77). Two is the city, especially New York, which provides the imagination with its raw material: "We have seen the city; it is the gibbous / Mirrored eye of an insect. All things happen / On its balcony and are resumed within" (*SP*, pp. 82–83). And, three, the one I want to focus on now, is the poet's style—for how else does an artist make himself an example if not in his own style? And what better way for Ashbery to describe his own style than by reference to this Mannerist painter whose work is in many ways a tantalizing parallel to his own?

> The consonance of the High Renaissance
> Is present, though distorted by the mirror.
> What is novel is the extreme care in rendering
> The velleities of the rounded reflecting surface
> (It is the first mirror portrait),
> So that you could be fooled for a moment
> Before you realize the reflection
> Isn't yours.
>
> [*SP*, p. 74]

Mannerism is almost a synonym for virtuosity and, true to our priggishness, we are apt to shun it as vulgar and inauthentic. But the idea of *maniera* in early art criticism implied almost the opposite. It was borrowed from the literature of manners, where it was something to boast about. If you had *maniera*, you had style. You had grace, sophistication, savoir faire. So when it was applied to the work of Parmigianino, say, it originally meant much the same thing: here was grace, here was elegance, here was "the stylish style."[6] So stylish was his style that Parmigianino eventually became a verb, *imparmiginare*, "to sub-merge expression of the subject in elegance and delicacy." I cannot make a verb so sonorous from "Ashbery," but the meaning of *imparmiginare* suggests what parallels are being dangled before us. To submerge the subject in an elegance that knows just where and how far it is breaking the rules—this is not the mannerism we speak of when we want to say someone is "affected." This is Mannerism given its due capital, the style of the savoir faire.

Getting back to poetry, there is a pleasurable symmetry to be had from thinking that the same times that produced Mannerism in painting would also produce it in her sister, poetry—the same times, if for English we allow for a cultural lag long enough to include the author of "To His Coy Mistress." In his book on Renaissance style, Wylie Sypher makes a nice case for this lag and for the similarities at either end of it. Of the "Coy Mistress" he writes: "Marvell's sharp but unsustained attack—brilliant, sensitive, private—is like the loose and surprising adjustment and counter-adjustment of figure to figure in Parmigianino's paintings, with their evidence of subjective stress."[7] Isn't it another pleasant symmetry that the prize-winning *Self-Portrait in a Convex Mirror* begins with just this Marvell peeping over its first title and ends with just this Parmigianino reflected in its last? Of course, the idea of guilt by association is something of an outrage (though less outrageous, one sees, in criticism), and it would be a tenacious conspiracy that could span centuries to include Ashbery, Marvell, and Mazzola. Yet the choice of titles was Ashbery's, not ours, and one has as evidence against him his remarks on the arbitrary titles of Tanguy's pictures: "Yet the fact that most of them are titled implies that a choice has been made, and that the purpose of this choice is to extend the range of the picture's meaning by slanting it in a certain direction."

Now in poetry there are a number of figures that are likely to be found in a stylish style. Not surprisingly, they are also found in "the sublime." Not surprisingly, because only so far as these figures are reckless with the sublime will they betray a subjective stress analogous to the self-consciousness of Mannerism—as Mannerism betrayed its stress by recklessness with the High Renaissance. Longinus named these figures with some big words, and, because it is more convenient in discourse to name a thing than to have to describe it over and over, I am going to introduce them by their big names and perpetuate the error, in a way.

1. First is *periphrasis*, who himself likes to name things. But periphrasis is never able to land on a name outright; instead he goes at it around Robin Hood's barn, and arriving at one haystack of the thing he names *that*. Therefore periphrasis is especially good at naming unnameable things, like attitudes.

> a kind of fence-sitting
> Raised to the level of an esthetic ideal.
>
> [*DD*, p. 18]

2. Periphrasis has a cousin, *apophasis*, who names things by unnaming them. Apophasis is like Peter being interrogated; his denials prove a great deal.

> the soul is not a soul
>
> [*SP*, p. 69]

3. Third is that rogue *paranomasia*, who likes to make fun of the things he names. We know him most often as pun, but he is agile in a variety of circumstances.

> You walk five feet along the shore, and you duck
> As a common heresy sweeps over.
>
> [*HD*, p. 38]

4. Another prankster is *polyptoton*. He likes to keep us in the dark as to your pronouns, so one cannot be sure if I will be doing the talking, let alone what tense we might have been in.

45

But I was trying to tell you about a strange thing
That happened to me, but this is no way to tell about it,
. . . . . .
And one is left sitting in the yard
. . . . .
As though it would always happen in some way
And meanwhile since we are all advancing
It is sure to come about in spite of everything
On a Sunday, where you are left sitting
In the shade.

[*SP*, p. 19]

5. *Hyperbole* is a show-off. He more than names, he swaggers
—and therefore he sometimes gets mixed up. Longinus thought
the better hyperboles would conceal themselves, but what fun is
it getting all dressed up if you can't go to town?

                                you my friend
Who saved me from the mill pond of chill doubt
As to my own viability, and from the proud village
Of bourgeois comfort and despair, the mirrored spectacles of
      grief.

[*HD*, p. 6]

6. But the real virtuoso is *hyperbaton*, mad for taking chances
—the most reckless of them all. Hyperbaton will mix words that
should never be mixed, like someone who invites rival lovers to
the same cocktail party just to watch the sparks fly. Even more
exhilarating, he will climb a great slide of words and let go, sure
as gravity that chance will bring him out to truth at the bottom.

They all came, some wore sentiments
Emblazoned on T-shirts, proclaiming the lateness
Of the hour, and indeed the sun slanted its rays
Through branches of Norfolk Island pine as though
Politely clearing its throat, and all ideas settled
In a fuzz of dust under the trees when it's drizzling:
The endless games of Scrabble, the boosters,

46

> The celebrated omelette au Cantal, and through it
> The roar of time plunging unchecked through the sluices
> Of the days, dragging every sexual moment of it
> Past the lenses: the end of something.
>
> [*HD*, p. 2]

His recklessness makes hyperbaton a public danger. Longinus says, "He carries his audience with him to share in the dangers of his long inversions." But like other public dangers he is powerfully convincing, since his conclusions seem not thought up but passionately wrung from him, almost against his will.

In addition to these six, there are other figures, or near-figures, that lack such elegant and accurate names. They are likewise more interesting as they are twisted away from the ideal. Longinus took up one of them, diction, but the chapters in which he discussed it are largely lost, so we will have to continue on our own.

7. *Diction* can be a matron or a streetwalker, depending on how she decides to dress. At her most vulgar she could hook even Emerson. This girl is adept with clichés, and she can arrange them to put out a stinging accuracy.

> We hold these truths to be self-evident:
> That ostracism, both political and moral, has
> Its place in the twentieth-century scheme of things.
>
> [*DD*, p. 31]

8. *Irony* is getting to be a brat. She may be forthright as satire or burlesque, but, since she is often timid in the nature of brats, she also likes to sow her discord on the sly. One of her amusements might be called *épater les critiques*, including Harold Bloom (as in "The Other Tradition"), Ruskin ("The Gazing Grain"), or even Horace ("And *Ut Pictura Poesis* Is Her Name"). Nor is irony above biting the hand that writes her, as when she prompts Daffy Duck in Hollywood to despair of his own avian self-portrait in a convex mirror.

I scarce dare approach me mug's attenuated
Reflection in yon hubcap.

[*HD*, p. 31]

9. *Surrealism* is an ingenious housewife, forever rearranging
the furniture, and she is also fed up with being thought French.
She knows her Emerson ("Bare lists of words are found suggestive, to an imaginative and excited mind") and she can squeeze
an analogy out of the barest list. She had a field day in *The
Vermont Notebook*, but often she gets stuck in the house, where
she understandably insists on the sad variety of woe.

And a sigh heaves from all the small things on earth,
The books, the papers, the old garters and union-suit buttons
Kept in a white cardboard box somewhere.

[*SP*, p. 2]

Last will come prophecy, but before we can consider her without interruption we have to take time out so those two laggards,
parergon and paralipomenon, can make their appearance.

10. *Parergon* likes to enter from offstage or even to speak offstage when you least expect it—as if to imply that it is by no
means settled who are the principals and who are the walk-ons in
the play. Being ornamental enough to attract attention, parergon also likes to turn up in unlikely locations so you will question where the real action is taking place.

A few black smudges
On the outer boulevards, like squashed midges
And the truth becomes a hole, something one has always
known,
A heaviness in the trees, and no one can say
Where it comes from, or how long it will stay—

[*HD*, pp. 60–61]

11. *Paralipomenon* has never been easy to keep track of either
and is continually being neglected or overlooked. When re-

covered as a supplement, however, paralipomenon gets its revenge—because the whole rest of the text is now characterized as much by what it left out, and may have left out still, as by what it included. Paralipomenon may come at the beginning, midsection, or end, but the revenge is sweetest when it comes as an afterthought.

>   My wife
>   Thinks I'm in Oslo—Oslo, France, that is.
>   [*SP*, p. 4]

12. Now on to *prophecy*, who enters sometimes as parergon or paralipomenon, but who also appears in so many other shapes we will have to extend her gender, Tiresias fashion. He and she are almost a summary of the other figures, but a summary never quite in the picture, and they are therefore sad with yearning. No matter how deeply she may yearn to influence the action, he also knows they must remain forever outside that action, emblematic only, like the prophetic figures who appear in the background of *The Marriage of St. Catherine* or the *Madonna of the Long Neck* (both by Parmigianino).

>   Wait by this
>   Mistletoe bush and you will get the feeling of really
>   Being out of the world and with it.
>   [*HD*, p. 5]

So, although prophecy never gives up the attempt, his or her voice arrives oddly anomalous to its source or object, as letters on trays or as fools shouting into the night.

>   words like disjointed beaches
>   Brown under the advancing signs of the air.
>   [*DD*, p. 94]

By introducing these dozen figures in such an offhand manner, I do not mean to imply that we are to take them lightly.

When they are brought into play, it is usually because there is some serious work for them to do. The elegance of combining many refined figures, and of stretching each of those in a way that would shiver the woodlots in Concord, is that it makes possible the reproduction in poetry of a world very much like the one in which the poet lives—a world where no attitude can hide from another, but all are revealed and commented on at once. It is largely the abundance of these dozen that makes the Ashbery style exasperating to some readers and makes them fear they are being taken in. But when the playful figures are for serious work, and when an abundance of them appears in one poem, then that may be a very serious poem indeed. One would not like to see this indulgence extended to poets across the board. But when we turn to a book like *Houseboat Days* we see how high is the high seriousness of which the stylish style is capable.

We should not leave the matter of John Ashbery's style without some mention of his unabashed borrowings from all over the place. These do not seem to annoy people very much; no one expects honor among thieves. On the contrary, people who are otherwise baffled may pick out the borrowings with pleasure. They are like the people one sees in a museum who have just come into the gallery, spied a famous picture whose reproduction they have seen many times, and are now congratulating each other on its presence, saying, "It's here! It's here!" This is good fun; we have all enjoyed it, and we can extend it to poetry. Take "Melodic Trains," where we have been waiting in the station and are suddenly asked, "How do they decide how much / Time to spend in each?" Now that question is a nugget of wonder, and nuggets of that kind have been polished to such perfection by James Schuyler that one finds it hard to resist pocketing them for himself. If this one was borrowed from Schuyler it is only one example of how the New York School is quarried for Ashbery's poetry, though Ashbery would not find such a comment very meaningful. Nor do I, in terms of the long-range meanings in his work that I am after today. But his New York School friendships and collaborations with Schuyler, Frank O'Hara, and Kenneth Koch are factual and momentous. Had you collected Pontormo and Parmigianino around a table in 1525 and informed them of their Mannerist fellowship, they probably would have responded, "Not very meaningful." They would have been right, and so would you.

Ashbery's affinities for certain European writers, writers in the big lump known as surrealism, are also fact. His "Into the Dusk-Charged Air," with its Rousselian list of every river in the encyclopedia, was published in the same summer as his translation of the first chapter from Roussel's *Impressions of Africa*. He has also translated from another favorite, Giorgio de Chirico, the painter who can make sentences that sound remarkably Ashberian. It was from de Chirico that Ashbery borrowed the title *The Double Dream of Spring*. But we could go on like this at length, citing Hesiod, the Book of Common Prayer, "An Ordinary Evening in New Haven," even the books for which he once wrote jacket copy at Oxford University Press—among them Henry Steele Commager's *Freedom, Loyalty, Dissent* and an edition of Schumpeter's *History of Economic Analysis*. After all, if there is a disposition called negative capability that will take in a host of attitudes, it will take in a host of other writers too. In an interview Ashbery was asked: "What types of diction are you aware of incorporating into your poetry?" The answer was: "As many kinds as I can think of."

One gets the exasperation in that answer. One also gets its truth. A poet cannot make a style so canny, to express a world so wide, and remain totally unaware of how he is doing it. In evidence, we have his inclusion of Wyatt and Surrey in "Grand Galop." Wyatt is famous for importing the sonnet to England, and Surrey is famous for domesticating it. Famous now, but one may forget that people who were reading English poetry in those days found the sonnet curious, its iambic pentameter baffling. To some of them, I venture, it didn't even sound like

English. Here too the parallels are tantalizing, as they must have been to the poet who wrote "Grand Galop," who has imported a good deal into the American language, and who knows what it feels like to be thought curious. In fact, the parallels must be sweetly tantalizing to Ashbery, for everyone knows that the odd little sonnet turned into a monument of English form.

> But if one may pick it up,
> Carry it over there, set it down,
> Then the work is redeemed at the end
> Under the smiling expanse of the sky
> That plays no favorites but in the same way
> Is honor only to those who have sought it.

[*SP*, p. 15]

We have interrupted the poet making a style, and his eyes are wide open. It is the first test of the savoir-faire style that you know how far you have come. Harder to know is where you are going: the Mannerists perhaps thought they were taking the High Renaissance higher. Like Ashbery, they knew how to make a style but could not know the sense of its effect. That is for the rest of us to say.

Now that I have put style and context asunder, I would like to get them back together where they belong. You can entertain them separately according to your interests, but what makes poetry ultimately meaningful is that style and context come together as a whole. To believe this, of course, is to believe meaning resides in poetry at all, a belief we have shriveled a great deal. We may let people find their meanings in our movies, but not in our poetry, and the wonder is we do not realize we do this at our own expense. Instead, we are dogged by revelations like the one Mallarmé visited on Degas. The painter, in search of advice, has confessed to having some ideas for poems, only to be notified by Mallarmé that poems are *words*, not ideas. One wonders, will Degas take this seriously, or will he perhaps reflect that his friend's remark is also made of words? No, the remark and others like it have been taken so trimly to heart, for both poetry and painting, that one still hears intelligent people praise a picture by saying things like, "The importance of the painting is the paint." Or one hears them praise a poem by saying, "The poem's only meaning is to be." It is all right for the painter or poet to protect himself by saying such things. But the rest of us really ought to be less timid. In the paint and the words is symbolized something more: the artist's sense of the world.

It is for his sense of the world that we remember Emerson, or Stevens (from whom I borrowed the phrase). It is his sense of the world that can make the poet a prophet of the commonwealth—someone, Stevens wrote longingly, who is "the axis of his time."

> What is the radial aspect of this place,
> This present colony of a colony
> Of colonies, a sense in the changing sense
>
> Of things? A figure like Ecclesiast,
> Rugged and luminous, chants in the dark
> A text that is an answer, although obscure.

That is Stevens, in canto xix of "An Ordinary Evening in New Haven," but the question and its project likewise fixed on John Ashbery at the start and have stayed itching at him ever since. If no other poet lives so ruthlessly into the present, I think it is also true that none is so relentlessly in pursuit of the up-to-date, the radial aspect of right now. In poem after poem, we are returned to the timeliness (and thus datedness) of fashion—of pyrography, of Mannerism, of names like Linda, Pat, or Sheila. In poem after poem, we are returned to the problem of defining the present—"Is anything central?" "What time of day is it?" The anxiety is catching and, like the figure of hyperbaton that is often used to express it, it takes the reader along for the ride. I suspect that this anxiety, unidentified as it first is to many readers, is another of the things which can make Ashbery initially uncomfortable to read.

In retrospect, however, the itch is easy enough to identify. It was there to make *Three Poems* a torment and a transport, and if one remembers that the three were written at the end of the peculiar 1960s, then he can see Ashbery itching for the present in their very titles: "The New Spirit," "The System," "The Recital." We are talking now about a poet who writes with the stereo on. "The New Spirit" was written to Elliott Carter's *Concerto for Orchestra*—which premiered in 1969 and which in turn owes something to the poem *Winds*, by St.-John Perse. Carter says his concerto was inspired by the poem's prophetic descriptions of a United States swept by transforming and obliterating winds, winds like the "self-propagating" ones that now blow through "The New Spirit"—winds "fresh and full, with leaves and other things flying."

> Something *is* happening. The new casualness had been introducing itself, casually of course, but suddenly its credentials lay everywhere.... It wasn't the lily-pad stage yet, but there was buzzing everywhere as though the news had already broken out and was flooding the city and the whole country. [*TP*, p. 45]

Is it outlandish to suggest that a poet so preoccupied with the buzzing news might aim to be the Ecclesiast of whom Stevens wrote? Of course in today's climate you are not likely to announce the embarrassing ambition to be the axis of your time. But you might reveal it anyway in a playful manner that, like the hand in Parmigianino's self-portrait, both protects and advertises: "Little by little / You were the mascot of that time" (*TP*, p. 33). Or you might state it outright by pretending its parody.

> How to explain to these girls, if indeed that's what they are,
> These Ruths, Lindas, Pats and Sheilas
> About the vast change that's taken place
> In the fabric of our society, altering the texture
> Of all things in it?
>
> [*SP*, p. 42]

How to explain? You adjust a style to the context of your life and chant a text that is an answer, though obscure: your sense of the world.

I am not pretending an Ashbery who argues a programmatic poetry. There are different sorts of prophets. We might speak of the visionary prophet who does have some program, however vague, and nothing would please him more than to fix it on the future, or at least on his readers. We might also speak of the vatic prophet whose enterprise is to recognize the world as is and give notice to the rest of us. The visionary looks to another world and in proportion may be optimistic and inexact. But the vatic looks to the world around and within him and in proportion may be accurate to despair. His predicament is by virtue of his "negative capability" the predicament of others; to use Ashbery's own word, he exemplifies.

> It is the lumps and trials
> That tell us whether we shall be known
> And whether our fate can be exemplary, like a star.
>
> [*SP*, p. 45]

It would be a mistake to expect programs from a poet busy with the lumps and trials. But if it is an example we are after, then we can read it in his fate or—which is the same thing for a poet—his sense of the world. If by means of his context he has given accurate notice of our predicament, then how he extricates himself from that predicament through style will be an example—as it is put so touchingly—like a "star."

I have already characterized the Ashbery context as an exploded one, as an apposite analogue for the tumultuous context of real lives as they "truly" behave. And whoever has been even momentarily bewildered in his own life by the blandishments of this bit of life-style or that may be willing to agree. Certainly the cultural tumult as experienced in Hollywood by Daffy Duck is little stranger than the tumult being experienced by other people as well—for evidence of which I submit this remarkable testimony by Jerry Rubin: "In five years, from 1971 to 1975, I directly experienced est, gestalt therapy, bioenergetics, rolfing, massage, jogging, health foods, tai chi, Esalen, hypnotism, modern dance, meditation, Silva Mind Control, Arica, acupuncture, sex therapy, Reichian therapy, and More House—a smorgasbord course in New Consciousness."[8] Now there is a course equally confused as—if less elevated than—the duck's. Perhaps such smorgasbord clutter does indeed describe our culture. But I would lift a few lines from John Ashbery's "Fragment" in order to say that, if this is a culture, it is one of "incomplete, good-natured pictures that / Flatter us even when forgotten with dwarf speculations / About the insane, invigorating whole they don't represent" (*DD*, p. 93).

The problem here is that the American self is hardly content to understand either self or world as an incomplete picture; the Emerson whose self could discern from particulars the perfect whole has long since carried the day. It was Emerson who first spoke of our new consciousness, and he said he could state it with precision: *the individual is the world*. The burden of this consciousness, of course, is that when one's self is the world it behooves one to find it as fast as possible. More than an ordinary burden, the search becomes a duty as enormous and private as salvation once was. Unfortunately, however, the individual who is bent on redeeming his transcendent self from today's particulars will confront an embarrassment à la Rubin or Duck—there are too many particulars.

> Like a rainstorm, he said, the braided colors
> Wash over me and are no help. Or like one
> At a feast who eats not, for he cannot choose
> From among the smoking dishes.
>
> [*SP*, p. 3]

Yet the individual who is precisely the world has no recourse; he must go on discovering himself via each and all ad infinitum. As a result, his inner life must come eventually to mirror the chaos of the culture around him, while his connections to reality—

which he had thought to strengthen—fail of direction and at-
rophy. He is Daffy Duck at the corner of Pistachio Avenue and
Highland Fling Terrace, and he finds everything getting choked
"to the point of silence."

He might also be Parmigianino, lost in alchemy—because I
don't think it is implausible for us to compare the embarrassment of riches that confronts the individual today with the cultural chaos that likewise threatened him immediately after the
High Renaissance. Arguably, this is a comparison Ashbery is
making for us in "Self-Portrait in a Convex Mirror." One should
remember that the poet is also an art critic. He was critic for the
Paris *Herald Tribune* for five years and executive editor of *Art
News* for nine. By the time he was named art critic for *New York*
magazine in 1978, his by-line had already appeared over more
than five hundred reviews, articles, and catalog notes. He is
surely familiar with many self-portraits—baroque, academic,
surreal, pop—and could have picked any one of them to stare at,
but he chose the one in a convex mirror: "Our time gets to be
veiled, compromised / By the portrait's will to endure. It hints at
/ Our own which we were hoping to keep hidden" (*SP*, p. 79).
To make something of that hint, why shouldn't we turn to art
history? If we did we could find in Arnold Hauser, for example,
the suggestive description of Mannerism as "the new spirit"
that sought to redeem itself from cultural anarchy.[9] We would
find that Hauser locates the birth of the modern artist in this
new spirit. And, still following Hauser, we would find that this
spirit engenders among artists a proportion of cranks, eccentrics
and psychopaths that will increase thereafter day by day. Given
this view, it is not surprising that the very figures in Parmigianino's pictures suggest a progression toward private
idiosyncrasy. In either *The Marriage of St. Catherine* or the
Madonna of the Long Neck, for example, one can see the several
figures gaze in as many several directions—apparently intent as
individuals on their separate psychological moments, and with
no center to socialize their attentions. Before his life is out, Fran-

cesco himself will lapse into melancholy, entirely neglect his appearance, and devote his energies to alchemy. One can imagine him like Daffy Duck, a character for whom everything is getting choked to the point of silence.

Taken by himself, such a character today would appear to be a candidate for psychotherapy. In fact, the chaotic and impulse-ridden personality recurringly described in Ashbery has its near look-alike in the personality being described in the literature on pathological narcissism. So for our convenience—and to the horror of the trained clinician—I am going to introduce that personality by reducing it to two parts. On the one hand we see in this personality a grandiose—what I would call an Emersonian—conception of the self.[10] And on the other we see an experiencing of reality as fragmented, chaotic, and inauthentic. Obviously the dilemma is built right in and leads almost as a matter of course to the narcissist's sense of his own formlessness, to the chronic sense that one's feelings are no longer associable in any accurate way with action: the very sense of society has petered out. This is the distress we can hear being sounded in the "Fantasia on 'A Nut-Brown Maid'" by each of those two characters, *He* and *She*, who never quite manage dialogue. And it is the distress sounded in "The System" by the voice that has just lamented how the things of reality do not speak to him, but have meaning only for themselves.

> It could be . . . that there is no such thing as a void, only endless lists of things that may or may not be aware of one another, the "sad variety of woe." And this pointless diversity plunges you into a numbing despair and blankness. The whole world seems dyed the same melancholy hue. Nothing in it can arouse your feelings. [*TP*, p. 84]

In that voice we have the paradigmatic complaint of the narcissist on the couch: he cannot feel, he is a blank, there is no "other" of sufficient salience to rouse him from himself.

I did not trot out this complaint from *Three Poems* in order to prove Ashbery the prophet of the clinically disordered. It is true that the journals for some time have carried reports of the increased incidence of narcissistic analysands. It is true some of these reports have further concluded that narcissism has become the dominant symptomatology of the late twentieth century, as hysteria was of the nineteenth. But what makes this shift in symptomatology of interest to us and to social commentators—among them Christopher Lasch, Richard Sennett, and now Hans Morgenthau—is the degree to which it may be promoted or exacerbated by the cultural and social context.[11] In other words, if clinical narcissism is truly encouraged by some general cultural event that has overtaken our society, then that event is going to affect the rest of us in the same direction, if not to the same degree. We may not all require the couch; but we must all understand ourselves within the confines of a common cultural aspect. The poet who shows us where those confines are, via his context, has indeed brought accurate notice of our commonwealth and its predicament.

One has to admit, however, that it is not exactly fun to be returned to a predicament—which may explain why there are those who feel trapped in an Ashbery poem. Fun would be to participate in an escape instead. So here is where we bring style back into the picture; for how does a poet engineer his escape except through style? Let me make my case in sequence, starting with the proposition that one good way to get loose from a predicament is to examine your assumptions and attitudes, for these may be all that hold you there. But—and the poet knows this instinctively—people are not persuaded from their attitudes by logic. They are seduced from them by style. This is why the poet gets to be, as Stevens termed him, "the appreciatory creator of values and beliefs." It is not that you truly create the alternative attitudes; it is that you make them stylish enough to make them desirable. It is as though poetry were an emotional enabling legislation that you could enact single-handedly for the public benefit. If true, that would make you of an exalted species

indeed, and, as we might expect from John Ashbery, he is the
first to say it isn't so.

> There was no life you could live out to its end
> And no attitude which, in the end, would save you.
>
> [RM, p. 21]

It seems the poet is not accepting our nomination of him for
prophet, for the Ecclesiast invoked by precursor Stevens. But
only at first, because the demurrer we just quoted pops up in a
poem called—of all things—"The Ecclesiast." We have seen before how one line comments on another, one poem on the next,
and now we see a title encroaching on the poem beneath it. We
have seen before that we cannot take Ashbery at his word; we
must take him at all his words. Taking him that way here, one
might read this poem to say something like this: There are no
life-saving attitudes and those are the ones I sing. Truly, poetry
cannot help itself: for to say beautifully that there are no attitudes is still to create an attitude. And to call the poem in
which you do so "The Ecclesiast" is to let ambition's cat ever so
slyly out of her bag.

Having found his ambition out, we are in a position to observe
Ecclesiast as he turns his style to the problem at hand: how to
get loose from the general predicament of which the narcissist
seems at once product and avatar. Given the Ashbery view of
our culture, there is not much to be done about the individual's
experience of reality as fragmented and inauthentic—reality *is*
fragmentary. Even a poet cannot synthesize the storm of "information" that besieges the Daffy Ducks or Jerry Rubins. To
pretend otherwise, to opt for a poetry that polishes one Incan
rock, would be to renege altogether on the vatic enterprise. But
when it comes to the other side of the narcissist dilemma—that
grandiose and Emersonian self—we are indisputably back in the
realm of the poet's competence. Whatever self one harbors by

the grace of Emerson is harbored, after all, by the grace of poetry. And what poetry has done it can also alter. What if, for example, Emerson overrated the self? What if it is not the world? Why then the world or parts of it must lie elsewhere, and as there is an elsewhere there is a way to wriggle free.

> Each person
> Has one big theory to explain the universe
> But it doesn't tell the whole story
> And in the end it is what is outside him
> That matters, to him and especially to us
> Who have been given no help whatever
> In decoding our own man-size quotient and must rely
> On second-hand knowledge.
>
> [*SP*, pp. 81–82]

Put them side by side with Emerson, and the preceding lines from "Self-Portrait in a Convex Mirror" will read as an outright rebuttal. I remember, however, that I promised us seduction, not a public argument. So before we decide to be disappointed, I am going to suggest we play those Ashbery lines over again—keeping in mind this time that seduction is almost by definition successful in gestures which go at first unnoticed. And I am going to suggest therefore that we stop when we get to one of those gestures: "man-size quotient." Right there, in one stylish subversion, is the grandiose self undone. Long after one has forgotten exactly where the lines occurred, or exactly what it was they said, one will be able to recall the tone—the seductive attitude—imparted to them by that phrase: man-size quotient. Long after one has forgotten the phrase itself, one will remember the skill with which our friend, paranomasia, shifted attention to his pun, *man-size*—which in the language of commercial packaging promises "more" but which in the context of the transcendent self can only suggest a diminished, if equitable, amount. Emerson, still teaching his doctrine of "the infinitude of the private man," has been upstaged not by argument, but by style. He has been upstaged by a gesture that—to bring back the verb *imparmiginare*—simply subverted the subject by expressing it, but by expressing it with such stylish savoir faire that its premises have begun to slip.

Having seen what paranomasia can accomplish in the way of seduction, one will want to keep an eye on the other stylish figures we meet in Ashbery as well. For, as it turns out, they can all be pressed into service toward the same end—seducing the American self away from its High Emersonian model.[12] A few highlights from that model should serve to give us an idea of what we are on the lookout for.

1. To begin with, the grandiose self must have its unique integrity if it is to be considered intrinsically worthy. "Nothing is at last sacred," wrote the author of *Self-Reliance*, "but the integrity of your own mind." We have already seen how apophasis can reduce this notion with a single coy negative: the soul is not a soul. We may not have noticed, however, how polyptoton has been up to much the same project, blurring personal pronouns in a manner to suggest that identity, far from being integral, is likewise blurred.

> How many people came and stayed a certain time,
> Uttered light or dark speech that became part of you
> . . . until no part
> Remains that is surely you.
>
> [*SP*, p. 71]

2. Equally important to the grandiose self is an analogue for its own greatness. Emerson settled on nothing less than Nature, declaring that "The Universe is the externization of the soul," and in so doing he set himself up for hyperbole, who now finds the sport irresistible. We hear from Ashbery of "*angst*-colored skies," of "pain in the cistern," even of a "jock-itch sand-trap." After such externizations as these, one becomes conditioned to accept the following.

> Yes, friends, these clouds pulled along on invisible ropes
> Are, as you have guessed, merely stage machinery...
>
> [*HD*, p. 50]

3. Since the self is analogous to the Universe, it is more than grandiose; it must be unbounded. Sure enough, Emerson was true to his analogy: "There is no outside, no inclosing wall, no circumference to us." But where do parergon and paralipomenon come from, for example, if not from outside some circumference? Each time they appear, they teach us their revisionist lesson.

> the soul is a captive, treated humanely, kept
> In suspension, unable to advance much farther
> Than your look as it intercepts the picture.
>
> [*SP*, pp. 68–69]

4. Since it knows no bounds, a grandiose self must necessarily dwell in an area of unlimited possibility. Said the unforgiving Emerson: "Men cease to interest us when we find their limitations. The only sin is limitation." Against the enormity of this judgment, it will be necessary to marshal a host of figures: surrealism to collapse the space that potential must have in order to flourish; periphrasis to warn that what is possible may nevertheless be unnameable and unknown; irony, pop diction, and paranomasia to remind us that potential has gone already stale and there is nothing to be discovered new. Instead, we are only "free to come and go within a limited area, a sort of house-arrest of the free agent intentionally cut off from the forces of renewal," (*TP*, p. 20).

5. Finally, a self wrought on the universal scale must also be a self which is always in control, responsible by its own order for making the world orderly. "There is no chance and no anarchy in the universe," was Emerson's statement on the matter. And to pull the rug out from under this assertion, who could do better than hyperbaton, whose very presence insists on chance?

Hasn't the sky? Returned from moving the other
Authority recently dropped, wrested as much of
That severe sunshine as you need now on the way
You go.

[RM, p. 27]

Once you have watched those figures as they perform in concert, it may seem ironic that the poetry of John Ashbery could
ever be dismissed as private, as a hermetic celebration of the
self. For to see the performance from where we have been sitting
is to witness the poet at work on an attitude that in fact diminishes the scope of the American self.[13] How to get loose
from our narcissist predicament? Why, one need only style the
self as the exiguous facture it truly is. At that moment, the
universe must cease to be the externization of the soul. At that
moment, it is possible to regard the exploded context of our
culture not as a mirror of the self, but as a public theater for
action. And at the moment the world is a theater, one is free.
Our cultural clutter, so threatening to the grandiose self, becomes for man-size persons the mulch for their serious
business—play.

This mulch for
Play keeps them interested and busy while the big,
Vaguer stuff can decide what it wants—what maps, what
Model cities, how much waste space. Life, our
Life anyway, is between.

[HD, p. 34]

In those lines, as elsewhere, one senses how Ashbery too has
paid his Emersonian dues. Didn't he too struggle to match "the
big, vaguer stuff" and come out on top, struggle to beat the dire
sin of limitation: Didn't he, like others, discover that the big,
vaguer stuff was getting the better of it, that whoever would
match the stuff without invites a commensurate vagueness
within? Yes, he must have done so. But what makes the poet an

example like a star is that he has won through these lumps and trials to the stylish, seductive expression of an alternative attitude. Let the big stuff decide what it wants; the life of the self, kept to proportion, may be spryly lived "between." Here is an attitude at last fitted to the actual country Americans live in now. If the poetry that delivers it has caused a commotion, this is because its arrival is not a private, but a public event.

2

"Fragments of a Buried Life": John Ashbery's Dream Songs

MARJORIE PERLOFF

—I wrote about what I didn't see. The experiences that eluded me somehow intrigued me more than the one I was having, and this has happened to me down through the years.

John Ashbery in an interview[1]

Of Raymond Roussel, that enigmatic writer whom Cocteau called "the Proust of dreams," Ashbery remarks: "What he leaves us with is a work that is like the perfectly preserved temple of a cult which has disappeared without a trace, or a complicated set of tools whose use cannot be discovered. But even though we may never be able to 'use' his work in the way he hoped, we can still admire its inhuman beauty, and be stirred by a language that seems always on the point of revealing its secret, of pointing the way back to the 'republic of dreams' whose insignia blazed on his forehead."[2]

In praising what he calls Roussel's "mysteries of construction," Ashbery seems to be casting a sidelong glance at those of his own readers who have complained that his poetry refuses to yield up its "secret," that this "complicated set of tools" has no "use." Robert Boyers's recent strictures in the pages of the *Times Literary Supplement* are typical: "If we take meaning to refer to the possibility of shared discourse in which speaker and auditor may participate more or less equally," then "Ashbery is an instance of a poet who, through much of his career, eliminates meaning without achieving any special intensity.... Meaning is often left out of an Ashbery poem... to ensure the continuity of a quest for which ends are necessarily threatening."[3]

This is to regard *meaning* as some sort of fixed quantity (like two pounds of sugar or a dozen eggs) that the poet as speaker can either "leave out" or proffer to the expectant auditor with whom he is engaged in "shared discourse." But what if there are other ways of "meaning"? Ashbery's penchant for trompe l'oeil, for "shifting sands," for rooms whose "fourth wall is invariably missing" (*HD*, p. 9), is born of a conviction that "the magic world really does exist" (*TP*, p. 16), that to escape "the familiar interior which has always been there ... is impossible outside the frost of a dream, and it is just this major enchantment that gave us life to begin with." But, he adds in the next breath, "Life holds us, and is unknowable" (*TP*, p. 11).

Dream is thus regarded as the source of our energy, our élan, of life itself; and yet that life remains curiously "unknowable." This paradox is at the heart of Ashbery's poetry and accounts for his preoccupation with dream structure rather than dream content. Not *what* one dreams but *how*—this is the domain of Ashbery, whose stories "tell only of themselves," presenting the reader with the challenge of "an open field of narrative possibilities" (*TP*, p. 41). For these are not dreams "about" such and such characters or events; the dream structure *is* the event that haunts the poet's imagination. It follows that Ashbery is especially sensitive to the process of moving in and out of dream, of "waking up / In the middle of a dream with one's mouth full / Of unknown words," as he says in a poem called "No Way of Knowing" (*SP*, p. 55). Or, to put it in the words of a recent Ashbery title, one's visions are "Lost and Found and Lost Again" (*HD*, p. 36).

Accordingly, Ashbery's dream poems lack the finish of, say, Yeats's "A Dream of Death," or the air raid sequence in Eliot's "Little Gidding," or, for that matter, of *The Dream Songs* of John Berryman. Here is "Dream Song #89," which belongs to the series called "Opus Posthumous":

> In a blue series towards his sleepy eyes
> they slid like wonder, women tall & small,

of every shape & size,
in many languages to lisp 'We do'
to Henry almost waking. What is the night at all,
his closed eyes beckon you.

In the Marriage of the Dead, a new routine,
he gasped his crowded vows past lids shut tight
and a-many rings fumbled on.
His coffin like Grand Central to the brim
filled up & emptied with the lapse of light.
Which one will waken him?

O she must startle like a fallen gown,
content with speech like an old sacrament
in deaf ears lying down,
blazing through darkness till he feels the cold
& blindness of his hopeless tenement
while his black arms unfold.[4]

Here we have the poet's retrospective account of a dream in
which a procession of fair women comes to the tomb of Henry
(the poet's alter ego) and engages in a macabre marriage-death
ceremony in the tomb. The "one" special woman, evidently a
former sweetheart, steps forward and brings "Henry almost
waking" back to life: his "black arms unfold" to embrace her,
and in his longing, he feels, for the first time, "the cold & blindness of his hopeless tenement."

Despite certain verbal and syntactic oddities ("crowded
vows," "and a-many rings fumbled on") and confusing pronouns (the women "tall and small" become "you"), Berryman's
Dream Song has a coherent conceptual and sequential structure:
this happened, and then this, and therefore that. In Freudian
terms, the dream is motivated by Henry's secret guilt feelings
about a particular woman and takes the form of wish fulfillment:
not only do women "of every shape & size" "lisp 'We do'" in
Henry's ear, but the "one" whom he has loved makes a "sacrament of speech" that comes "blazing thru darkness" to his
tomb.

This is dream filtered through the rationalizing consciousness of a poet who wants to convey particular feelings—in this case, the longing to be loved—to his audience. The poem may be admired for its wit and poignancy or for the immediacy of its personal drama, but there is surely nothing *dreamlike* in Berryman's Dream Song. For the words that come to us in dreams are characterized by their inability to express the full meaning we wish to convey; behind each word lies a range of nonverbal meanings or inarticulate feelings.[5] Fidelity to the dream process precludes the kind of ex post facto formulation we are given here. Or, to put it another way, a Berryman "dream" looks as if it has already *gone through* a certain amount of psychoanalytic interpretation. Compare Ashbery's "On the Towpath," which appears in *Houseboat Days* (1977):

> At the sign "Fred Muffin's Antiques" they turned off the road
> into a narrow lane lined with shabby houses.
>
> If the thirst would subside just for awhile
> It would be a little bit, enough.
> This has happened.
> The insipid chiming of the seconds
> Has given way to an arc of silence
> So old it had never ceased to exist
> On the roofs of buildings, in the sky.
>
> The ground is tentative.
> The pygmies and jacaranda that were here yesterday
> Are back today, only less so.
> It is a barrier of fact
> Shielding the sky from the earth.
>
> On the earth a many-colored tower of longing rises.
> There are many ads (to help pay for all this).
> Something interesting is happening on every landing.
> Ladies of the Second Empire gotten up as characters from
>   Perrault:
> Red Riding Hood, Cinderella, the Sleeping Beauty,
> Are silhouetted against the stained-glass windows,

A white figure runs to the edge of some rampart
In a hurry only to observe the distance,
And having done so, drops back into the mass
Of clock-faces, spires, stalactite machicolations.
It was the walking sideways, visible from far away,
That told what it was to be known
And kept, as a secret is known and kept.

The sun fades like the spreading
Of a peacock's tail, as though twilight
Might be read as a warning to those desperate
For easy solutions. This scalp of night
Doesn't continue or break off the vacuous chatter
That went on, off and on, all day:
That there could be rain, and
That it could be like lines, ruled lines scored
Across the garden of violet cabbages,
That these and other things could stay on
Longer, though not forever of course;
That other commensals might replace them
And leave in their turn. No,

We aren't meaning that any more.
The question has been asked
As though an immense natural bridge had been
Strung across the landscape to any point you wanted.
The ellipse is as aimless as that,
Stretching invisibly into the future so as to reappear
In our present. Its flexing is its account,
Return to the point of no return.

[*HD*, pp. 22–23]

The poem begins on a realistic note, but as soon as the name-less "They" turn off the road "into a narrow lane lined with shabby houses," the "normal" world of "Fred Muffin's An-tiques" dissolves. Like Dorothy in *The Wizard of Oz*, stepping over the rainbow into the technicolor country of the munchkins, the protagonist finds himself in a strange new world in which events unfold without any logic. The towpath that begins at

Fred Muffin's antique shop leads inexplicably into some sort of desert ("If the thirst would subside just for awhile") in which time has come to a standstill. But in this empty and silent desert, there are, oddly, "roofs of buildings," and we learn that "the pygmies and jacaranda that were here yesterday / Are back today, only less so." What are exotic tropical trees (jacaranda) and pygmies doing here and why were there more of them yesterday? We never know, nor do we have time to care; for now "a many-colored tower of longing rises," and we are transported into a fairy-tale region where "Ladies of the Second Empire gotten up as characters from Perreault ... Are silhouetted against the stained-glass windows." Is this a medieval castle or some sort of Disneyland mirage? Ashbery lets us see it either way: his focus here, as in so many of his poems, is on the moment of metamorphosis, "l'heure indicible," as Rimbaud called it, when one object dissolves and another begins to take form. So the shadowy "white figure" who "runs to the edge of some rampart / In a hurry" (the white rabbit of *Alice in Wonderland*? a white nymph? Snow White?) suddenly crumbles like a punctured ballon and "drops back into the mass / Of clockfaces, spires, stalactite machicolations."

What does such "dropping back" signify? Perhaps the white figure has been struck by a missile, cast through one of the "machicolations" of the parapet. Perhaps, on the other hand, these spires and stalactites are mere decorations on a frosted wedding cake, bits of spun sugar that delight the poet's senses. The meaning of what has happened remains, in any case, "a secret." And, as the sun fades "like the spreading / Of a peacock's tail," the charming Perreault figures "silhouetted against the stained-glass windows" appear in a new light. The poet now refers, with some irritation, to the "vacuous chatter / That went on, off and on, all day." The many-colored tower of longing gives way to a rain-soaked "garden of violet cabbages." The dreamer still hopes that other "commensals"[6] might replace the "ruled lines" made by rain sweeping across the kitchen garden, but he knows that what Yeats called "Those images that yet / Fresh images beget" are dissolving.

How to recapture the "many-colored tower of longing"? "The question has been asked," but there is no answer. One would like to remain inside the dream "As though an immense natural bridge had been struck across the landscape to any point you wanted." But the "ellipse is . . . aimless"; its "flexing" marks a "Return to the point of no return."

What are we to make of this strange narrative in which unspecified persons perform unspecified and unrelated acts against the backdrop of a constantly shifting landscape whose contours dissolve before our eyes? When, moreover, did these things happen? In the moment of genesis, of metamorphosis that is the source of the poet's life-force, the past is catapulted "into the future so as to reappear / In our present." But what is the relation of such explosive displacements to the time signal of the fading sun?

In discussing Roussel's poem *La Vue*, Ashbery says: "the poet, like a prisoner fascinated by the appearance of the wall of his cell, remains transfixed by the spectacle before his eyes."[7] So it is for both poet and reader of *On the Towpath*. Like Proust's magic-lantern show in which Geneviève de Brabant and Golo appear and disappear on the brightly lit screen, enchanting the young Marcel, Ashbery's Dream Song unfolds a series of palpable, arresting images that seem to arrive out of nowhere, creating moments of stark confrontation and illumination. The dream content is fluid, mobile, unanchored, but its form is surprisingly fixed. And here a remark Ashbery made about Gertrude Stein's *Stanzas in Meditation* provides an interesting clue:

> *Stanzas in Meditation* gives one the feeling of time passing, of things happening, of a "plot," though it would be difficult to say precisely what is going on. Sometimes the story has the logic of a dream . . . at other times it becomes startlingly clear for a moment, as though a change in wind had suddenly enabled us to hear a conversation that was taking place some distance away. . . . But it is usually not events which interest Miss Stein, rather it is their

"way of happening," and the story of *Stanzas in Meditation* is a general, all-purpose model which each reader can adapt to fit his own set of particulars. The poem is a hymn to possibility.[8]

"On the Towpath" is just such a "hymn to possibility." It is "difficult to say precisely what is going on," but the "way of happening" can be delineated. Ashbery's is the landscape of desire, and the poet's visionary journey takes him through deserts and cities, tropical forests and medieval castles in quest of the "secret [that] is known and kept." But the dreamer knows, even if he cannot formulate statements about it, that the source of such visionary images is always and only in the self. Bits of everyday reality—"Fred Muffin's Antiques," lanes "lined with shabby houses," the "many ads" that "help pay for all this"— weave in and out of the poet's consciousness, serving as reminders that to dream is to be on the verge of waking up. The bridge "Stretching invisibly into the future" "reappear[s] in our present"; it "Return[s] to the point of no return." The moment of genesis is over.

But—and this thematic motif appears in poem after poem— the experience of dream is the *only* way of knowing we have. In a poem called appropriately "No Way of Knowing," the poet observes:

> The body is what this is all about and it disperses
> In sheeted fragments, all somewhere around
> But difficult to read correctly since there is
> No common vantage point, no point of view
> Like the "I" in a novel. And in truth
> No one never saw the point of any....
> There is no way of knowing whether these are
> Our neighbors or friendly savages trapped in the distance
> By the red tape of mirage.
>
> [*SP*, p. 56]

Given such uncertainty, poetry becomes the continual attempt to reveal that "Something interesting... happening on every landing" of the "many-colored tower of longing," an attempt just as continually blocked as reveiling occurs. "Language," as Ashbery says of Roussel, "seems always on the point of revealing its secret," but the longed-for disclosure never comes.

This pattern of opening and closing, of revelation and reveiling, of simultaneous disclosure and concealment is the structural principle of the Ashbery lyric. Like Duchamp's *Large Glass*, such an enigma text endlessly generates the impulse that makes the reader yearn for completion and understanding. As Roger Cardinal puts it in an interesting essay called "Enigma," "the receiver knows that a signal *is* being emitted, but his connection with the transmitter seems to be on a faulty line." It is in this sense that Roussel's work is like "a complicated set of tools whose use cannot be discovered." To read such a text is, in Cardinal's words, "like being given a key only to learn that the locks have been changed."[9]

To create such "mysteries of construction" is by no means easy, as anyone knows who has read the countless imitations of Ashbery currently breaking into print. Too much disclosure produces contrivance; too much concealment, unintelligibility and boredom. In Ashbery's early poems, these twin dangers are not always avoided. Consider the well-known "The Instruction Manual," which appeared in *Some Trees* (1956). Ashbery recalls that he wrote this poem when he was working for McGraw-Hill in New York as a writer and editor, not quite of instruction manuals but of college textbooks: "The poem really ends with me returning to the boring task I have to do, where the poem began. It leads back into me, and is probably about the dissatisfaction with the work I was doing at the time. And my lack of success in seeing the city I wanted most to see, when I was in Mexico. Mostly because the name held so much promise: Guadalajara. So I wrote about what I didn't see."[10]

"The Instruction Manual" begins:

> As I sit looking out of a window of the building
> I wish I did not have to write the instruction manual on the
> uses of a new metal.

I look down into the street and see people, each walking with
     an inner peace,
And envy them—they are so far away from me!
Not one of them has to worry about getting out this manual on
     schedule.
And as my way is, I begin to dream, resting my elbows on the
     desk and leaning out of the window a little,
Of dim Guadalajara! City of rose-colored flowers!
                                                    [ST, p. 14]

Bored with the dreary instruction manual he has to prepare, the
poet conjures up vivid and exotic images of Guadalajara, with
its "flower girls, handing out rose- and lemon-colored flowers,"
its bandstand musicians "in their creamy white uniforms," "its
houses of pink and white, and its crumbling leafy terraces." The
poem's structure is that of a travelogue: here is the poorer quar-
ter, here is the market, here is an old woman sitting in a patio,
and so on. Finally, the narrator exclaims:

How limited, but how complete withal, has been our
     experience of Guadalajara!
We have seen young love, married love, and the love of an
     aged mother for her son.
We have heard the music, tasted the drinks, and looked at
     colored houses.
What more is there to do, except stay? And that we cannot do.
And as a last breeze freshens the top of the weathered old
     tower, I turn my gaze
Back to the instruction manual which has made me dream of
     Guadalajara.
                                                    [ST, p. 18]

The reality-dream-reality structure of "The Instruction Manual" is a simplified version of the "greater romantic lyric" as
Meyer Abrams and others have defined it. A determinate
speaker in a particularized setting (looking out of the window of
the building) is moved by a certain stimulus—in this case the
pages of the instruction manual—to a reverie or daydream.
"Such a poem," writes Abrams, "usually rounds upon itself to

end where it began, at the outer scene, but with an altered mood and deepened understanding which is the result of the intervening meditation."[11] Although Ashbery's speaker does not achieve the epiphany usually found in greater romantic lyric (his dream of Guadalajara is a pleasant escape fantasy rather than an integral psychic event), "The Instruction Manual" does have the out-in-out form characteristic of Romantic poems like "Tintern Abbey" or "Frost at Midnight" or Keats's odes. Its neat division into three acts—Before the Dream, the Dream, and After the Dream—makes it one of Ashbery's most accessible poems; and, not surprisingly, this is one of his rare anthology pieces.

But such clear-cut boundaries between reality and dream have always been alien to Ashbery's sensibility, and even in *Some Trees* he rarely makes things so easy for himself or for his reader. In the opening poem, "Two Scenes," the interplay of fact and fantasy is much more complex:

I

We see us as we truly behave:
From every corner comes a distinctive offering.
The train comes bearing joy;
The sparks it strikes illuminate the table.
Destiny guides the water-pilot, and it is destiny.
For long we hadn't heard so much news, such noise.
The day was warm and pleasant.
"We see you in your hair,
Air resting around the tips of mountains."

II

A fine rain anoints the canal machinery.
This is perhaps a day of general honesty
Without example in the world's history
Though the fumes are not of a singular authority
And indeed are dry as poverty.
Terrific units are on an old man
In the blue shadow of some paint cans
As laughing cadets say, "In the evening
Everything has a schedule, if you can find out what it is."

[*ST*, p. 9]

The opening line, "We see us as we truly behave," immediately recalls the Wallace Stevens of "What We See Is What We Think," but Ashbery's "new ways" of seeing the world and ourselves are purposely left mysterious: "Two Scenes" is like a Stevens meditation in which the particulars refuse to add up. Why does the train come "bearing joy"? Who is the "you" of "We see you in your hair"? And so on. Ashbery's predilection is already for concrete, presentational images—what he was to call, with reference to Reverdy, "living phenomena"—whose signification is purposely left blurred and open.[12] We can invent any number of stories in which a "train comes bearing joy," possibly carrying a group of "laughing cadets" into the mountains, possibly passing a canal where "Destiny guides the water pilot." "Everything has a schedule, if you can find out what it is," but the trouble is that you can't find out. The only certainty is that, as in the later "On the Towpath," everything shifts ground: the sparks that illuminate the table go out; the "Air resting around the tips of mountains" gives way to a "fine rain anoint[ing] the canal machinery," and when the rain dries up strong fumes appear, perhaps from "the blue shadow" of the old man's paint cans. In its fidelity to "a way of happening" rather than to "what happens," "Two Scenes" anticipates Ashbery's later work.

But before that later work came into being, Ashbery wrote the poems collected in *The Tennis Court Oath* (1962). Here the balance often tips the other way: disclosure is so totally blocked that the reader is all but excluded from the world of the text; his connection with the transmitter seems to be not on a faulty line that allows for expectation and suspense, but on no line at all. "Leaving the Atocha Station" begins:

> The arctic honey blabbed over the report causing darkness
> And pulling us out of there experiencing it
> he meanwhile... And the fried bats they sell there
> dropping from sticks, so that the menace of your prayer
>   folds...
> Other people...   flash

the garden are you boning
and defunct covering... Blind dog expressed royalties...
comfort of your perfect tar grams nuclear world bank tulip
Favorable to   near the night pin
loading formaldehyde.   the table torn from you
Suddenly   and we are close
Mouthing the root   when you think
generator   homes enjoy leered

[*TC*, p. 33]

It is amusing to watch Ashbery's inventiveness, his modulation of images from "arctic honey" to "fried bats" to "garden are you boning," "Blind dog," and "world bank tulip." It reads rather like a Dada collage or *cadavre exquis* made by jumbling and cutting up the lines from *The Waste Land:*

"Oh keep the Dog far hence, that's friend to men,
"Or with his nails he'll dig it up again!"

But the words in the poem remain excessively discrete, refusing to group themselves into larger configurations. The curtain does not open on one side, allowing us to see, if only for a moment, before the gesture of disclosure is suspended. Here the theater remains dark, and we who sit in the audience begin to be restless and bored. Occasionally the curtain does flutter for a moment, as when Ashbery indulges in such clever wordplay as "air pollution terminal." But it is not enough to hold our attention.

"These Lacustrine Cities," the opening poem of Ashbery's next volume, *Rivers and Mountains* (1966), is probably the first of the great Dream Songs. I have argued elsewhere that in this remarkable poem, we meet "cities" that resemble no cities we have ever seen and yet seem remarkably "real."[13] In the verbal landscape of the poem, desert and mountain, violent sea and tapering branches, swans and beacons can coexist, creating new configurations that remind me of those little balls of paper one drops into water, which slowly open up and become intricate and beautiful Japanese flowers. The strangeness of the images is underscored by the indeterminacy of conjunctions and pronouns. "These Lacustrine Cities" is full of connectives—"although," "for instance," "until," "then," "but," "yet"—that create expectations of causality, of relatedness that the narrative never fulfills. Its pronouns, moreover, have no precise referents: "you" may or may not be the same person as "I" or "we," and in any case we don't know who this "you" is. The "all-inclusive plans made for you" in the fourth stanza sound vaguely ominous, for there is talk of sending "you" to the "middle of the desert." But according to the dream logic that governs this poem, such a "private project" need never be carried out, and when we next meet the nameless "you," he is building "a mountain of something" (*RM*, p. 9).

Reading a text like "These Lacustrine Cities" is thus rather like overhearing a conversation in which one can make out individual words or phrases but has no clear idea what the speakers are talking about. *Three Poems* (1972), perhaps the most important source for understanding Ashbery's poetic as well as his characteristic procedures, is full of such "conversations." Here is a representative passage from the first section, "The New Spirit." The subject, in a very general way, is the rebirth of the self that comes when one falls in love:

At this point an event of such glamor and such radiance occurred that you forgot the name all over again. It could be compared to arriving in an unknown city at night, intoxicated by the strange lighting and the ambiguities of the streets. The person sitting next to you turned to you, her voice broke and a kind of golden exuberance flooded over you just as you were lifting your arm to the luggage rack. At once the weight of the other years and above all the weight of distinguishing among them slipped away. You found yourself not wanting to care. Everything was guaranteed, it always had been, there would be no future, no end, no development except this steady wavering like a breeze that gently lifted the tired curtains day had let fall. And all the possibilities of civili-

79

zation, such as travel, study, gastronomy, sexual fulfillment—these
no longer lay around on the cankered earth like reproaches, hide-
ous in their reminder of what never could be, but were possibilities
that had always existed, had been created just for both of us to
bring us to the summit of the dark way we had been traveling
without ever expecting to find it ending. Indeed, without them
nothing could have happened. Which is why the intervening
space now came to advance toward us separately, a wave of music
which we were, unable to grasp it as it unfolded but living it. That
space was transfigured as though by hundreds and hundreds of
tiny points of light like flares seen from a distance, gradually merging into one wall of even radiance like the sum of all their possible
positions, plotted by coordinates, yet open to the movements and
suggestions of this new life of action without development, a fixed
flame. [TP, p. 37]

This prose sounds deceptively reasonable and straightforward. One sentence follows another imperturbably: "At this
point... ," "At once... ," "And all the possibilities... ," "Indeed. ..." The tone is quiet, the language chaste, subdued, and
given to abstraction: "glamor," "radiance," "the ambiguities of
the streets," "the possibilities of civilization," "reproaches hide-
ous in their reminder of what never could be," "the summit of
the dark way." Adverbs of time abound: "all over again," "at
night," "no longer," "gradually," "yet"; and similes, rarely
used in the early work, are prominent: "These no longer lay
around on the cankered earth like reproaches," "Hundreds of
tiny points of light like flares seen from a distance," "one wall of
even radiance like the sum of all their possible positions."

One would think that Ashbery had emerged from his
shadowy cave and decided to face the sun. But the seeming
continuity of the paragraph is deceptive. The syntax of the opening sentence, for example, looks straightforward: a simple
subject-predicate unit followed by a subordinate result clause.
But the "result" makes no sense because we do not know the
"name" that "you forgot... all over again." In the preceding
section, Ashbery has alluded to the sudden disappearance of

Rumpelstiltskin, "furious that you guessed the name," but in the new context there is no certainty that the reference is still to the Grimm fairy tale.

Forgetting "the name" leads, in any case, to a startling dream in which the poet finds himself arriving in an unknown city at night, intoxicated by the "strange lighting." Something happens as if in slow motion: "The person sitting next to you, her voice broke and a kind of golden exuberance flooded over you just as you were lifting your arm to the luggage rack." In this privileged moment, "At once the weight of the other years and above all the weight of distinguishing among them slipped away." The effect is Proustian, but with a difference: in Ashbery's poem, the connection between stimulus and response is never established. The gesture of lifting one's arm to the luggage rack is not comparable to the tasting of the *petite madeleine* or the tying of the shoestrings, particular actions that bring back to life a buried past in which these same actions had occurred. In "The New Spirit" we have, as in "These Lacustrine Cities," parts that belong to no whole, an absent totality. For we never learn what it is that has happened or why time suddenly comes to a stop.

Even familiar things become unfamiliar in this context. The breeze that gently lifts "the tired curtains day had let fall," for instance, is, of course, the Romantic symbol for rebirth, an influx of inspiration, a renewal of creativity. Yet here it is hard to say who has been reborn or what changes result on account of the "correspondent breeze." The "possibilities of civilization" now lie open to the poet and his other self; "without them," he declares, "nothing could have happened." But then nothing does "happen." "Which is why the intervening space now came to advance toward us separately, a wave of music which we were, unable to grasp it as it unfolded but living it." Is the "it" the "intervening space" and, if so, how do two separate beings whose identity resembles a wave of music, "grasp it as it unfolded" and "live it"?

The logic of dream allows such enigmatic events to occur. We cannot identify the "summit of the dark way" or the "intervening space," but for Ashbery getting there, wherever *there* is, is surely all the fun. As he says in "The System," "The apotheosis never attracted you, only those few moments in the next-to-last act where everything suddenly comes momentarily clear, to sink again into semi-obscurity before the final blaze" (*TP*, p. 94). To submit to experience, however inchoate, is, for this Paterian poet, to witness "those few moments" when space is "transfigured as though by hundreds of tiny points of light like flares seen from a distance, gradually merging into one wall of even radiance."

It should be apparent by now that Ashbery's poetry does not, as is so often supposed, render the psychic life of its maker in all of its random and contradictory character. Such psychic life as is admitted to Ashbery's verbal universe is, on the contrary, highly structured and condensed. Again and again we come across stories that "become startlingly clear for a moment, as though a change in wind had suddenly enabled us to hear a conversation that was taking place some distance away." And this momentary clarity, like a flare seen from far away, is consistently dispelled, leaving the reader waiting anxiously for the next installment.

In his recent poems, Ashbery's landscapes of desire are increasingly presented in the guise of what Frank O'Hara called "charming artifice." Medieval romance, Elizabethan pageant, comic books, Arthur Rackham fairy tale, Disney World T-shirts, flowered wallpaper, frosted wedding cakes, "stage machinery," "grisaille shepherdesses," "terrorist chorales"[14]—all these coalesce in the dream theater of *Houseboat Days*, on whose dust jacket, designed by R. J. Kitaj, we find a portrait of a graceful lady in a long-sleeved dress, immobile at the oar of a stylized houseboat, silhouetted against the shadowy flat forms of mountain, lake, and cloudy sky.

Not surprisingly, the finest poem in the collection is called

"Pyrography"; the process of burning designs on wood and leather with a heated tool here becomes the process of imprinting burning traces of memory and vision on a consciousness so fluid and amorphous that the "heated tool" is likely to slip on its surface. The poem begins:

> Out here on Cottage Grove it matters. The galloping
> Wind balks at its shadow. The carriages
> Are drawn forward under a sky of fumed oak.
> This is America calling:
> The mirroring of state to state,
> Of voice to voice on the wires,
> The force of colloquial greetings like golden
> Pollen sinking on the afternoon breeze.
> In service stairs the sweet corruption thrives;
> The page of dusk turns like a creaking revolving stage in
>   Warren, Ohio.
>
> [HD, p. 8]

The scene is present-day Chicago, the heart of the nation ("This is America calling"), but curiously it is also a fairy-tale world in which "The carriages / Are drawn forward under a sky of fumed oak." This contrast of old and new is nicely reflected in the stanza's meter, which oscillates between the formality of "In service stairs the sweet corruption thrives," a perfect iambic pentameter line with inverted word order and heavy alliteration, and the prosaic inflection of "The page of dusk turns like a creaking revolving stage in Warren, Ohio."

In the second stanza, the "we" who are also "they" set out on a journey across the great American continent, first by boxcar through the "gyrating fans of suburbs" and "the darkness of cities"; then the scene suddenly dissolves and the travelers are moving up the Pacific coast to Bolinas, where "The houses doze and seem to wonder why." Along the way they meet, in an echo of Baudelaire's "Le Voyage," the "disappointed, returning ones," but "the headlong night" beckons and it is too late to take warning and turn back. Indeed, as the journey continues, one proceeds not westward or north to Canada, but into an imaginary world. A city has evidently been erected, "built... Partly over with fake ruins in the image of ourselves: / An arch that terminates in mid-keystone, a crumbling stone pier / For laundresses, an open-air theater, never completed / And only partially designed" (*HD*, p. 9). Where are we? Like Rimbaud's "Villes," or Ashbery's own "lacustrine cities," these cities cannot be specified; they emerge as part of a theater decor upon which the curtain may fall any minute. So the poet asks:

> How are we to inhabit
> This space from which the fourth wall is invariably missing,
> As in a stage-set or dollhouse, except by staying as we are,
> In lost profile, facing the stars.
>
> [*HD*, p. 9]

This question has haunted Ashbery from the beginning. He has known all along that "Everything has a schedule, if you can find out what it is," the difficulty being that you cannot find out. Just so, the question posed in "Pyrography" is rhetorical, for the poet knows that the only way to inhabit a "space from which the fourth wall is invariably missing" is to accept it as the "stage-set or dollhouse" it really is—to realize that, in Yeats's words, "Man can embody truth but he cannot know it."

And yet one longs to counter the "strict sense / Of time running out, of evening presenting / The tactfully folded-over bill." And so one continues to journey, despite all warnings from "the disappointed, returning ones," this time into the haunted landscape of the past:

> A long period of adjustment followed.
> In the cities at the turn of the century they knew about it
> But were careful not to let on as the iceman and the milkman
> Disappeared down the block and the postman shouted
> His daily rounds. The children under the trees knew it
> But all the fathers returning home
> On streetcars after a satisfying day at the office undid it:

The climate was still floral and all the wallpaper
In a million homes all over the land conspired to hide it.
One day we thought of painted furniture, of how
It just slightly changes everything in the room
And in the yard outside, and how, if we were going
To be able to write the history of our time, starting with today,
It would be necessary to model all these unimportant details
So as to be able to include them; otherwise the narrative
Would have that flat, sandpapered look the sky gets
Out in the middle west toward the end of summer.

[HD, pp. 9–10]

Here memories of Ashbery's Rochester childhood blend with
"Märchenbilder" and present-day images to create a hallucin-
atory picture of absence. Everyone seems to know "it"—
whatever "it" is—but "it" must be kept from the iceman,
milkman, and postman. Fathers, "returning home / On street-
cars after a satisfying day at the office undid it"; "the wallpaper /
In a million homes conspired to hide it." This mysterious "it,"
the poem implies, must be included in all accounts of "the
history of our time." Without "these unimportant details," the
narrative "Would have that flat, sandpapered look the sky gets /
Out in the middle west toward the end of summer." And of
course we already know *that* look from the opening lines of the
poem.

The journey, it turns out, is not only a journey across the
American continent or back into "cities at the turn of the century," but the eternally present "journey" one lives through
each day of one's life. Change is the keynote: thus the "still
floral" climate instantly dissolves into the floral wallpaper found
"In a million homes all over the land"; the "painted furniture"
"just slightly changes everything in the room," and one cannot
"save appearances / So that tomorrow will be pure" (*HD*, p. 10).
Such rationalistic schemes invariably fail, for "The parade is
turning into our street." As in Rimbaud's "Parade," our dreams
are haunted by a procession of unidentifiable and hence

frightening figures in "burnished uniforms." And now the scenic dissolves come faster and faster: the "street" gives way to the image of "The land / pulling away from the magic, glittering coastal towns." Cottage Grove and Bolinas, boxcars and trams, boats and circling kites—all coalesce and their fragments are etched, as if with a heated tool, into the contours of the poet's psyche. And the poem concludes:

> The hunch is it will always be this way,
> The look, the way things first scared you
> In the night light, and later turned out to be,
> Yet still capable, all the same, of a narrow fidelity
> To what you and they wanted to become:
> No sights like Russian music, only a vast unravelling
> Out toward the junctions and to the darkness beyond
> To these bare fields, built at today's expense.
>
> [*HD*, p. 10]

"Pyrography," which is to say *poetry*, thus involves a continuous attempt at "unravelling / Out toward the junctions," an attempt just as continuously blocked as the stage-set suddenly disappears from sight. Just when the language "seems . . . on the point of revealing its secret," the mirror clouds over. For the designs burned into the surface by the pyrographer's tool lose their sharp outlines after a time. Yet the artist continues to erect his crumbling stone piers and open-air theaters, and to invent "forgotten showtunes" for his "Street Musicians," in an effort to redeem the "bare fields, built at today's expense." As Ashbery says of the sculptor Arp: "Everything in fact, is real from the moment he imagines it."[15] Or, to put it the other way around:

> The phenomena have not changed
> But a new way of being seen convinces them they have.
>
> [*TP*, p. 39]

3 / The Metaphysical Subject of John Ashbery's Poetry

JOHN KOETHE

A conception of the self can inform a poet's work in a variety of ways. Perhaps the most familiar is through its possession of a distinctive "voice," which basically amounts to a projection of a personality—either the poet's actual personality or one he assumes. There can be as many voices as there are personalities, but it does not follow that differences between two poets' voices reflect a difference in the *conception* of the self that informs their work. For example, Robert Lowell's characteristic voice is quite different from John Berryman's, and the personalities their poems project are correspondingly different. But it strikes me that these distinctive personalities represent selves of essentially the same *kind:* they *are* personalities, that is, they are or are to be regarded as actual psychological egos as much a part of the real world as the historical circumstances, incidents, feelings, and relationships with which they become engaged. Poetry that is characterized primarily by its voice embodies, it seems to me, a psychological concept of the self: the self is a real entity among other real entities, maybe more important than most of them, but, like them, a part of the world it is trying to tell us about.

But poetry can also involve conceptions of the self not so directly tied to the poet's own distinctive personality or voice. It can force us to consider the *position* of the "speaker"—or what I would prefer to call the "subject"—of the poetry with respect to the incidents, objects, thoughts, and personalities (including the poet's own) it describes. And sometimes this position seems drastically different from the vantage point in the world that the poem presents and that is occupied by the psychological subject of the poem. In reading poetry informed primarily by the psychological notion of self embodied in the poet's voice, we are struck by questions like "How does he sound?" or "Whose voice is it?" (and a sense that the answers to these questions are indeterminate tells against the poetry). But for poetry involving a less psychological conception of the self or subject, the important question is not so much what the voice sounds like, as *where it comes from*; and a mark of the success of this sort of poetry is that this question seems to *have* a determinate answer, even when we find ourselves unable to formulate it.

Remembrance of Things Past serves to illustrate the difference between the conceptions of a psychological ego and a non-psychological subject. The character Marcel has a particular personality and lives *in* time and in tension between Swann's way of domesticity and the Guermantes' of social circulation. And we can think of the novel as Marcel's autobiography, whose theme is the fusing of the two ways over the course of time. But the vantage point of the narrator is an atemporal one from which the moments of his life do not succeed one another, but coexist simultaneously. We are supposed to read the novel twice, the second time not as autobiography, but as the narrator's attempt to circumscribe the atemporal position Marcel comes to occupy at the end. Had someone other than Proust written a novel to this point, the personality of the protagonist and the incidents of his life would have been different: the psychological ego embodied in the work would not have been Marcel's. Yet the *subject* of this hypothetical novel could have been the same: a *different* voice could have emanated from the same durationless position occupied by Proust's narrator.

Now it seems to me that a distinctive quality of John Ashbery's poetry, a source of much of its power, is that the conception of the self it embodies is not primarily a psychological one. I say not *primarily* psychological, because his work *is* possessed of an authentic individual voice, gently reticent, delighting equally in the abstract, the literal and the silly, and usually heard through a haze of humor:

> And so we too
> Came where the others came: nights of physical endurance,
> Or if, by day, our behavior was anarchically
> Correct, at least by New Brutalism standards, all then
> Grew taciturn by previous agreement. We were spirited
> Away *en bateau*, under cover of fudge dark.
> It's not the incomplete importunes, but the spookiness
> Of the finished product.
>
> ["Daffy Duck in Hollywood," *HD*, p. 33]

This passage captures some of Ashbery's characteristic "twang." He does actually sound something like this in conversation, and one reason his imitators are usually unconvincing is that this tone, however cool and detached, works to project a genuine human voice and personality, in whose absence it seems (like any strong poet's style in someone else's mouth) willed, mannered, and depersonalized.

But even though Ashbery's work embodies the presence of a particular psychological ego, it is almost unique in the degree to which it is informed by a nonpsychological conception of the self or subject: a unitary consciousness from which his voice originates, positioned outside the temporal flux of thought and experience his poetry manages to monitor and record (*almost* unique in this respect: I sometimes feel something similar to be true of Elizabeth Bishop's work, though—and this is part of the point—her *voice* is decidedly different from his). The sense of the presence of a unified subject that conceives these poems is very strong, almost palpable. Among the stylistic indications that this subject is not a particular personality are Ashbery's characteristic use of pronouns: it seems a matter of indifference whether the subject is referred to as "I," "you," "he," "she," "it" or "we,"[1] shifts between which often occur rapidly within the course of the same poem:

SHE
But now always from your plaint I
Relive, revive, springing up careless,
Dust geyser in city absentmindedness,
And all day it is writ and said:
We round women like corners. They are the friends
We are always saying goodbye to and then
Bumping into the next day. School has closed
Its doors on a few. Saddened, she rose up
And untwined the gears of that blank, blossoming day.
"So much for Paris, and the living in this world."
But I was going to say
It differently, about the way
Time is sorting us all out, keeping you and her
Together yet apart, in a give-and-take, push-pull
Kind of environment. And then, packed like sardines,
Our wit arises, survives automatically. We imbibe it.

[*HD*, pp. 72–73]

This from "Fantasia on 'The Nut-Brown Maid,'" a long poem written in the form of a dialogue between "HE" and "SHE," two identities that are not really differentiated by the poem at all. The references of "HE" and "SHE," the pronouns within the passage above, and Ashbery's pronouns generally, are anaphoric. But these references are never given *in* the poem: they seem to belong to a world outside it, and there is a strong sense that any distinctions between them would be basically arbitrary.

"Time is sorting us all out." Another stylistic clue to the nature of Ashbery's subject is the pervasive sense of temporal dislocation that characterizes his work: the grammatical past tense is often used to indicate the present of the poem, even when this present is the moment of writing itself (as David Kalstone has observed, "Tense will shift while the poem refers

to itself as part of the past."[2]) Another passage from "Fantasia"
both illustrates and offhandedly tries to explain this tendency:

HE
To him, the holiday-making crowds were
Energies of a parallel disaster, the fulfilling
Of all prophecies between now and the day of
Judgment. Spiralling like fish,
Toward a distant, unperceived surface, was all
The reflection there was. Somewhere it had its opaque
Momentary existence.
But if each act
Is reflexive, concerned with itself on another level
As well as with us, the strangers who live here,
Can one advance one step further without sinking equally
Far back into the past? There was always something to see,
Something going on, for the historical past owed it
To itself, our historical present. Another month a huge
Used-car sale on the lawn shredded the sense of much
Of the sun coming through the wires, or a cape
Would be rounded by a slim white sail almost
Invisible in the specific design, or children would come
Clattering down fire escapes until the margin
Exploded into an ear of sky. Today the hospitals
Are light, airy places, tented clouds, and the weeping
In corridors is like autumn showers. It's beginning.
[*HD*, pp. 86–87]

Time's job of "sorting us all out" is always in progress but never
gets completed, for the subject cannot "advance one step further
without sinking equally / Far back into the past." Ashbery's
subject seems possessed by an impulse, which it knows has to
be frustrated, to *reify* itself, to find or create some *thing* with
which it can identify totally:

I shall use my anger to build a bridge like that
Of Avignon, on which people may dance for the feeling
Of dancing on a bridge. I shall at last see my complete face

91

> Reflected not in the water but in the worn stone floor of my
> bridge.
>
> ["Wet Casements," *HD*, p. 28]

"I shall at last see"—the tone is wistful and resigned. The attempt at reification yields only a personality or image that is "other," "A portrait, smooth as glass, . . . built up out of multiple corrections / [which] has no relation to the space or time in which it was lived" ("Definition of Blue"). The subject inhabits "the sigh of our present" ("Blue Sonata") and is timeless, while any representative of it in the real world is time-bound, part of "The present past of which our features, / Our opinions are made." It can only be a *surface:*

> But your eyes proclaim
> That everything is surface. The surface is what's there
> And nothing can exist except what's there.
>
> ["Self-Portrait in a Convex Mirror," *SP*, p. 70]

The note of desperation in the poetry that attends the subject's impulse to reify itself does not arise because the surface representation leaves out something real:

> there are no words for the surface, that is,
> No words to say what it really is, that it is not
> Superficial but a visible core.
>
> [*SP*, p. 70]

This "Wooden and external representation / Returns the full echo of what you meant / With nothing left over" ("Clepsydra," *RM*, p. 33). Rather, the trouble is that the subject and its "Wooden and external representation" occupy fundamentally different *positions.* The latter, like the psychological ego or self, *is* a thing, existing in the real world of past, present, and future; whereas the subject of Ashbery's poems—what I shall call the "metaphysical subject"—seems to inhabit a durationless "now," existing in a condition of "drifting . . . toward a surface which can never be approached, / Never pierced through into the timeless energy of a present" (*HD*, p. 28). And what both drives and frustrates his poetry is the attempt to fuse the two positions, an attempt conducted in the full knowledge that it cannot possibly succeed: "Why, after all, were we not destroyed in the conflagration of the moment our real and imaginary lines coincided, unless it was because we never had a separate existence beyond that of those two static and highly artificial concepts whose fusion was nevertheless the cause of death and destruction not only for ourselves but in the world around us?" ("The Recital," *TP*, p. 114).

At this point we might be tempted to conclude that the moral of Ashbery's work is that the whole concept of the self is delusory. This would be a mistake. It is true only to the extent that by "I" one understands an individual psychological ego or personality: the referential and temporal vagaries of his poetry are simply incompatible with the speaker's being a real person in the world, with a particular, individual biography. What is striking about Ashbery's work is that despite these distortions and pressures to which his "self" is subjected, surely sufficient to dismantle any *personality*, one never loses the sense that a perfectly definite point of consciousness is behind the whole enterprise. Later I want to compare the concepts of the self that inform Ashbery's work and Frank O'Hara's: both of them try to undermine the notion of the self as a permanent and objective personality, but I think one (among many) of the significant differences between them involves the different philosophical conceptions of the self alternative to that of the psychological ego to which their works have affinities.

The reification of the self as the psychological ego represents what might be called a Cartesian conception of the self. According to this conception the self *is* an object in the world among other objects (Descartes identifies it with the mind, a *res cogitans* or "thinking thing"); and as an object in the world we can experience it (introspectively), hold beliefs about it, and frame descriptions of it—at least as much as we can for any object in the world (e.g., the sun). Of course, for Descartes the mind or self is a spiritual or mental substance, unlike, say, the sun, which is a physical or material substance; but this just means that our world of acquaintance and experience contains substances of two sorts, mental and material, and does not affect the main point of this conception of the self—that it *is* a substance or thing, and part of the world of substantial things.

Descartes's is not the only view of the self found in the Western philosophical tradition. Hume's critique of the Cartesian conception boils down to the idea that experience simply fails to acquaint us with any single persisting thing we might mean by "I," but rather discloses only the various sensations and passions we mistakenly ascribe to a persisting "self" whose experiences we take them to be:

> But self or person is not any one impression, but that to which our several impressions and ideas are supposed to have reference. If any impression gives rise to the idea of self, that impression must continue invariably the same, thro' the whole course of our lives; since self is supposed to exist after that manner. But there is no impression constant and invariable. Pain and pleasure, grief and joy, passions and sensations succeed each other, and never all exist at the same time.... For my part, when I enter most intimately into what I call *myself*, I always stumble on some particular perception or other, of heat or cold, light or shade, love or hatred, pain or pleasure. I can never catch *myself* at any time without a perception, and never can observe anything but the perception.... I may venture to affirm of... mankind, that they are nothing but a bundle or collection of different perceptions, which succeed each other with an inconceivable rapidity, and are in perpetual flux and movement.[3]

According to Hume's conception there is literally *no such thing* as the self. The illusion that there is is partly grammatical and partly due to resemblances between the perceptions comprising the bundle. What is real are the perceptions themselves; but what is illusory is the persisting Cartesian ego whose perceptions we take them to be.

A third conception of the self derives from Kant and emerges in a somewhat modified form in Schopenhauer and Wittgenstein. Consciousness, Hume's "bundle of perceptions," possesses a unity that cannot be reduced to relations of resemblance among its constituents; but Descartes's error, according to Kant, consisted in confusing this unity of conscious experience with the experience of a unitary substance, a self or subject. We can have no *concept* of such an ego, for to us it is "nothing more than the feeling of an existence without the least concept... , only the representation of that to which all thinking stands in relation":[4] "We do not have, and cannot have, any knowledge whatsoever of any such subject. Consciousness is, indeed, that which alone makes all representations to be thoughts, and in it, therefore, as the transcendental subject, all our perceptions must be found; but beyond this logical meaning of the word 'I,' we have no knowledge of the subject in itself, which as substratum underlies this 'I,' as it does all thoughts."[5] Schopenhauer's modification was to reify this purely logical notion of the transcendental ego, yet to construe it not as a substantial thing in the world, but "as an indivisible point"[6] outside space and time, on whose existence the world of experience and representation rests. And it is this somewhat murky conception of the self that lies behind Wittgenstein's obscure remarks toward the end of the *Tractatus*:

> I am my world. (The microcosm.)
> There is no such thing as the subject that thinks or entertains ideas.
> If I wrote a book called *The World as I found it*, I should have to include a report on my body, and should have to say which parts were subordinate to my will, and which were not, etc., this being a

method of isolating the subject, or rather of showing that in an important sense there is no subject; for it alone could *not* be mentioned in that book.—

The subject does not belong to the world; rather, it is a limit of the world.

Where *in* the world is a metaphysical subject to be found?

You will say that this is exactly like the case of the eye and the visual field. But really you do *not* see the eye.

And nothing *in the visual field* allows you to infer that it is seen by an eye. . . .

The philosophical self is not the human being, not the human body, or the human soul, with which psychology deals, but rather the metaphysical subject, the limit of the world—not a part of it.[7]

I am not going to try to assess these three philosophical approaches to the notion of the self or subject. But I do think they provide useful devices for making sense of different poets' bodies of work, since the conception of the self that informs the work of a particular poet usually has stronger affinities with one among these three traditional views than with the others. The most familiar conception of the self is that of the Cartesian ego: it is this conception that, I think, grounds any poetry introspective to a significant extent and characterized by a distinctive sense of personality or voice. While there is usually a degree of alienation of the self from the world, that self is still seen as *part* of the world, a part to which the poet has a privileged means of introspective access, and a part whose experiences and nature the poetry ventures to depict (even though the expression may involve a variety of voices and personae—e.g., Berryman's Henry).

The conception of the self underlying Ashbery's poetry is, I believe, that of the transcendental or metaphysical subject; and I think this helps account for the radical difference between his poetry and that of most other poets for whom the self is a main theme, including ones who have managed to capture some of his characteristic tone and voice. I have already noted some of the reasons for this way of looking at his work: the extreme referential, temporal, and spatial dislocations and transitions in his poems that make it impossible to read them as an autobiographical record of the experiences of a time-bound, self-identical Cartesian ego; his subject's characteristic impulse to identify or produce an adequate representation of itself while simultaneously distancing itself from every such image, which all become "other" as soon as they become concrete or clear enough (and in this connection note David Kalstone's observation that "Alive in its present, and determined as a Jack-in-the-Box, that self pops up when any moment of poetic concision threatens to obliterate it;"[8]) and, most important, the fact that despite these tendencies we are aware, reading his poems, of an undeniable "feeling of an existence without the least concept [of it]"[9] (to use Kant's characterization of the transcendental subject), together with the impression that it is from the vantage point of this ineffable existence that his poetry monitors the details of the world, among which are his own personality:

> Each detail was startlingly clear, as though seen through a
>   magnifying glass,
> Or would have been to an ideal observer, namely yourself—
> For only you could watch yourself so patiently from afar
> The way God watches a sinner on the path to redemption,
> Sometimes disappearing into valleys, but always on the way.
>   [“The Bungalows,” *DD*, p. 72]

Of course Ashbery's is not the only poetry infused with a conception of the self different from the traditional Cartesian one. Frank O'Hara's is another. In the course of discussing O'Hara's poem "Music," Marjorie Perloff observes that

the pronoun "I" and its cognates appear ten times in the space of twenty-one lines. Yet, unlike the typical autobiographical poem with its circular structure (present-past-return to the present with renewed insight), "Music" does not explore the speaker's past so as to determine what has made him the person he is; it does not, for that matter, "confess" or "reveal" anything about his inner

psychic life. The role of the "I" is to respond rather than to confess.... As in Pasternak's *Safe Conduct,* one of O'Hara's favorite
books, the "I" fragments into the surfaces it contemplates. Hence
the poet can only tell us what he does... , how he *responds* to
external stimuli... , and what he *recalls.*... But he makes no
attempt to reflect upon the larger human condition, or to make
judgments upon his former self, as Robert Lowell does in the *Life
Studies* poems.... It is a matter of reifying a feeling rather than
remembering another person or a particular event; in so doing,
that feeling becomes part of the poet's present. [10]

This strongly recalls Hume's statement that "when I enter most
intimately into what I call *myself,* I always stumble on some
particular perception or other, of heat or cold, light or shade,
love or hatred, pain or pleasure. I can never catch *myself* at any
time without a perception, and never can observe anything but
the perception."[11] Many critics have remarked on the diversity
among the poets who constitute what used to be called "the
New York School"; and certainly in O'Hara and Ashbery the
differences in form, voice, and projected personality alone are
enormous. But I think the deeper distinction between them involves a difference between the views of the self their works
embody. Neither's poetry offers an autobiographical record of
the history of a Cartesian mind; but O'Hara's affinity is with
Hume's "no self" view, on which the very notion of a self is
delusory, corresponds to no reified perception or passion encountered in experience, and has to be dismantled:

> I could not change it into history
> and so remember it,
>   and I have lost what is always and everywhere
> present, the scene of my selves, the occasion of these ruses,
> which I myself and singly must now kill
>   and save the serpent in their midst. [12]

The vantage point of O'Hara's voice is always situated in real
time, in fact, at the moment of writing. But Ashbery's vantage
point is an atemporal one from which even the moment of actual

utterance seems remote (here compare Kalstone on Ashbery: "Tense will shift while the poem refers to itself as part of the past,"[13] with Perloff on O'Hara: "It is a matter of reifying a feeling . . . ; in so doing, that feeling becomes part of the poet's present."[14]) Ashbery's impulse is not so much to dismantle the various emblems with which the self might mistakenly try to identify as to try to see them, from the vantage point of the metaphysical subject, as what they really are, things among other things, and so to transcend them:

> So that now in order to avoid extinction it again became necessary to invoke the idea of oneness, only this time if possible on a higher plane, in order for the similarities in your various lives to cancel each other out and the differences to remain, but under the aegis of singleness, separateness, so that each difference might be taken as the type of all the others and yet remain intrinsically itself, unlike anything in the world. Which brings us to the scene in the little restaurant. You are still there, far above me like the polestar and enclosing me like the dome of the heavens; your singularity has become oneness, that is your various traits and distinguishing works have flattened out into a cloudlike protective covering whose irregularities are all functions of its uniformity, and which constitutes an arbitrary but definitive boundary line between the new informal, almost haphazard way of life that is to be mine permanently and the monolithic samenesses of the world that exists to be shut out. For it has been measured once and for all. It would be wrong to look back at it, and luckily we are so constructed that the urge to do so can never waken in us. We are both alive and free. ["The System," *TP*, pp. 101–2]

There is a curious and exhilarating sense of liberty in Ashbery's work, quite independent of his penchant for syntactic license (which occasionally serves to strain the more genuine sense of freedom his poems convey). I think it is significant, in this connection, that the idea of the transcendental or metaphysical subject was originally invoked by Kant in an effort to reconcile our awareness of that freedom we conceive ourselves as possessing with the fact that any merely psychological ego or personality must, as an object in the natural world, be constrained by the natural laws that govern this world. Writing recently of an artwork by Owen Morrel called *Asylum*, which he characterizes as a "private and transcendental experience,"[15] Ashbery quotes with evident sympathy the artist's own description of the piece: "If the room/cell becomes the confines of the light/energy of the mind, the open wall points to the future beyond the self—to no mind or one mind. *Asylum* becomes a gateway to a specific kind of freedom available to those who open the right door."[16]

In the last analysis the conception of the metaphysical subject merely serves to make palpable that "specific kind of freedom," that sense that "We are both alive and free," which is Ashbery's poetry's most distinctive characteristic, and the one that makes it so valuable.

4

The Shield of a Greeting:
The Function of Irony in
John Ashbery's Poetry

DAVID LEHMAN

John Ashbery readily confides that *The Vermont Notebook* was written in Massachusetts. This could hardly come as much of a surprise to one familiar with Ashbery's deadpan humor, playfulness, and wit; and by now, several years since *Self-Portrait in a Convex Mirror* won America's triple crown of book awards, anyone who reads poetry at all must be aware of Ashbery's lifelong courtship of a decidedly ornery muse, whose wish to defy augury is her most constant feature. Not that Ashbery aims to shock or outrage; after all, the reader as unsuspecting bourgeois is largely an anachronism; and at any rate Ashbery's flamboyance is of a quieter sort. Nevertheless, the indisputable fact that *The Vermont Notebook* has as little (or, in its guise as chronicle of holy absence, as much) to do with Massachusetts as with Vermont does warrant an explanation—just as even the most sophisticated student of prose poetry may yet find it noteworthy and at first perhaps mildly startling that a book of lengthy prose meditations should be entitled *Three Poems*, a banner that turns out upon inspection to be at once modest and grand, efficiently making its point about the suitability of the cool element of prose as a poetic medium. In both cases, the tension between title and text is meaningful beyond its ability to perplex, like a joke of silence. "I am not what I am," these titles whisper, reminding one of René Magritte's famous picture of a pipe, under which is written "ceci n'est pas une pipe."

This habit of upsetting our legitimate or impertinent expectations is suggestive of a predilection to advance, dialectically, by contraries, digressions, hesitations, abandonments. "We shall very soon have the pleasure of recording / A period of unanimous tergiversation in this respect," Ashbery writes in "The Bungalows" (*DD*, p. 71), forcing us to trace this unfamiliar word to its Latin root, *tergiversari*, "to turn the back"; the word has acquired the additional meanings of "evasion," "ambiguity," and "equivocation." All apply here. In his awareness of discrepancies, his strenuous attempt to take cognizance of different layers of consciousness and competing "realities," and above all in the intensity with which he records the various "tergiversations" of the act of writing, Ashbery seems to invest irony with a special importance, as "a kind of fence-sitting / Raised to the level of an esthetic ideal," to quote from "Soonest Mended" (*DD*, p. 18). But we must proceed cautiously here: irony in its narrow rhetorical sense—that is, saying the opposite of what one means or, in Ashbery's formulation, "Saying It to Keep It from Happening"—is broadened by the poet to such an extent that we are compelled to revise our received notions of what exactly irony is, consists of, means.

When I speak of Ashbery's irony, I do not mean the activity of balancing contradictory truths, at least not in the way the New Critics commended. Ashbery does not reconcile contradictions; rather, he presents them in a state of more-or-less peaceful coexistence, as though they were parallel lines that cannot be expected to meet in the finite realms we inhabit. And we may come to feel grateful that they cannot:

> The lies fall like flaxen threads from the skies
> All over America, and the fact that some of them are true of
> course
> Doesn't so much not matter as serve to justify
> The whole mad organizing force under the billows of correct
> delight.

> [*SP*, p. 20]

The maddeningly humorous elements of this passage contribute significantly to its effect: the use of the double negative, the jargon phrase "the fact that," the off-handed "of course," the unexpected adjectives ("mad organizing force," "correct delight"): all seem apposite for the oxymoronic "true lies." Ashbery's irony is never mere whimsy or humor; for all his alertness to the comic potential of the American vernacular, for all his affection for truths that seem funny when named or understood, it is not a simple laugh the poet is playing for. For Ashbery, even the most elaborate ironic gesture is scarcely an end in itself; it is directed at the aim of a redemptive enchantment, an ultimately affirming apprehension of "the real reality, / Beyond truer imaginings," in all its puzzling variousness and delightful disorder. Like the "frozen gesture of welcome" in an extended right hand, the many ironies in Ashbery's fire may thus be viewed as "conventions" to be used "For kindling. The sooner they are burnt up / The better for the roles we have to play" (*SP*, p. 82). Far from being gratuitous and merely clever affectations, as critics of the so-called New York School of poetry sometimes charge, these mechanisms of a reflexive irony—like the parallel development of a highly self-reflexive language—figure as an indispensable part of the most significant and attractive aesthetic strategy available to an American poet today.

Like Stevens, whom he resembles in other telling ways, Ashbery pursues a "supreme fiction," knowing it cannot be expected to lodge in a single utterance; it can only inform the notes toward one, those acts of investigation which can be renewed but not repeated. The search resembles a climb up a winding staircase that diminishes in size as it approaches the heavenly destination, although with Ashbery that point as well as the upper levels of the staircase are likely to have vanished in clouds that faithfully reappear after rains: height, even absolute height, is not particularly blessed; but movement is, even when the end and the beginning are one, or especially then. An

Ashbery poem exists in a flow of continuous movement, a continuous present, "each day digging the grave of tomorrow" (*DD*, p. 68) for only the present is here to stay. Consequently, there is a strong cognizance of genesis, as though every moment were the speaker's first, every utterance a "Dazed waking of the words with no memory of what happened before, / Waiting for the second click" (*DD*, p. 66); to begin, for Ashbery, is to register a pause marking the awareness of beginning, and all that it implies. The initial poems of Ashbery's books—"These Lacustrine Cities," "The Task," "As One Put Drunk into the Packet Boat," "Street Musicians"—wipe the slate clean of previous markings, establishing a condition of "absolute clearance"; these poems seem to veer self-consciously into the present, taking or announcing steps that are "forward" in the geography of time, not necessarily in the sense of "better" or "more mature," but always closer to the trap of "death's capacious claw" (*RM*, p. 21).

According to Valéry, poems are not completed but abandoned; in Ashbery's formulation, completion *is* abandonment, and pushing on requires casting off, with violence if necessary. Poetry is architecture of a sort,

> For it all builds up into something, meaningless or meaningful
> As architecture, because planned and then abandoned when
>   completed,
> To live afterwards, in sunlight and shadow, a certain amount
>   of years.
>
> [*DD*, p. 72]

In early career, Ashbery was especially fastidious in putting into practice that aspect of his antiprogrammatic program that calls for "the abandonment of such archaic forms as these" (*DD*, p. 76)—and any form becomes "archaic" once published. ("But today there is no point in looking to imaginative new methods / Since all of them are in constant use," *DD*, p. 53; "You can't say it that way any more," *HD*, p. 45). Frequent reversals of direction seemed essential, all explanations postponed to a mythical future time when "the purpose of the many stops and starts will be made clear" (*DD*, p. 30). If *Some Trees*, Ashbery's first book, reveals the hand of the virtuoso practitioner of rare and exotic forms, who would make new the sestina and canzone and pantoum and eclogue, all the while placing the planet of Wallace Stevens on his dinner plate, serving up multicolored metaphysical questionings to us, then his next book must be an exercise in the inchoate, the inarticulate, and finally the disintegrated consciousness, and sure enough *The Tennis Court Oath* is famous for its poems like "Europe" that make no sense at all yet "tease us out of thought." It is as if, at this point in Ashbery's career, when he was living in Paris and must have felt the exile from his native language far more keenly than the expatriation itself, what empowered his lines was a treatment of English as though it were a crazy foreign tongue; it is also as if, in order to expel the forces of silence, he must first let them destroy as many of his ranks as necessary to test his capacity to speak. It is a baptism by fire extinguisher:

> Everything is being blown away;
> A little horse trots up with a letter in its mouth, which is read
>   with eagerness
> As we gallop into the flame.
>
> [*TC*, p. 58]

Perhaps never before has originality been so highly valued as now, and it is a measure of Ashbery's poetic power that he has converted this pressure into something of a modus operandi, a means by which his writing, as though self-engendered, can realize its autonomy and comment on its past. Adhering to a policy of restless doing, turning his back to the lair of preexistent patterns (whether fashioned by himself or by others), Ashbery has devised and taken a series of exhilarating gambles. *The Ten-*

nis Court Oath—which may be described as a dark night, not of the soul, but of a soulless language—is the very embodiment of a risk, an unflinching stare into the abyss of meaninglessness and incoherence; the Ashbery of *Three Poems* countered with the rather different risk of a deliberately flat, prosaic diction. In an agnostic's universe, such risk-taking as Ashbery favors has its built-in attractions. "Most reckless things are beautiful in some way," Ashbery has remarked, "and recklessness is what makes experimental art beautiful, just as religions are beautiful because of the strong possibility that they are founded on nothing. We would all believe in God if we knew He existed, but would this be much fun?"[1] It is the wager, not the outcome of the wager, that matters, just as the process of arriving at a truth is—as an article of faith among contemporary artists—itself a central truth. The process has led Ashbery to conceive of his works as fresh responses to earlier responses. If the initial assumption was "There are no questions / There are many answers,"[2] it has since been refined into the realization that "the whole question of behavior in life has to be rethought each second," for "not a breath can be drawn nor a footstep taken without our being forced in some way to reassess the age-old problem of what we are to do here and how did we get here" (*TP*, p. 61). Whatever else the poems may be "about," they record their own process of becoming, with the confidence that such attentiveness "takes in the whole world, now, but lightly, / Still lightly, but with wide authority and tact" (*SP*, p. 1).

Charged with the impulse to be somehow all-inclusive, to take in the whole world of flux on a single city balcony, Ashbery's long poems—from "Europe" and "The Skaters" to "The System" and "Self-Portrait in a Convex Mirror"—propose a paradox of absence as a governing principle. "This leaving-out business," as Ashbery calls it in "The Skaters," places the burden of composition on strategic omission; the emphasis is on the "fundamental absences" displaced by "carniverous" lines that "devour their own nature" (*RM*, p. 39) in the same way that the impatient future erases the present, "And the past slips through your fingers, wishing you were there" (*SP*, p. 8). Time is the great, the cosmic ironist; with the clocks of our poems we can say "how it feels, not what it means" (*HD*, p. 29); we can exist

> only in the gap of today filling itself
> as emptiness is distributed
> in the idea of what time it is
> when that time is already past.
>
> [*SP*, p. 7]

The specific method of erasure differs from case to case. A literally "spaced out" poem like "Europe" comes instantly to mind as an example of "distributed emptiness"; with its use of collage and cut-up techniques, the poem may strike the reader as a literary counterpart to Rauschenberg's famous erasure of a de Kooning drawing. In the opening of "Soonest Mended," Ashbery's recognition of "fundamental absences" takes a rather different form:

> Barely tolerated, living on the margin
> In our technological society, we were always having to be
> rescued
> On the brink of destruction, like heroines in *Orlando Furioso*.
>
> [*DD*, p. 17]

Here the enjambment calls attention to the word "margins" and, by extension, to the whiteness into which the word trails off, the vacant lot in which we do our "living"; the very lining recapitulates the theme of "marginal" existence. On the other hand, the winding syntax and plethora of qualifying clauses in "The System" give an effect of self-erasure, the mind warning itself not to take any of its pronouncements as final, absolute, beyond revision; there can be no last word. At times, Ashbery's lines act like the rungs of a mysterious ladder—as soon as one is vacated it vanishes entirely, superseded, erased by the inevitable next step:

> One must bear in mind one thing.
> It isn't necessary to know what that thing is.
> All things are palpable, none are known.
>
> [*SP*, p. 22]

In the manner of musical composition, Ashbery's poetry communicates the syntax rather than the content of an argument or a story; meaning inheres between the words, not in them. (Ashbery seems to presuppose as a given the validity of Chomsky's contention that language is "structure dependent," that the meaning of any sentence resides somewhere below, or beyond, its semantic surface.) The poet is thereby permitted to write about everything and nothing at once, to welcome and negate the world simultaneously, to make of the reader an active participant who must fill in the gaps in order to complete the composition. Faithful to a dream logic of its own fashioning, the writing presents a multiplication of metaphors that—by seeming to disregard their ostensible referents or leaving these crucially undefined—illuminate the "deep grammar" of a reality that can never be realized by ordinary means of denotation. Consider in the following how the simile takes over; what it was meant to modify is, as it were, buried:

> And as the plant grows older it realizes it will never be a tree,
>
> Will probably always be haunted by a bee
> And cultivates stupid impressions
> So as not to become part of the dirt. The dirt
> Is mounting like a sea. And we say goodbye
>
> Shaking hands in front of the crashing of the waves.
>
> [*TC*, p. 26]

Notice how a single word ("cultivates") organizes an entire stanza, and how a figure of speech ("like a sea") compels the reality ("of the crashing of the waves") to come immediately into being, like a hunger capable of providing the food it calls for.

Significantly, "The New Spirit" opens with a statement that clarifies the paradox of inclusion-by-absence:

> I thought that if I could put it all down, that would be one way. And next the thought came to me that to leave all out would be another, and truer, way.
>
>   clean-washed sea
>   The flowers were.
>
> These are examples of leaving out. But, forget as we will, something soon comes to stand in their place. Not the truth, perhaps, but—yourself. It is you who made this, therefore you are true.
>
>   [*TP*, p. 3]

The subjective "I" passes through the editorial "we" to merge, and reverse roles, with the "you" who emerges in "their" place. This novel use of pronouns is but one way in which Ashbery's prose poetry follows logically from the procedures and strategies of his earlier work. But if, to cite another Ashberry title, there is "Plainness in Diversity," it is the discontinuity that meets the eyes first, and *Three Poems* may also be read as a reaction against certain tendencies in the earlier work, a growing out of them, as children outgrow their clothes and adults their friends. To a certain extent, Ashbery's decision to write poetry in prose was a formal choice mandated by the desire to do something new and different, to avoid falling into his own footsteps, to invite a "new spirit" to descend at the behest of a linguistic act of volition. Moreover, with its verbal hedonism and fustian use of clichés, the prose poetry of *Three Poems* signified a new expansiveness and openness to experience on the part of one who had previously established a reputation for his syntactical dislocations, his deployment of words and phrases isolated from their familiar contexts, as though the writer had operated, scalpel in hand, on an anesthetized body of language. If, as Delmore Schwartz has suggested, "the normal state of affairs occurs when poetry is continually digesting the prose of its time,"[3] *Three Poems* may be regarded as a brilliant effort to appropriate for poetry the humblest and most public forms of speech in current use and thus to redeem them. As such, the book appears to be an equal and opposite response to the fragmented, "pulverized" utterances of *The Tennis Court Oath*, a volume as revolutionary as its title suggests, which still arouses savage indignation in some quarters, even among the poet's partisans.

As I have implied from the outset, Ashbery's titles, like those of Stevens and Auden, command attention in their own right. There is seldom the same relation twice between title and text in Ashbery's poetry, or rather it seems that the relation is constantly fluctuating. A portrait of the author of *The Double Dream of Spring*, the "insatiable researcher of learned trivia" (p. 77), emerges from the titles alone of that work, as "Each new diversion adds its accurate touch to the ensemble" (p. 53). A number of the poems have simple, pastoral headings ("Summer," "Spring Day," "Evening in the Country," "Clouds," "The Bungalows"). The book itself takes its title from a de Chirico painting; the use of paintings, real or imaginary, as points of departure for poems that discover themselves by meditating on objets d'art, and thus displacing them, is a device Ashbery continues to exploit to advantage. The volume's keynote poem, "The Task," exemplifies his inclination to rehabilitate the titles of famous or recondite literary works—in this case, William Cowper's poem that began as a mock-heroic account of a sofa and ended as a meditation of epic proportions. "Variations, Calypso and Fugue on a Theme of Ella Wheeler Wilcox" demonstrates the fun Ashbery has with clichés and with bad poetry. "Sortes Vergilianae," a phrase Sidney drops in his *Apology for*

Poetry, "refers to the ancient practice of fortune-telling by choosing a passage from Vergil's poetry at random" (*DD,* p. 95). Against this concession to chance, we turn to the "French Poems," which Ashbery wrote in French, then translated into English, "with the idea of avoiding customary word-patterns and associations" (*DD,* p. 95). Then there is "Fragment," the longest and arguably the most ambitious poem in the book—the joke being that any poem is merely a fragment of some larger discourse, as any incident, regardless of its intensity and significance, is a mere fragment of one's life.

Ashbery chooses his titles in a novel manner—the title is assigned *before* the poem is written. The account he gives of his procedures is instructive:

> I really can't explain why I enjoy using preexistent titles like "Civilization and Its Discontents" except that I must have a sort of cuckoo instinct that makes me enjoy making my home in somebody else's nest. But for me the title of a poem is really much more than the word title conventionally suggests; it's also the subject of the poem, implicitly, and sometimes contrary to one's impressions otherwise of the text. That's probably something that I originally got from reading Stevens. The title almost amounts to the "given" for me; it indicates a space in which I will work. In addition to introducing the poem, it introduces me to the poem.
>
> Very often my poems diverge from the areas or concerns the title has announced, and I think it's possible in this way to add a further dimension to poetry. I mean, one can write a poem "To A Waterfowl" that has nothing to do with waterfowls, and the reader is obliged to consider the poem as somehow related to the subject indicated only in the title and not in the text itself.[4]

The variety of sources for Ashbery's titles bespeaks more than versatility; it testifies to the poet's ability to avail himself of any or all information—from comic books to *Märchenbilder,* from popular songs to *Paradise Lost*—as though to indicate that everything is relevant, if not necessarily wise or pleasing; it is all "intelligence" in the espionage sense. "Polyphony and polyto-

nality are privileges which I envy composers for having,"
Ashbery has said, referring to the presence of a choir of distinctive voices in his poetry—the voice of the prose rationalist and
skeptic, the voice of the romantic taxicab driver, the voice of the
dwarf, the voice of a tiresome old man telling us his life story,
the sociologist's voice, the voice of Daffy Duck aping the voice of
John Milton.

It would be useful to compare Ashbery's sense of the past as a
gift with Eliot's uncanny ability to spot the ideal epigraph in
plays by Marlowe and Shakespeare, as if the quoted lines
existed primarily as predictions of the present moment. Consider "Lost and Found and Lost Again," one of the many short
poems in *Houseboat Days*. The title is taken from "East Coker,"
part 5, where Eliot describes the practice and perils of poetic
composition. "Each venture," he says, "Is a new beginning, a
raid on the inarticulate / With shabby equipment always dete-
riorating / In the general mess of imprecision of feeling, / Undis-
ciplined squads of emotion." Writing is a futile act, but a com-
pulsory one—"the fight to recover what has been lost / And
found and lost again and again."[5] By appropriating this phrase
as the title of his poem, Ashbery alludes to these problems of
authorship, of wresting meaning from language. But the title is a
mere fragment of Eliot's poem, unacknowledged, sequestered
from its former surroundings, and therefore it is literally the
pre-text for a work that modulates mysteriously from the image
of "an object whose loss has begun to be felt / Though not yet
noticed" to a new raid on the inarticulate, bringing back "these
colors and this speech only" (*HD*, p. 36). If the poem serves as a
gloss on Eliot's lines, it is surely the most enigmatic one on
record, an exemplification rather than an interpretation, designed to make the reader forget its source before tracing it
down, before forgetting all over again (so that it too is "Lost and
Found and Lost Again").[6] Thus, where Eliot evokes the past to
dramatize the imaginative poverty of the historical present,
Ashbery's larcenies are accompanied by forgetfulness; where

Eliot's sense of tradition is applied as a corrective to the modern world, Ashbery's glad-handed "other tradition" furnishes him with so much raw material, no strings attached, nothing to acknowledge or be faithful to:

> And one is left sitting in the yard
> To try to write poetry
> Using what Wyatt and Surrey left around,
> Took up and put down again
> Like so much gorgeous raw material.
>
> [*SP*, p. 19]

Ashbery is evidently fond of "the other tradition." There is a poem by that title in *Houseboat Days;* the phrase also appears in a crucial passage in *Three Poems.* And indeed Ashbery seems committed to an alternative literary tradition, a tradition of eccentricity; he has advocated a revival of interest in such neglected authors of our recent past as Pierre Reverdy and Max Jacob, Henry Green, Raymond Roussel, Gertrude Stein, John Wheelwright, and the Australian hoax poet Ern Malley. It may be argued that every "school" of poetry, to the extent that it is a viable movement, with epigones and commentators, performs just this sort of critical service, in an attempt to alter and re-create the taste of its readership; this was one of Wordsworth's major intents and achievements in the preface to the *Lyrical Ballads.* It is in this sense that, for all its inadequacy, the term "New York School of poets" does have real value. For Ashbery, together with such confreres as Kenneth Koch and Frank O'Hara, has helped to make possible an influence without angst; they have opened up an avenue of access to works of a highly experimental and liberating nature, which we are urged to read or misread creatively—in them we may see "images that yet / Fresh images beget." But "the other tradition" is also to be understood in a second sense, as describing the pronounced "otherness" of Ashbery's own poetic enterprise, the way he focuses our attention on "unrelated happenings that form a kind of sequence of fantastic reflections," outside time yet obeying its rules, independent of "the world of accident" yet enacting its characteristic motion:

> It is this "other tradition" which we propose to explore. The facts of history have been too well rehearsed (I'm speaking needless to say not of written history but the oral kind that goes on in you without your having to do anything about it) to require further elucidation here. But the other, unrelated happenings that form a kind of sequence of fantastic reflections as they succeed each other at a pace and according to an inner necessity of their own—these, I say, have hardly ever been looked at from a vantage point other than the historian's and an arcane historian's at that. The living aspect of these obscure phenomena has never to my knowledge been examined from a point of view like the painter's: in the round, bathed in a sufficient flow of overhead light, with "all its imperfections on its head" and yet without prejudice of the exaggerations either of the anathematist or the eulogist: quietly, in short, and I hope succinctly. [*TP*, p. 56]

With the subsidiary interest of focusing attention on the neglected but important subject of titles, it is worth taking a closer look at the cover of *The Vermont Notebook* and how it modifies our judging of the pages it introduces. Ordinarily, what gives vitality to such "notebook" forms as the diary or journal is the methodical if fragmentary recording of the minutiae of everyday life, the attention paid to exact particulars of time and place. Naturally the thought is more valuable than where or when it was thought or with whom, but these are named often enough not only because they matter but because writers are charmed to keep an eye out for their future biographers. (In his more exuberant letters, Scott Fitzgerald went so far as to leave sufficient space for them to make marginal comments at their ease.) What then are we to make of *The Vermont Notebook* with its cheerful irrelevance, its long, seemingly inconsequential inventories, its random double takes of a land of chain stores and split-levels and thirty-two flavors? And, especially, how are we to regard the deliberate falsification of data in the title, the subversive change of name not to protect the innocent, for no one is guilty, nor to cloak an otherwise naked history, since there isn't any to speak of?

To be sure, there is a local tradition of humor of this sort. In the title poem of his collection *New Hampshire,* Frost qualifies his admiration for that state with a sly Yankee wit that prompts him to confess, in the final line of the poem, "At present I am living in Vermont." And in Stephen Vincent Benét's erstwhile high-school classic, the devil has by dint of the eloquence of Daniel Webster been banished from New Hampshire, a triumph completed by the nose-thumbing one-sentence paragraph that concludes the story: "I'm not talking about Massachusetts or Vermont."

But if there are precedents for Ashbery's sleight-of-hand, they seem somehow less profoundly whimsical (or whimsically profound). It is not with folksy interstate rivalry but with the geography of the mind that Ashbery is concerned, with jolting and thereby rescuing the names and places from their too-familiar positions on the worn and sloppily folded road maps long ago deposited in the glove compartments of our lives. By such a process, the Massachusetts of the world becomes on paper a fantasy of Vermont. This is a statement that may with equal veracity be taken either as an epistemological fact or as an aesthetic prerogative (or both). God speaks, and the word becomes deed, automatically and immediately; man speaks, and yesterday's actions turn into the distortions and ambiguities of today. Since the premier mental activity that is language cannot but transform what it was supposed only to describe—since true imitation, in the Aristotelian sense, is impossible—why not evade the challenge to subordinate word to world, accept the autonomous life of words as a given, and convert a metaphysical dilemma into a literary celebration? If the act of writing is an act of imposture, so be it. "If all the green of Spring was blue, and it is," Stevens wonders in "Connoisseur of Chaos," is there not a law to be based on "the immense disorder of truths"? In a similar spirit, Ashbery pays heed to that passage in *Either/Or* where Kierkegaard advises the aesthete to exalt the arbitrary and form icons out of the happily fortuitous. Thus it is a zodiac rearranged by chance that marks the serene close of "The Skaters":

> The constellations are rising
> In perfect order: Taurus, Leo, Gemini.
>
> [*RM*, p. 63]

With similar logic, "To a Waterfowl" is composed exclusively of lines culled from an anthology of great poems; the following couplet is half Spenser, half Stevens, ergo all Ashbery:

> Calm was the day, and through the trembling air
> Coffee and oranges in a sunny chair.[7]

Thus, too, the reader of "And You Know" is invited to the names of places rather than the places themselves, to travel

> not to a better land, perhaps,
> But to the England of the sonnets, Paris, Colombia,
>   and Switzerland,
> And all the places with names, that we wish to visit.
>
> [*ST*, pp. 57–58]

The trip looks good on paper, but the imagination can never be home free; it is checked by doubts, as snowstorms upset airplane schedules; it is besieged by nagging reminders of an outside reality that can never be wholly transcended or forgotten. Our metaphoric journeys must halt to accommodate metaphysical musings, though they call into question certain of our most cherished assumptions. Is motion itself an illusion, for example? Does the perception of change amount to a hardened case of wishful thinking? Is motion, paradoxically, a requisite for stasis?

The train is still sitting in the station.
You only dreamed it was in motion.

[*RM*, p. 61]

Now there is no question even of that, but only
Of holding on to the hard earth so as not to get thrown off.

[*DD*, p. 17]

One must move very fast in order to stay in the same place, as the
Red Queen said, the reason being that once you have decided
there is no alternative to remaining motionless you must still learn
to cope with the onrushing tide of time and all the confusing
phenomena it bears in its wake, some of which perfectly resemble
the unfinished but seemingly salvageable states of reality at
cross-purposes with itself that first caused you to grow restless, to
begin fidgeting with various impractical schemes that were in the
end, we have seen, finally reduced to zero. [*TP*, pp. 90–91]

An unremitting skepticism puts all in doubt, and it remains for
the genius of irony to cancel out the opposing natures of good
dreams and nightmares so that, in the consciousness of the survivor of the unpredictable vagaries of sleep, the wide-awake
world seems magical *because* quotidian and not in spite of this
condition:

The west wind grazes my cheek, the droplets come pattering
    down;
What matter now whether I wake or sleep?
The west wind grazes my cheek, the droplets come pattering
    down;
A vast design shows in the meadow's parched and trampled
    grasses.
Actually a game of "fox and geese" has been played there, but
    the real reality,
Beyond truer imaginings, is that it is a mystical design full of a
    certain significance,
Burning, sealing its way into my consciousness.

[*RM*, p. 54]

117

Like the game of "fox and geese" that denies the vast design only to be assimilated into it, the intrusion of an ironically self-deprecatory persona—the voice that interrupts a lyrical reverie to say "But no doubt you have understood / It all now and I am a fool" (*TC*, p. 26) or to ask, "Any more golfing hints, Charlie?" (*RM*, p. 58)—indicates a profound distrust of both the visionary moment and the grand utterance, a distrust that is ultimately and triumphantly absorbed by the "combination / Of tenderness, amusement and regret" (*SP*, p. 69) that it both undercuts and underscores. To the extent that his lines occur "as between invisible quotation marks,"[8] Ashbery's poetry denies his own consciousness, then reconstitutes it as a sort of Aeolian lute, played upon by continually changing winds. To the extent that all the voices are aspects of "the self that must sustain itself on speech" (in Wallace Stevens's phrase), Ashbery's poetry points toward a new mimesis, with consciousness itself as the model; we are offered "epistemological snapshots" (*HD*, p. 28) of a mind in motion, as though "A single implication could sway the whole universe on its stem" (*SP*, p. 26).

Three Poems, which Ashbery has called his own favorite among his works, is singular in this regard. In their matter, they resemble nothing more than Thomas Traherne's *Centuries of Meditation;* in their use of a convoluted, Jamesian syntax, they owe something perhaps to Auden's *The Sea and the Mirror*. But where Auden presents an oration by a stentorian Caliban, Ashbery gives us the prose poem as extended meditation, as the internal soliloquy of a sorely distracted Hamlet willing to put the verbal antics he is famous for at the service of a poignant indecisiveness. It is one thing for Traherne, writing in the seventeenth century, to apply his vigorous and altogether admirable prose style to the contemplation of the soul, its heavenly origins and earthly orbit; it is quite another thing for a contemporary American poet, and a radically innovative one at that, to chart the progress of the soul without any of the conveniences of religious belief, to construct out of the everyday world a heaven without the furniture of theology. The protean quality of prose diction enables the poet to capitalize on a tension between the language of philosophical abstraction and the pedestrian turn of phrase, with the result that the great and the humble intersect; prosaic existence is animated to the point where it can convey, not without humor, a spiritual reality:

> As a lost dog on the edge of a sidewalk timidly approaches first one passerby and then another, uncertain of what to ask for, taking a few embarrassed steps in one direction and then suddenly veering to another before being able to ascertain what reception his mute entreaty might have met with, lost, puzzled, ashamed, ready to slink back into his inner confusion at the first brush with the outside world, so your aspirations, my soul, on this busy thoroughfare that is the great highway of life. [*TP*, p. 91]

The analogy is surprising enough to begin with, but the incongruities are compounded as the sentence goes on. While "a lost dog" evokes inflated rhetoric ("to ascertain what reception his mute entreaty might have met with"), the soul and its aspirations collapse into the double cliché that ends the sentence. In the process, the "heroic" Homeric simile is burlesqued, subverted, and (thereby) renewed.

It is probably not too much of an exaggeration to say that no one ever gets anywhere in an Ashbery poem, though many are traveling; if Keats perennially froze his characters as they were the moment before the moment of fated action, destined always to be postponed but existing in a definite form as an aspiration, Ashbery's fictional *selves* and *others* seem sometimes jolted out of time altogether; they exist within "the segment of chance / In the circle of certainty":

> Sadness of the faces of children on the platform,
> Concern of the grownups for connections, for the chances
> Of getting a taxi, since these have no timetable.
> You can get one if you can find one though in principle
>
> You can always find one, but the segment of chance
> In the circle of certainty is what gives these leaning

Tower of Pisa figures their aspect of dogged
Impatience, banking forward into the wind.

[*HD*, pp. 24–25]

More often than not, the journeys these characters embark on are incomplete; they are interrupted before they get off the ground, delayed, postponed, resumed, then interrupted again, with an arbitrary *finis;* in a crucial way, they are unbegun, like a false dawn or the illusion of spring in February, to take examples from *Three Poems.* "Everything has a schedule, if you can find out what it is," Ashbery had written in *Some Trees* (p. 9), but it can only be ascertained after the fact, if at all, for it is according to an inscrutable law of coincidence that events unfold.[9] "Every invitation / To every stranger is met at the station," he writes in the recent "Unctuous Platitudes" (*HD*, p. 12), but they remain strangers to one another, to us, and to their own destinies; the observer is therefore at liberty to see them as in themselves they really are not, to cite Wilde's emancipatory revision of Arnold's famous formula. Merely to watch these passengers behind smudged train windows, to see their mouths move and not hear what they say, is an activity of the most august imagination, as Theseus tells us in Ashbery's play *The Heroes:*

> Let me tell you of an experience I had while I was on my way here. My train had stopped in the station directly opposite another. Through the glass I was able to watch a couple in the next train, a man and a woman who were having some sort of conversation. For fifteen minutes I watched them. I had no idea what their relation was. I could form no idea of their conversation. They might have been speaking words of love, or planning a murder, or quarreling about their in-laws. Yet just from watching them talk, even though I could hear nothing, I feel I know those people better than anyone in the world.[10]

The theme of travel, coupled with the ironic afterthought that true motion is an impossibility, recurs with a haunting frequency throughout Ashbery's career, so much so that the captivated reader is likely to suspect that fastidious study of all the "journeys" will reward him with the revelation of the figure in Ashbery's carpet, the vital clue to his enigma. And surely it is a casual procession of enigmatic truths that awaits scrutiny: the detour turns out to be the right road after all; it is only by divagations that we find true directions out; we cannot stop, yet we never arrive. Ashbery's poetry resists paraphrase so adamantly that again I yield to the temptation to let it speak for itself:

> There is no going back,
> For standing still means death, and life is moving on,
> Moving on towards death. But sometimes standing still is also
> life.
>
> [*DD*, p. 72]

> So the journey grew ever slower; the battlements of the city
> could now be discerned from afar
> But meanwhile the water was giving out and malaria had
> decimated their ranks and undermined their morale,
> You know the story, so that if turning back was unthinkable,
> so was victorious conquest of the great brazen gates.
>
> [*DD*, p. 76]

> It was not the time for digressions yet it made them inevitable, like a curtain at the end of an act. It brought you to a pass where turning back was unthinkable, and where further progress was possible only after it had been discussed at length, but which also outlawed discussion. Life became a pregnant silence, but it was understood that the silence was to lead nowhere [*TP*, pp. 62–63]

Or take the cheerful dummies who flock together in the ever-ever land of *A Nest of Ninnies,* the wonderful comic novel written collaboratively by Ashbery and James Schuyler. Although the locale of the novel constantly shifts, the characters cannot escape the rain that follows them everywhere, as a kind of geographical fixture, a hint that for all their traveling they have not really managed to leave. As in Henry Green's novels, the dead-pan rendering of dialogue with minimal narrative interference is used by the authors of *A Nest of Ninnies*—the title taken from a seventeenth-century "jestbook"—to let the characters define themselves; they do so with a charming innocence that makes their central concerns, faithfully and fondly reported, seem somehow beside the point, though it is difficult to say what the "point" might be. There are no climaxes, no conclusions, no "development," though plenty of "change." As John Koethe has observed, the landscape of the novel "while at times actually urban or international, remains confidently suburban throughout."[11] Or in the words of "Self-Portrait in a Convex Mirror," "all time / Reduces to no special time" (*SP*, p. 79).

In his quasi-narrative and "journey" poems, Ashbery activates an extraordinary array of stop-action devices, from what he calls "the 'it was all a dream' syndrome" to the Brechtian interruption, the curtain dropping only to lift again an instant later, reversing the roles of spectators and actors, never letting us forget that what we have been experiencing is spectacle, artifice, "the cold, syrupy flow / Of a pageant" (*SP*, p. 82). When Theseus penetrates to the heart of the maze, what does he encounter? "A stupid, unambitious piece of stage machinery" in lieu of the sought-after minotaur.[12] Ditto the "clouds pulled along on invisible ropes," in "The Wrong Kind of Insurance"; they too are "merely stage machinery"

> And the funny thing is it knows we know
> About it and still wants us to go on believing
> In what it so unskillfully imitates.
>
> [*HD*, p. 50]

In "The New Spirit," Ashbery had proposed the act of writing as a metaphor for the act of living, the text as a metaphor for the self-determination of one's destiny; metaphor itself was to be "no longer a figure of speech but an act" (*TP*, p. 51). But in "The Recital," which serves as the coda to *Three Poems*, the inevitable feeling of resignation prevails, with the realization that "no art, however gifted and well-intentioned, can supply what we were demanding of it: not only the figured representation of our days but the justification of them" (p. 113). Energized by an intense consciousness of itself, the poetry mediates between the conflicting falsehoods of life, on the one hand, and the "decoys" of the imagination on the other. Of the seventy-four lines of "The Instruction Manual," only the first six and the last six concern the narrator, but these are sufficient to establish a Chaucerian effect—to reveal that his charming story of lovers in Guadalajara is nothing more than an elaborated comic-book balloon containing the daydream of a man in an office who wishes he were not employed to write copy "on the uses of a new metal." The imaginative escape from the sedentary life is necessarily a round-trip arrangement. "What more is there to do, except stay? And that we cannot do" (*ST*, pp. 14–18).

The unbegun journey to the unattainable place is the explicit subject of both "And You Know" and "The Skaters." In the former, the romantic flight to "heavenly Naples, queen of the sea, where I shall be king and you will be queen," takes place, in the future tense, on the globe of an old schoolroom, on the "fond" teacher's desk. It is a trip that must be postponed until the realization sets in that the voyage is an impossible one— until, in other words, we are no longer children with a ready access to magical and enchanted lands. "It is too late to go to the places with the names (what were they, anyway? just names)." As the students leave "the humid classroom, into the forever," the poem switches its point of view: *we* suddenly turn into *they;* and "they" have abandoned "us," "left us with the things pinned on the bulletin board," emptied of their former significance. Such is "the erratic path of time" (*ST*, pp. 56–59). On a grander level, "The Skaters" similarly enlarges its focus to admit reality's ironic intrusion. The poem presents the quintessential poetic journey, the quest for a suitable desert isle somewhere between heaven and no place, as an epic metaphor for the false starts and unknown destinations of the embattled imagination, with its struggles for escape and transcendence. The anthem of departure is the familiar but no less spooky laugh, no less funny for its urgency and anxiety. No sooner is the island reached than the poet must cut the ground out from under himself and us; it has taken pages of delay, frustration, and indecision to arrive at this point, and still the poet feels obliged to remind us of how inaccessible the paradise of poetry will always be; how pedestrian are our visions:

> In reality of course the middle-class apartment I live in is
>   nothing like a desert island.
> Cozy and warm it is, with a good library and record collection.
> Yet I feel cut off from the life in the streets.
> Automobiles and trucks plow by, spattering me with filthy
>   slush.
> The man in the street turns his face away. Another
>   island-dweller, no doubt.
>
> [RM, p. 56]

In dealing with "reality at cross-purposes with itself," Ashbery says in "The System" (TP, p. 91), he is inevitably tempted "to resume the stoic pose, tinged with irony and self-mockery" (p. 83). Nowhere does the poet examine this impulse more thoroughly and openly than in the much-admired "Self-Portrait in a Convex Mirror." One does not do justice to this remarkable poem by saying it is a meditation on a painting by Parmigianino; it is so much more. Gazing at the painting, the poet comes virtually to inhabit its room, to make its quarters his own. Translated across the barriers of media and centuries, the portrait is reconstructed so that Ashbery's own image, modified by "the turning seasons and the thoughts / That peel off and fly away at breathless speeds" (SP, p. 71), stares out at us. Because a convex lens magnifies the size of foreground objects, what dominates the picture is the model's curved right hand,

> Bigger than the head, thrust at the viewer
> And swerving easily away, as though to protect
> What it advertises.
>
> [SP, p. 68]

The hand, which "holds no chalk," tells of the mixed feelings that characterize Ashbery's attitude toward the written word, an ambivalence occasioned by the need to keep in precarious balance the claims of the world and the demands of the self. The title poem of *Some Trees,* we are reminded, ends with the rhyme of "reticence" and "defense" (*ST*, p. 51). Yet it is a reticence that speaks urgently and eloquently: while it "protects," the hand also "advertises"; it is first "shield," then "greeting," and finally it is both in one, "the shield of a greeting" (*SP*, p. 82), an apotropaic gesture that signifies acceptance and acquiescence as much as resistance. The hand is not extended in self-defense; on the contrary, it is forever recording its struggle to move freely and easily out of its "globe," as if it were an unfinished sculpture desperate to escape from its enslavement to the rock that encases it:

> One would like to stick one's hand
> Out of the globe, but its dimension,
> Which carries it, will not allow it.
> No doubt it is this, not the reflex
> To hide something, which makes the hand loom large
> As it retreats slightly.
>
> [*SP*, p. 69]

The poem is a hall of mirrors—all objects reflect back this primal situation of hand and globe. If the hand repeats itself in daily life as "a frozen gesture of welcome," the spherical mirror translates into "a globe like ours, resting / On a pedestal of vaccuum, a ping-pong ball / Secure on its jet of water" (p. 70). (It is also a balloon, a crystal ball, a bubble-chamber, reptile's eggs, the wrong end of a telescope, and "the gibbous / Mirrored eye of an insect"; in a diabolical pun, Parmigianino's "chamber" is looked at through the "chamber" of a gun.) Entering the painting by a process of speculation—"From the Latin *speculum,* mirror," Ashbery explains—is an experience equivalent to Keats's union with the nightingale; in both there is the possibility of a momentary transcendence, the "waking dream" of a paradise that might have been. All our efforts to prolong the experience are in vain; we must vacate it "even as the public / Is pushing through the museum now so as to / Be out by closing time. You can't live there" (p. 79). Only during "our moment of attention"—only during the creative process—does the work of art afford the poet "exotic / Refuge within an exhausted world" (p. 82).

As Parmigianino's "serene" gesture is "neither embrace nor warning," but "holds something of both in pure / Affirmation that doesn't affirm anything" (p. 70), Ashbery's ironic gesturing permits him to celebrate "purely"—to celebrate as an intransitive verb—to affirm without approval, as it were. Ashbery might enjoy being told that he has the courage of his ambiguities. At home with an essential homelessness among ideologies and programs, adrift yet secure in the houseboat of his days, he has resisted the temptation to fill up vacancies with reassuring convictions. That, in the words of another Ashbery title, there is "No Way of Knowing"—that, as he writes in "The System," "the term ignorant is indeed perhaps an overstatement, implying as it does that something is known somewhere, whereas in reality we are not even sure of this"—is arguably not only a tolerable but an enviable condition, allowing for a transcendent "open-mindedness": "*that*, at least, we may be sure that we have—and are not in any danger, or so it seems, of freezing into the pious attitudes of those true spiritual bigots whose faces are turned toward eternity and who therefore can see nothing" (*TP*, pp. 74–75). What Ashbery calls "a tongue-and-cheek attitude" permits him to find a certain congeniality in situations of maximum uncertainty, as these lines from "Decoy" suggest:

> There is every reason to rejoice with those self-styled prophets
> of commercial disaster, those harbingers of gloom,
> Over the imminent lateness of the denouement that,
> advancing slowly, never arrives.
>
> [*DD*, p. 31]

The "Decoy" of the poem's title refers both to the mind and to the object of its contemplation, a world of disparate and seemingly unrelated phenomena, deceiving appearances, and devious locutions. While the married couple "Waking far apart on the bed" at the conclusion of the poem do much to illustrate the riddlelike premise with which the poem begins, they do not rob it of its essential mysteriousness and humor:

> We hold these truths to be self-evident:
> That ostracism, both political and moral, has
> Its place in the twentieth-century scheme of things.
>
> [*DD*, p. 31]

The poignant finale of the poem occurs as neither an indictment nor a defense, "without prejudice of the exaggerations either of the anathematist or the eulogist" (*TP*, p. 56). The lamented distance between husband and wife is a deliberately hedged bet, a crucial instance of ironic "open-mindedness":

> There was never any excuse for this and perhaps there need be none.

In the *perhaps* is the signature of John Ashbery.

5/

Ashbery's Dismantling of Bourgeois Discourse

KEITH COHEN

> Suppose that the intellectual's (or the writer's) historical function, today, is to maintain and to emphasize the *decomposition* of bourgeois consciousness. Then the image must retain all its precision; this means that we deliberately pretend to remain within this consciousness and that we will proceed to dismantle it, to weaken it, to break it down on the spot, as we would do with a lump of sugar by steeping it in water.
>
> Barthes, *Roland Barthes*, trans. Richard Howard

In the metaphysical soap opera that is John Ashbery's poetry, a critical scrutiny of language plays a major role. I will argue that Ashbery aims consistently at the glibness, deceitfulness, and vapidity of bourgeois discourse and in his poems subjects this discourse to a process of disintegration. What some may relegate in his early work to the area of language games and gratuitous surrealistic effects is an integral part of a very serious attack, through language, on basic assumptions, institutions, and modes of thought in contemporary America.

A political regime maintains power as much through controlling ideological production (the superstructure) as through controlling the means of material production (the infrastructure). Within the broad realm of superstructural—or simply cultural—activities, language plays a crucial role: it is one of the fundamental ways the individual subject's consciousness is formed, being the primary medium through which social interaction takes place. Without this indoctrinating process of subjective consciousness, it would be difficult, if not impossible, for a ruling class to maintain power.

In advanced capitalist societies, the sources of what the Frankfurt School critics call the "consciousness industry" are contained in their most undiluted form in the mass media— radio, television, movies, journalism, advertising, and "popular" entertainment generally. Such a high instance of group consciousness reflected in the mass media suggests the irrelevance of the traditional distinction between high and low culture—a distinction that, though perhaps valid through the early twentieth century, certainly does not apply to United States society since World War II. If political regimes have tended to maintain their power at the superstructural level mainly through high culture—early aristocracies through rigorously codified courtly poetry, later aristocracies through classical music and portrait painting—the modern-day bourgeois regimes of advanced Western societies, it seems, must seek to dominate the discourse of many media across the cultural spectrum. Nevertheless, in the cultural homogenization characteristic of our own society, certain popular areas of subject formation seem to be more flagrantly dominated by bourgeois ideology than others.

One such area is that of Hollywood cartoons. Careful scrutiny of that arm of American film production will demonstrate that, even more clearly than fiction films of the same period, these animation shorts that traditionally accompany features reflect in a quite transparent manner the leading social myths of the day. From Betty Boop to Superman, the major anxieties of American life come into prominence: the puritanical ethos spread thinly across the Prohibition era, the shameless utopian fantasies promulgated during the Depression years, the national inferiority complex and anguish of competition during World War II. According to John Ashbery's aesthetic, these pronouncements of the obvious, reflectors of what is already there, are integral parts of the cultural scene. For anyone growing up with frequent exposure to such productions, in fact, these pronouncements might seem to take on the weight of destiny ("Destiny guides the water-pilot, and it is destiny," *ST*, p. 9).

In "Daffy Duck in Hollywood" (*HD*, pp. 31–34), Ashbery seems to outline, among other things, just such a position against any strict division between "high" and "low" culture. More specifically, the poem seems to be a celebration of the way Hollywood manages to incorporate everything—from classical opera to pop music, foreign culture to American Gothic—and spew it back transformed within its narrow vision of things. I say "celebration" because, as we shall see, there is no clear denunciation of this process itself.

The first concatenation of the most diverse cultural artifacts appears after the first line of the poem. Somehow La Celestina's rendition of "something mellow from / *Amadigi di Gaula*" triggers an association with or draws into its aura the following:

> a mint-condition can
> Of Rumford's Baking Powder, a celluloid earring, Speedy
> Gonzales, the latest from Helen Topping Miller's fertile
> Escritoire, a sheaf of suggestive pix on greige, deckle-edged
> Stock.
>
> [*HD*, p. 31]

Note the way the enumeration of each item includes a word that is linguistically alien to that object's "proper place" in the cultural spectrum. "Mint condition" is generally applied to extremely rare, old objects—hardly the case with Rumford's baking powder. "Celluloid earring" bears its own internal incompatibility at the level of the signified: as with a plastic corsage or fake pearls, we generally regard any earring as not genuine unless it is made from a rare or semiprecious material. (*Movies* are made of celluloid.) The writing of Helen Topping Miller, presumably a minor poet or writer of not particularly high caliber, is sardonically referred to as coming from a "fertile / Escritoire"; here a foreign word is used to construct a purpose-fully hackneyed metaphor for creative fecundity. "Suggestive pix" is obscure: pornographic pictures come to mind; but in any case the slang of "pix" strikes a sharp dissonance with the delicate, refined connotation of "greige, deckle-edged / Stock." The humor here is that, in looking at pornography, one rarely examines the quality of the paper. It is the model, the original one is after.

In the same manner, Ashbery seems to be suggesting in the poem, Hollywood's celluloid has the power of reducing everything it can record to the same level of mediocrity. In other words, the nondifferentiating medium tends to result in a nondifferentiated subject. This superficiality and lack of strict specificity are reflected in these lines that seem to be a description of a Hollywood landscape:

> You meet
> Enough vague people on this emerald traffic-island—no,
> Not people, comings and goings, more: mutterings,
> splatterings,
> The bizarrely but effectively equipped infantries of
> happy-go-nutty
> Vegetal jacqueries, plumed, pointed at the little
> White cardboard castle over the mill run.
>
> [*HD*, pp. 31–32]

Most important is the way Ashbery's language reflects the gigantic disproportions among Hollywood's cultural objects by constantly shifting, zooming up to the heights of the stilted and parachuting down to the fracas of slang.

> I scarce dare approach me mug's attenuated
> Reflection in yon hubcap, so jaundiced, so *déconfit*
> Are its lineaments.
>
> [*HD*, p. 31]

This is an example of the radical modulation taking place between the elevated, or the phony elevated ("I scarce dare"), and the dialectic ("me mug's"). The platitudes of popular music are recorded here ("'Up / The lazy river, how happy we could be?'"), as well as cartoon characters ("Walt, Blossom, and little / Skeezix"), who waddle among references to the Princesse de Clèves, Lethe, and Tophet. And these mixed enumerations, like the one at the beginning of the poem, titillate as much by their phonic misalignment as by their denotative irreconcilability.

After pointing out all that is potentially mystifying in the visions Hollywood offers us—its knack for producing identification, its powers of "fabulation," the speaker of the poem then does a take-off on that master manipulator of identification processes, Milton's Satan:

> While I
> Abroad through all the coasts of dark destruction seek
> Deliverance for us all, think in that language: its
> Grammar, though tortured, offers pavilions
> At each new parting of the ways.
>
> [*HD*, p. 33]

Here we arrive at what might best be called the nonnegative valuation of the spectacle Ashbery has been describing. The greatness of Hollywood is that, even at the moment you realize you are being conned, you succumb to the artificial glory, romp amid the discordant array of cultural objects, feel uplifted by the phony appeal of the archaic or exotic effects.

Toward the end of the poem, Ashbery will elaborate slightly: "why not / Accept it as it pleases to reveal itself?" (p. 34). And later: "Not what we see but how we see it matters." The transforming power of the movies, in other words, resides not in what they reveal to us but in how they prod us to see. Viewed in the right way, the most mediocre of B movies presents a compelling vision of things. And, if any validating data were necessary to corroborate such a conclusion, we could simply take a look at the pervasiveness of nostalgia for the grand Hollywood period of the thirties and forties. In retrospect especially, it seems, these productions take on an unexpected charm and depth.

In "Daffy Duck in Hollywood," then, cultural homogenization is reflected in the hodgepodge of discourses, the mixing of
distinct levels of language. But since the movies as subject matter turn out to be, for all their mystifying powers, lovable trin-
kets on America's commercialized landscape, it is necessary to
go beyond Ashbery's sensitivity to the simple slipperiness of
language. After all, it will be difficult to maintain that Ashbery is
launching an ideological critique through language without further specifying the methods and objects of attack.

Before going further I should add that the position I am adopting here represents a rather loose adaptation of a line promulgated by the French critics associated with *Tel Quel*. It may for
that reason not be irrelevant that Ashbery was friends with the
editors of that journal—Marcelin Pleynet, among others—
during the ten years he spent in Paris. Roughly, the *Tel Quel*
critics begin by maintaining that a poet's calling into question
the mutely accepted dogma of a ruling regime through language
differs sharply from a poet's manifest political position or social
attitude, as distilled from his or her work. The latter amounts to
nothing more than what Marxists call *Tendenzliteratur*, literature
that exhibits a certain political line, and the disengagement of
this message from the work can be accomplished by the most
vulgar thematic methodology. The poet who attacks through
language, on the other hand, uses the medium of the craft itself,
with its built-in rules and ready-made attitudes, at once to pin
down and to dissect the habits of a particular ideology.[1]

The object of attack in Ashbery's case is, at the most general
level, bourgeois discourse. Now the earmarks of bourgeois discourse are not themselves a complete mystery. It would be a
mistake, in other words, to further mystify matters by claiming
that the dominant discursive habits of bourgeois culture are so
insidious as to defy the critic's identification. Roland Barthes
has, in fact, cataloged the earmarks of bourgeois discourse as it
infects Balzac's prose.[2] Not surprisingly, these traits have not
changed much since Balzac's time and are not difficult to see

transposed into another national language like our own. Among those that seem clearly to apply to Ashbery's critique are the utility of referential orientation, structural continuity, and closure of form. Such characteristics can be found in perhaps their rawest form in a poem such as "Decoy" (*DD*, pp. 31–32).

The title of the poem suggests from the outset some deception or, more specifically, a process by which we will be unwittingly lured into a trap. The first of these traps is the one that starts the poem off: "We hold these truths to be self-evident." To begin a poem with a famous phrase from the Declaration of Independence suggests all by itself a playful attitude toward both language and American values. Ashbery more than any contemporary poet is acutely sensitive to the words and cadences that ring in our ears. His opening line is just such a phrase. We might go further by saying that this phrase does not even signify on a primary level. It is so well known that it is at first meaningless and only serves to signify, at a second level, the document it comes from and the patriotic or "democratic" values we might vaguely associate with it. Like Eliot's "Here we go round the prickly pear," it conveys nothing but connotation.

The lines that follow present a series of "truths" that are, of course, by no means "self-evident"—in fact not moral or ethical truths at all, but rather statements of social reality.

> That ostracism, both political and moral, has
> Its place in the twentieth-century scheme of things;
> That urban chaos is the problem we have been seeing into and
>   seeing into,
> For the factory, deadpanned by its very existence into a
> Descending code of values, has moved right across the road
>   from total financial upheaval
> And caught regression head-on.
>
> [*DD*, p. 31]

Rather than presenting mankind's "inalienable rights," Ashbery's declaration lists conditions that preclude equality and individual freedom. Working against the possible expectation,

raised by the first line, of a rejoicing over the continuity of democratic institutions, Ashbery makes an indictment of the forms
of social injustice these institutions have spawned. Ostracism,
urban blight, dehumanizing and life-endangering factory conditions are phenomena we witness or read about every day. They
chart the discrepancy that has formed, according to what
Ashbery terms a "descending code of values," between the original intent behind these founding documents and the everyday
reality that amounts to a parody of such intentions.

While the opening line is a well-known refrain of patriotic
nostalgia, phrases such as "seeing into" aim at contemporary
double-talk. Such a phrase is typical of the bureaucratic rhetoric
that seeks to cover its tracks and obscure its motives. Politicians
are forever "seeing into" those important matters that concern
voters. Yet, as we know from experience, "seeing into and seeing into" some more can often indicate the opposite: closing
your eyes, refusing to investigate, even covering up if necessary.

Laying blame with the corporate executives and their
bureaucratic and managerial lackeys, "The men who sit down to
their vast desks on Monday to begin planning the week's notations," Ashbery suggests that "those harbingers of gloom" who
are usually mocked as they chant about doomsday on street
corners have somehow given expression to the underlying feeling of the times. The level of sarcasm is difficult to gauge when
he says, "There is every reason to rejoice with those self-styled
prophets of commercial disaster." On the one hand, since conditions are so poor for the majority of people, we may as well
welcome the prospect of the end of the world. On the other
hand, the phrase "There is every reason" once again has the
ring of the politician's lingo, suggesting that this attitude, too, is
fraught with a certain calculation.

The tone of the poem as a whole raises complex issues. It
seems to adopt the calm self-righteousness that the poem
thematically seeks to impugn. The cloak of "seeing into" is dec-
orated with phrases associated with bureaucracy and gov-

ernmental double-talk: "scheme of things," "keeping the door open" (in the figurative sense), "on the average," "to sum up."

Linked to the slipperiness of this dominant tone is a slight shift beginning after the first long stanza. Directing his attention away from the material conditions of our socially chaotic world, Ashbery takes up a more pressing theme, but one intimately related to the first. Far more devastating than the physical conditions of our modern existence are the psychological conditions, the patterns of thought induced by the physical environment. Just as the men at the vast desks begin their calculations aimed at reaping the highest profits, so we all go on a profit-oriented expedition into our memory reservoirs:

> Seeking in occasions new sources of memories, for memory is profit
> Until the day it spreads out all its accumulation, delta-like, on the plain
> For that day no good can come of remembering, and the anomalies cancel each other out.
>
> [*DD*, pp. 31-32]

Underlying these ominous lines is the implicit comparison between the capitalist's financial investments and our everyday libidinal investments, staked largely in the past. Profit margins are thus measured by the number and density of one's memories, as though by remembering one eluded the present. This process is referred to as "pyramiding memoires," for, just as in high finance, the profits from one action are used to invest further in other actions. The point is that we are not merely the victims of men in gray flannel suits. We come to think the way they act, to conduct our personal lives the way they conduct their businesses. The key difference is that while their investments pay off in the future, ours are simply burrowings into the past.

In these terms, the title of the poem becomes more meaningful. Not only are the patriotic "truths" we memorize in grade school a trap to contain possible questioning, to channel our public feelings in a certain direction; the very modes of subjectivity encouraged in bourgeois society, the hallowing of sacred memories and the venerating of the past, are also decoys, means of channeling our private feelings in predictable directions and, worst of all, of turning those feelings against our own best interest.

"Decoy" is thus perhaps the clearest statement, both in theme and in tone, of the prison-house that bourgeois discourse condemns us to. The poem contains two diametrically opposed moments that may conveniently stand for what is at stake in the position I am ascribing to Ashbery. The first is the image of the executives "who sit down to their vast desks on Monday to begin planning the week's notations, jotting memoranda that take / Invisible form in the air." These executives or bureaucrats epitomize the function of language in bourgeois society: to be clearly referential, hence useful. The "notations" themselves do not designate a writing activity, but rather are objects of "planning." In other words, they are not so much signs of expression or communication as verbiage that leads directly to action, like so many commands. The temporal all-inclusiveness of this activity suggests the second earmark of bourgeois discourse: its structural continuity. These notations function not to open up the range of possibilities but rather to structure the week by a carefully planned process of *enchaînement*. Again, the writing itself is of no importance, only the "invisible form in the air" that it takes. All is aimed, finally, at containment: both of action and of time. Hence, a closure of form. While the memoranda may appear to be "turning and wheeling aimlessly," in fact they are "on the average directed by discernible motives." Nothing is open to chance. The objects of the notations (human subjects, presumably) are given no area within which to participate in decision-making, since the motives are unilateral, clear.

The other, opposite moment comes in the last, brief stanza:

> There was never any excuse for this and perhaps there need be none,

For kicking out into the morning, on the wide bed,
Waking far apart on the bed, the two of them:
Husband and wife
Man and wife.

[DD, p. 32]

These lines seem in no way related to the rest of the poem, except perhaps in tone. As such, the final lines exemplify an opening out of the form that bourgeois discourse seeks to avoid. Furthermore this stanza, unlike what precedes, is marked by the referentially obscure pronouns characteristic of much of Ashbery's work. Does "this" in the first line refer to what precedes or what follows? Any interpretation of the ending depends on this point; yet it cannot be decided definitively. And, finally, this fragment not only opens up the form of the poem, it also introduces a principle of *non*continuity. Who are these people? Why are they shown just waking up? Why don't they go to work? Both closure and continuity are made impossible.

In summary, then, the very grandiosity of the opening line, which alone implies referentiality (both to its "meaning" *and* to the document it comes from), continuity, and closure, is subverted by the final lines of the poem. While one might expect a married couple to exemplify those rights suppressed after the opening line—"life, love, and the pursuit of happiness"—this man and wife are oddly apart, uncannily antecedent to something that fails to follow. And it is precisely this nonsequitur, ingeniously built into the poem's form and meaning, that we experience once we begin to investigate the great decoys of American discourse.

Ashbery's critique of bourgeois discourse heads in many different directions. As we have seen, the voice of the poems seems at one moment to be mouthing the discourse, at the next moment to be mocking it. It is often difficult to pinpoint where the rote repetition stops and the critical distancing begins. In a sense, these two activities are seldom distinguished. It is like trying to differentiate between a well-molded graduate from Harvard Business School and a comedian's impression of a businessman. Indeed, throughout Ashbery's work there is this problem of determining exactly where the ax falls.

Building on the analysis of "Decoy," I will try to outline the way Ashbery's poetry moves toward a full-scale attack on bourgeois discourse. There is at the beginning of the process a subtle institution of a collective persona who speaks this bourgeois discourse with false consciousness—that is, with the intent of speaking truths while actually viewing the world just the way Marx described, as through a photographic lens, upside down. Different layers of speech can subsequently be discerned in this persona, so that the false consciousness is undercut by the poet. This process is not so much what is generally referred to as irony as it is a structuring of parallel stances that cannot be reconciled. Finally, within this framework of mouthing and mocking, or giving and taking away, various raw elements of bourgeois discourse, like so many revolving targets at a shooting gallery, are appropriated directly, without mediation, from the institutionalized speakers of that discourse. This inhabiting a bourgeois persona only to subvert his genuineness reaches its culmination, it seems to me, in *Three Poems.*

Let me make one theoretical digression before proceeding further. I have been speaking of Ashbery's attribution of a collective voice to monopoly capitalism in a way that might suggest, in spite of whatever subversion it operates subsequently, that the poet is thereby providing a quasi-mythic origin for that voice and hence *naturalizing* it in the way Barthes claims ideology always functions—that is, to make existing social and economic relations *appear* natural, inevitable.[3] But what is of prime importance here is the *mouthing*, not the *speaking*. In other words, Ashbery always makes us aware that there is a subject speaking, collective or individual, who has been mystified *already* by the naturalization processes of bourgeois ideology. It would be wrong, therefore, to conceive of Ashbery's poetry as giving a voice to monopoly capitalism. It is not monopoly capitalism speaking, but rather, as in ventriloquism, a subject using that voice, speaking that ideology, as though it were his own.

In *Three Poems* Ashbery makes very subtle use of pronoun shifters to establish both a collective voice and the effect of a splintering subject. "The System" (*TP*, pp. 53–106), his most accomplished long poem in this respect, is dominated in parts by a "we." Though the poem begins as a somber testimonial about "the one who had wandered alone past so many happenings and events" (p. 53), it is not long before the speaker of the poem is extending the process of soul-searching to some undefined group: "Yet so blind are we to the true nature of reality at any given moment" (p. 59). Since the general spiritual malaise, which seems to the speaker to be of such gravity that the reader is immediately put on guard, spreads its ramifications across every sector of material and psychological life, it is quite possible that this "we" stands for all of humanity.

Another pronominal designation enters in: "you." The sections dominated by the second person give a definite impression of some introspective subject speaking to himself as "you." The "I" does not disappear, however. Instead, there seems to be a positing of two distinct aspects of the self—something like the reasoning and feeling parts, or the reflective and the emotive (the more hackneyed, the more likely to describe this aspect of the poem). In other words, the "I" speaks knowingly, if hypothetically, to the "you," who becomes the self in action, not furnished with a voice to reply. "Let us assume for the sake of argument that the blizzard I spoke of earlier has occurred, shattering the frail décor of your happiness like a straw house" (pp. 82–83).

It is within the intricacies of this split I-you that the speaker reveals himself most candidly. On the one hand, we learn that the central subject has been given to adopting many masks: "The temptation here is to resume the stoic pose, tinged with irony and self-mockery, of times before" (p. 83). The final, vaguely delineated scene—in a poem notable for its lack of any clear visual imagery—is a movie of "your" life. "If you could see a movie of yourself you would realize that this is true. Movies show us ourselves as we had not yet learned to recognize us" (p. 102). In this context the "I" reveals himself most fully: "And it is here that I am quite ready to admit that I am alone, that the film I have been watching all this time may be only a mirror, with all the characters including that of the old aunt played by me in different disguises" (p. 105). A tone of final reckoning dominates here, suggesting that the greatest benefit of such introspective meditation is precisely in the subject's ability to split up into separate voices, to deploy separate vantage points, so that one part of the subject can look down paternalistically at another part, and so that the self can innocently melt into the vast body of humanity at large. Once the transparently reflected image of the mirror is returned to, "I am alone" again, and anguish sets in.

The meditation undertaken in "The System" is difficult to characterize. In the most general terms, it seems to be about the very notion of "life's progress." The speaker, whose tone of voice at the beginning sets up resonances with that of Dante in the *Inferno,* is at pains to locate the present anguish of the subject and to trace the origins of this present. I say this because of the preponderance of images relating to life's stream, the road of life, and so forth. But the more important themes of the poem, those that engage us in the complex shifting of voice, are concerned with ethical and moral questions largely associated with Protestantism.

In a humorous passage where he distinguishes between two kinds of happiness, the "frontal" and the "latent," Ashbery takes up one of the central questions of orthodox Protestantism, and of most other faiths as well: predestination. In describing the second kind of happiness the poet depicts a group who bestow their trust in a certain set of beliefs in the hope that these doctrines will bring them everlasting happiness. As he makes painfully clear, however, no such state is forthcoming, and deep down the people themselves suspect as much.

> Hence the air of joyful resignation, the beatific upturned eyelids, the paralyzed stance of these castaways of the eternal voyage, who imagine they have reached the promised land when in reality the ship is sinking under them. The great fright has turned their gaze upward, to the stars, to the heavens; they see nothing of the disarray around them, their ears are closed to the cries of their fellow passengers; they can think only of themselves when all the time they believe that they are thinking of nothing but God. Yet in their innermost minds they know too that all is not well; that if it were there would not be this rigidity, with the eye and the mind focused on a nonexistent center, a fixed point, when the common sense of even an idiot would be enough to make him realize that nothing has stopped, that we and everything around us are moving forward continually, and that we are being modified constantly by the speed at which we travel and the regions through which we pass, so that merely to think of ourselves as having arrived at some final resting place is a contradiction of fundamental logic, since even the dullest of us knows enough to realize that he is ignorant of everything, including the basic issue of whether we are in fact moving at all or whether the concept of motion is something that can even be spoken of in connection with such ignorant beings as we, for whom the term ignorant is indeed perhaps an overstatement, implying as it does that something is known somewhere, whereas in reality we are not even sure of this: we in fact cannot aver with any degree of certainty that we *are* ignorant. [*TP*, p. 74]

This profound skepticism, clearly verging on agnosticism, is not unusual in itself. It would be, perhaps, if the poem did not also contain moments when that other voice, the mystified one, will speak as though fatalism were a condition of life. " 'Whatever was, is, and must be'—these words occur again to you now, though in a different register, transposed from a major into a minor key" (p. 93). The effect in this case of Ashbery's dual-pitched voice is to show us both aspects of fatalism, the pitifully mystified voice of a subject seeking some divinely inspired *vouloir-dire*, and a demystified voice putting down such beliefs

with a skepticism that seems almost too easy. Yet what underlies this dual perspective is Ashbery's fundamental concern
about the whole process of mystification, be it religious or political. Even after we realize the deceptive nature of putting "our
faith in some superior power," we are left with our personal
histories. "Yes, in the long run there is something to be said for
these shiftless days, each distilling its drop of poison until the
cup is full; there is something to be said for them because there
is no escaping them" (pp. 66–67). What are the ultimate effects,
in other words, Ashbery seems to be asking, of doctrines and
ideologies that hold sway over our minds for long periods?

What is even more ominous in the poet's ruminations is the
question, never directly broached, What if these beliefs return,
as with the words "Whatever was, is, and must be," and thrust
their meanings on us by mere rhetorical force? In this respect we
begin to glimpse the deeper significance of the advertising jin-
gles, the platitudes, the clichés that seep into our discourse, into
our consciousness. Under the innocent veil of an infectious tune
or rhythm lie the claws of a message.

The force of mainstream dogma, like that of Protestantism,
and like that of its next of kin, the ideology of the bourgeoisie,[4]
can therefore be most devastatingly undercut by breaking the
continuity of its rhetoric. Hence the absolute necessity of a doubly focalized speaking subject in "The System." The mystified
mouthing of dogma must be shown to be dislocated and cut
short by another speaking. The shackles of past indoctrination
can be loosed only by breaking the spell cast by its verbalization
ringing in our ears. And only when we finally snap out of it,
presumably, can we head toward "the pragmatic and kinetic
future" that ends the poem.

Perhaps Ashbery's most powerful way of subverting bourgeois
discourse is to obfuscate anything resembling a natural system
of referentiality. What is amazing in "The System"—a title that
refers to the deceptive patness of this discourse and the tight-
ness of its closure, as when one speaks of a gangster's "system"

—is that, taken phrase by phrase, no other contemporary poem would seem so humdrum, so vapid. Each sentence seems another fatuous building block of a tiresome, transparent metaphysical argument. But the structure does not hold. The argument never manages to surface. It is in the strange, convoluted organization of these feathery building blocks that Ashbery, in the most magnificent instance of what he has called "the leaving out business,"[5] takes away from the discourse its ability to describe, denote, designate—in short, to refer at all.

Most characteristic of this process is a descending scale of metaphors, linked by the consciously stilted grammatical structure of "as though." Traditionally, "as though," like any comparison, is intended to clarify what is being expressed by presenting it in new terms, typically with the aid of a striking image. But in this case the opposite occurs. Partly because the image that follows is not clearly linked to what precedes, and partly because the string of comparisons has no clear common denominator or common inner relation, the reader is prevented from grasping the point of the comparison.

> Thus, in a half-baked kind of way, this cosmic welter of attractions was coming to stand for the real thing, which has to be colorless and featureless if it is to be the true reflection of the primeval energy from which it issued forth, once a salient force capable of assuming the shape of any of the great impulses struggling to accomplish the universal task, but now bogged down in a single aspect of these to the detriment of the others, which begin to dwindle, jejeune, etiolated, as though not really essential, as though someone had devised them for the mere pleasure of complicating the already complicated texture of the byways and torments through which we have to stray, plagued by thorns, chased by wild beasts, as though it were not commonly known from the beginning that not one of these tendrils of the tree of humanity could be bruised without endangering the whole vast waving mass; that that gorgeous, motley organism would tumble or die out unless each particle of its well-being were conserved as preciously as the idea of the whole. [*TP*, p. 58]

The central slippage here occurs around the notion of "organism," used, it seems, metonymically to characterize all of humanity. Note that the confusion might be metalinguistically ascribed to the speaker's vague use of "tree of humanity" and his inability to extend this metaphor in a consistent manner. The confusion begins when certain "aspects" of the "great impulses struggling to accomplish the universal task"—which themselves are not familiar terms from what precedes—are vegetabalized by the words "dwindle, jejeune, etiolated." At this point the "universal task," a stand-in for "the real thing," turns into what appears to be "a thorny path" (a cliché only imminent in the text) so as to lead us to the "tree of humanity." Our way becomes bromidically characterized as overgrown, full of "thorns" and "wild beasts." Suddenly it seems that we do not exist as part of this tree but rather pursue the tree, branch by branch. There is simply no way of connecting "not one of these tendrils" to what precedes other than by taking "tendrils" as a metaphor for "the byways and torments through which we have to stray."

I would conclude by asserting that what I have tried to identify as key processes of subverting bourgeois discourse in "The System" is simply a large-scale version, brought off in greater detail, of what occurs in many of Ashbery's poems. As early as a poem like "Idaho" (*TC*, pp. 91–94), Ashbery is experimenting with cliché-ridden discourses. In that poem he aims more particularly at novelistic discourse. The poem is built between two blocks, at the beginning and end, of parodies of pop-romance fiction, whose diegetic kernels are first sex, then suicide. What is important, though, is that the kernels are nothing more than that. They are not given the chance to develop, to unfold, to become plotted. Instead, fragmentary lines blistering with excessive punctuation marks intervene. In this explosion of cut-up phrases, the placid narrator of the prose has either disappeared or developed hiccups complicated by amnesia. The clearly referential, "well-made" action of bourgeois narrative is not allowed to continue. Something else happens, and, whatever it all means, it is clear that the operation of discontinuity it performs is at the level of the poem's apparatus itself—language.

A similar attitude toward language and its potential as vehicle for critique of the ideology it ordinarily reflects can be detected in other poems, such as "Album Leaf" (*ST*, p. 26) and "Variations, Calypso and Fugue on a Theme of Ella Wheeler Wilcox" (*DD*, pp. 24–29). In all these pieces, language is manipulated in such a way that continuity, utility, and closure are foregone, yielding to structured dysfunctioning.

Another important aspect of the splintered speaking voice is its connection with the contemporary notion of the "disintegrated subject" as propounded by psychoanalytic and social theory. Relying to a great extent, as described above, on a carefully controlled misuse of key shifters, Ashbery's vacillating voice is clearly not homogeneous, not unified, and is by no means integrated. The whole burden of "The System" is that a certain ideological mystification must by definition prevent integration.

Ashbery's multiple subject is one more means of creating his special brand of nonrepresentation. Without the postulation of a definite, anthropomorphic subject lurking behind the speaking voice, as in Pound's "persona," the degree of representation suggested by the words is constantly in flux. If we can never be sure where one voice or fragmented subject stops and another picks up, then any figuration at all ascribed to the poem is suspect. As with so many other ways artists have of manipulating the apparatus of their craft, this procedure ends up throwing into question some of the mutely accepted expectations and standards regarding poetry.

One of the most obvious of these is the tendency to define poetry in contrast to prose. Ashbery's *Three Poems* clearly gives the lie to such a definition, if it were really necessary. He seems to discover in the open yet solid contours of amply paragraphed prose the best vehicle for his shifting voice. It is as though the tradition of prose narrative provided the most recalcitrant version of the omniscient, inflexible voice, hence also the structure against which Ashbery's splintering process could have the greatest impact.

As with *The Cabinet of Dr. Caligari,* where we discover only at the end how totally crazed the old man narrating is, as with *The Murder of Roger Ackroyd,* where the narrator turns out to be the murderer, as with *The Turn of the Screw,* where the governess may have hallucinated any number of the strange appearances she claims to have witnessed, so with Ashbery's splintered speaker. He becomes not simply the nonintegrated subject, but the subversively canny schizophrenic. As we have seen in "The System," the truth lies in neither the mystified nor the demystified voice, but rather in the alternation, the interstices, the gaps between the two. And the society into which this subject cannot become integrated no more wants to tolerate him than he wishes to feel a part of the whole. For the society in question cannot deal with a speaking voice that will not mouth its ideology fully, without incision or deletion.

Thus Ashbery offers a twofold solution to the problem of appropriated language within a socioeconomic regime that relies crucially on language manipulation. First, he reappropriates that language in its crassest forms. Nothing, it seems, evades his scrutiny: movies, cartoons, advertising, the jargons of government and bureaucracy. These snippets of bourgeois discourse, so easily mouthed by the unsuspecting subject who thus plays into the heavily ideological process of character formation within the regime, are included only to be truncated, cut short; their power as touchstones of bourgeois ideology is thus completely undermined. They become part of what I have called Ashbery's structured dysfunctioning of bourgeois discourse. Their fragmented state presents a vision, albeit purely verbal, of the smashing of dominant ideology.

On the level of manifest content, I should add, the bourgeois regime never surfaces as such. Ashbery maintains the oblique view, despairing implicitly of the bourgeoisie by putting its discourse through the distorting echo chamber of his own idiolect. His position recalls in this regard a description he once gave of Frank O'Hara's poetry, which "does not attack the establishment. It merely ignores its right to exist."[6]

Second, Ashbery does not leave the speaking subject, mouthing bourgeois canons, in a state of total mystification. The discourse of the subject is divided up and multiplied. The condition of the subject in contemporary America, in other words, is one in which he or she cannot help but echo the resounding slogans of the bourgeoisie, but in which moments of critical scrutiny, comic debunking, and conscious self-demystification are possible. On the surface such a condition resembles schizophrenia. Such a model is resorted to not for prescriptive purposes, however, but simply as a more intense version of the splintered babbling that refuses ideological domination. The schizophrenic speaks for us as we might speak only in dreams.

Ashbery launches a frontal attack on the fundamental props of bourgeois discourse—continuity, utility, and closure—at the same time rejecting out of hand any notion of the homogeneous, integrated subject. It is as though speaking, along with all the subjacent processes that it implies—consciousness, the unconscious, contradictory feelings—were not possible in the monolithic manner often ascribed to it by contemporary sociology and linguistics. What may have appeared, moreover, in the early work as mere poetic effects intended to "épater le bourgeois," in the tradition of Dada and surrealism, turns out to be a far more carefully calculated projectile aimed at the nerve center of bourgeois automatism, the speaking voice.

To speak is to lie, or at least to be untrue in some subtle way. Writing, says the poet to himself, might be a way of putting together the necessarily splintered tones of discourse in a truer way. "I thought that if I could put it all down, that would be one way," he says at the beginning of "The New Spirit." Yet as *Three Poems* develops it becomes clear that the person speaking, the "I," is himself composed of many subsidiary subjects, one of which is a "recording angel," the "scriptor" posited by structuralist poetics. As Ashbery demonstrates at the end of "The System," the very notion of scribe, or copier, is often misconstrued in the writing process, because even in copying the data of everyday life there is invention. There is, among other things, deletion and fantasized addition. And so one is led to suspect that the scriptor, like a diffident attendant who has remained mute throughout the comedy, could present the whole picture and have the last word.

Now it seems as though that angel had begun to dominate the whole story: he who was supposed only to copy it all down has joined forces with the misshapen, misfit pieces that were never meant to go into it but at best to stay on the sidelines so as to point up how everything else belonged together, and the resulting mountain of data threatens us; one can almost hear the beginning of the lyric crash in which everything will be lost and pulverized, changed back into atoms ready to resume new combinations and shapes again, new wilder tendencies, as foreign to what we have carefully put in and kept out as a new chart of elements or another planet—unimaginable, in a word. [*TP*, p. 104]

6/

The Lonesomeness of Words: A Revaluation of *The Tennis Court Oath*

FRED MORAMARCO

The Tennis Court Oath remains, even after all these years, the most enigmatic of Ashbery's books, puzzling and outraging serious critics of his work as much as it did early reviewers.[1] The disjointedness of its language, its adaptation of collage techniques to literary forms, the abstract expressionist esthetic that informs its literary method, have combined to make the work impervious to more traditional forms of literary criticism, and admirers of the book are likened to connoisseurs of chaos rather than of poetry. I have elsewhere examined the influence and adaptation of painterly modes in Ashbery's work (in the September 1976 *Journal of Modern Literature*); here I would like to focus more particularly on the exclusively literary dimensions of Ashbery's early work and attempt to show that even what appear to be among the most opaque poems in the book yield to close reading and careful analysis.

Reading through the critical commentary on this volume, however, one wonders just what about this book so offends and enrages otherwise level-headed people. In Harold Bloom's enthusiastic and supportive overview of Ashbery's work, for example, *The Tennis Court Oath* is viewed as an appalling, grotesque mistake that detracts from Ashbery's overall achievement. Bloom describes the book as an "outrageously disjunctive volume" and a "fearful disaster." He writes that a "great mass of egregious disjunctiveness is accumulated to very little effect" and asks "how Ashbery could collapse into such a bog by just six years after *Some Trees,* and then touch a true great-ness in *The Double Dream of Spring* and *Three Poems?"* One must regretfully conclude, reading the whole of Bloom's essay, that the reason he regards this book so dimly is that it does not neatly fit into his reductionist scheme of "revisionary ratios," for he notes that *The Tennis Court Oath* "attempted too massive a swerve away from the ruminative continuities of Stevens and Whitman."² It *is* difficult to discuss *The Tennis Court Oath* in terms of "swerves," "kenosis," "daemonization," "clinamen," or any of the other terms in Bloom's lexicon, but it is not difficult to engage and respond to the book on its own terms. And those terms have to do with observing the poems as evoking or con-structing a reality generated solely by language itself.

The evocative power of language has absorbed Ashbery throughout his poetic career and is reflected in his literary en-thusiasms as well as in his own poetry. In 1962, the year *The Tennis Court Oath* was published, Ashbery also published an essay in *Art News Annual* called "Re-establishing Raymond Roussel," which was part of his then ongoing project to write a study of Roussel's work. Roussel is still only slightly known in this country, although now that most of his work has been trans-lated into English he has developed a small cult following. Roussel's poems, plays, and novels, written between 1897 and 1933, are surrealistic precursors of Robbe-Grillet and the French "new novelists" of the 1960s. Their basic mode is precise, in-credibly detailed description for its own sake. Roussel's plots, as Ashbery points out in the *Art News* essay, are merely pretexts for description.

What is most striking about Roussel's descriptions is that they do not attempt to describe an actual physical reality, but rather manufacture an exotic, surrealistic, fantastic reality in a totally matter-of-fact way through the generative potential of language itself. Ashbery writes:

> Sometimes he would take a phrase containing two words, each of
> which had a double meaning, and use the least likely meanings as

the basis of a story. Thus the phrase, *maison à espagnolettes* ("house with window latches") served as the basis for an episode in *Impressions d'Afrique* about a house (a royal family or house) descended from a pair of Spanish twin girls. [*Art News Annual* 1962, p. 104]

This technique is described more fully in a posthumous essay by Roussel entitled *Comment j'ai écrit certains de mes livres*, recently translated into English by Trevor Winkfield and published by Sun Books as *How I Wrote Certain of My Books* (1975).

Roussel's technique is worth examining closely in relation to Ashbery's early work, especially *The Tennis Court Oath*, because that work was written while he was deeply immersed in Roussel's life and writing, which surely stimulated the innovations recorded in that volume.[3] Roussel's essay begins by explaining that the creation of his work involved a "very special method" and suggests that other writers may be able to develop it further, hence he feels a "duty" to reveal it. Roussel continues:

> I chose two almost identical words (reminiscent of metagrams). For example, *billard* [billiard table] and *pillard* [plunderer]. To these I added similar words capable of two different meanings, thus obtaining two almost identical phrases. In the case of *billard* and *pillard* the two phrases I obtained were:
>   1. *Les lettres du blanc sur les bandes du vieux billard . . .*
>   [The white letters on the cushions of the old billiard table . . .]
>   2. *Les lettres du blanc sur les bandes du vieux pillard . . .*
>   [The white man's letters on the hordes of the old plunderer. . .]
> In the first, "lettres" was taken in the sense of lettering, "blanc" in the sense of a cube of chalk, and "bandes" as in cushions.
> In the second, "lettres" was taken in the sense of missives, "blanc" as in white man, and "bandes" as in hordes.
> The two phrases found, it was a case of writing a story which could begin with the first and end with the second. [*How I Wrote Certain of My Books*, p. 3]

We can see that by merely changing a single letter in the final word of the passage quoted, Roussel has altered the meaning of all the words that precede it. After citing many further examples of these pairs of matched words and phrases that occur throughout *Impression of Africa*, Roussel concludes by noting that "this method is, in short, related to rhyme. In both cases there is unforseen creation due to phonic combinations. It is essentially a poetic method" (ibid., p. 11).

Ashbery's method in *The Tennis Court Oath* is much closer to free association than is Roussel's, but he is clearly enchanted by the generative power of language, its ability to evoke a palpable sense of things, and the way the onward linguistic motion of a poem affects previous and future utterances in it. His "rhymed pairs" within poems are often the same word appearing in a slightly different context and evoking an altered world. Consider, for example, the first stanza of a poem called "A Life Drama":

> Yellow curtains
> Are in fashion
> Murk plectrum
> Fatigue and smoke of nights
> And recording of piano in factory.
> Of the hedge
> The woods
> Stained by water running over
> Factory is near
> Workers near the warmth of their nights
> And plectrum. Factory
> Of cigar. The helium burned
> All but the man. And the
> Child. The heart. Moron.
> Headed slum
> Woods coming back
> The sand
> Lips   hips   The sand poured away over
> The slum and the fountain
> Man and child
> Cigar and palace
> Sand and hips
> The factory and the palace. Like we

> Vote. The man and the rose.
> The man is coming back—take the rose.
>
> [*TC*, p. 39]

The poem begins with a color and object, and a comment on the social importance of that particular combination. You "see" something; it means something in a context. "Yellow curtains / Are in fashion" is not a "poetic statement" but a social observation. The two rather exotic words in the next line, however, alter the context of that observation by introducing mood, shape, and certainly sound. "Murk plectrum" is a chord sounded in the poem, ominous and portentous. The fashionable yellow curtains are irreversibly altered. And the gloomy plucking of that chord evokes an altogether different world in lines four and five—a world framed by the "linked" words "fatigue" and "factory" and containing the visual and aural imagery of smoke and music. We glimpse this world only slightly, as if observing it from afar, and the three lines that follow provide a kind of natural though fragmentary perspective—hedge, woods, and water consecutively "foregrounding" the initial imagery.

At this point in the poem, the diction introduced in the first eight lines begins to recur, with different associative possibilities. The lines

> Factory is near
> Workers near the warmth of their nights
> And plectrum. Factory
> Of cigar.

are variations on the initial verbal picture in the poem. We move in closer, as if looking at a blown-up detail from a painting. The word "factory," which has recurred three times to this point in the poem, is shown to have romantic potential in the first usage ("recording of piano in factory"), is rather neutrally evoked the second time merely to provide perspective ("Factory is near"), and is mundanely associated the third time, though the phrase "Factory / Of cigar" has exotic overtones not present in the clichéd usage "cigar factory." The line "Workers near the warmth of their nights" is a deliberate echo of "Fatigue and smoke of nights" but suggests coziness and community rather than exhaustion and industrialization. "Plectrum" sounds the chord again, and our piano factory becomes a "Factory / Of cigar."

Associations proceed: "cigar" (probably through association of shape with a dirigible) leads to helium, and the phrase "The helium burned" can stand alone as a sort of explosion in the midst of the stanza, or it may be connected with the following line—"The helium burned / All but the man," leaving a human presence in the midst of the fragmented imagery we have been surveying. We move into the human world: "the / Child. The heart. Moron." It does not take us where we expect to go. From the child and the heart we move not to feeling and emotional sensitivity, as might be expected, but to mindlessness—a vacuous devastated presence: "Moron / Headed slum." There is what appears as a reconsideration here:

> Woods coming back
> The sand
> Lips   hips   The sand poured way over
> The slum and the fountain

We have linguistic association through rhyme (lips hips), repetition (the woods again), echoes of previous lines with variation ("The sand poured over" echoes the earlier "Stained by water running over"), and pairs of words related in both likely and unlikely combinations:

> The slum and the fountain
> Man and child
> Cigar and palace
> Sand and hips
> The factory and the palace.

155

The final linking of standardization and splendor evokes the poles of human experience, the ordinary and the extraordinary, the mundane and the remote. The human presence is recalled again to conclude the stanza, "coming back" as the woods came back earlier, and paired with natural beauty:

> The man and the rose.
> The man is coming back—take the rose.

This process of linking, pairing, repetition, echoes—associative generation of a poetic world—continues throughout the poem. The "key" words have already occurred: plectrum, nights, piano, factory, woods, water, cigar, man, palace, rose. Like end words in a sestina—a form Ashbery is especially fond of—they recur continuously altered throughout the poem. It should be noticed that apart from "plectrum" they are extremely ordinary words with little connotative value. Brought together, however, they create a surrealistic world, the landscape of dream and nightmare. In the second stanza we find:

> The child and the rose and the cigar are there at the edge of the
>   fountain
> "The bath of the mountains" in a way.
> The factory to be screwed onto palace
> The workers—happy.

and

> The piano is seldom mute
> The plectrum on the lawn vanishes
>   . . . . .
> Walking at twilight by the path that leads to the factory
> The floor a pool. When the cigar
> Explodes.

This process has clear affinities with collage techniques, or Burroughslike verbal cut-ups, but its surest source is Raymond

Roussel, and the "Life Drama" of the poem is a Rousselian drama of words made entities, of description that seems to lead to thematic "meaning" but never quite arrives.

Ashbery's poetry in *The Tennis Court Oath* is an art of thwarted expectations—of words leading to but never reaching climactic insight. And yet there are, built into all this verbal architecture, passages that seem to soar outward from the purely verbal worlds of the poems themselves toward some ineffable perception—a perception necessarily limited by the words that describe it, as any perception one hopes to convey to others must be—which rings absolutely true and transcends the "wordplay" it is encased in. One such passage occurs in the middle of a poem called "How Much Longer Will I Be Able to Inhabit The Divine Sepulcher . . . ."

> And as the plant grew older it realizes it will never be a tree,
>
> Will probably always be haunted by a bee
> And cultivates stupid impressions
> So as not to become part of the dirt. The dirt
> Is mounting like a sea. And we say goodbye
>
> Shaking hands in front of the crashing of the waves
> That give our words lonesomeness, and make these flabby
> hands seem ours—
> Hands that are always writing things
> On mirrors for people to see later—
>
> [TC, p. 26]

One could analyze this passage in terms of poetic devices: linked interior and end rhymes like "tree" "be" "bee" "sea" "seem" "See"; subtle double meanings in words like "cultivates" "mounting" and "shaking"; implied comparisons between human and vegetal existence (trees "cultivating" impressions); clever metaphor and simile (dirt mounting like a sea)—but the lingering impression is the ineffability of the human contact with cosmic immensity: "Shaking hands in front of the crashing of the waves / That give our words lonesomeness." Those shaking hands suggest both camaraderie—our mortality links us all—and the fear and trembling that result from the confrontation with immensity of time and space.

What I have been trying to suggest is that despite all the innovations and avant-garde qualities in *The Tennis Court Oath*, many of the poems in the volume may be examined and responded to in a rather traditional literary fashion. The poem, "Our Youth" (*TC*, p. 41), for example, begins with a straightforward metaphor and a rhetorical question: "Of bricks... Who built it?" Youth, as the "foundation" of life, is likened to bricks, and the "construction" metaphor is extended into the question that follows. The metaphor is purposely "mixed" in the latter part of the line "Of bricks... Who built it? Like some crazy balloon" to evoke the paradoxical quality of our youth, at once the foundation for the remainder of our lives and as ephemeral as a deflated balloon. The stanza continues:

> When love leans on us
> Its nights... The velvety pavement sticks to our feet.
> The dead puppies turn us back on love.

Youth is evoked nostalgically in the first two lines here, love personified, its nights, perhaps of sexual initiation, leading us to two surrealistic images that contrast something lovely with something ugly. A "velvety pavement" is lovely, but because it sticks to our feet" one would like to get rid of it. The same juxtaposition occurs in the final line, with the values reversed: dead puppies "recall" love. What I see in the initial stanza of the poem are the contradictions of youth recalled from a distance. It is the formative stage of our life; it made us what we are, and yet we outgrow it, transcend it. It is memories—love, nights, dead puppies—the first impinging of traumatic events on our consciousness, that systematically slip into the subconscious to emerge in dreams—or nightmares—as velvety pavement clinging to our feet, as dead puppies "turning us back on love."

The second stanza elaborates on these evocations. The words "brick" and "crazy" recur with the same contradictory suggestiveness: solidity and ephemerality, the foundation for the present and the lost world of fresh emotional response.

> Where we are. Sometimes
> The brick arches led to a room like a bubble, that broke when
>   you entered it
> And sometimes to a fallen leaf.
> We got crazy with emotion, showing how much we knew.

The "brick" "bubble" association "rhymes" with the "brick" "balloon" association in the first stanza, and the cliché, "We got crazy with emotion" ironically counters the latter part of the line (also a cliché) "showing how much we knew." On the other hand, the fresh, emotional response to life, associated with youth, is imagistically likened to a lost world—a broken bubble, a fallen leaf.

The next two stanzas are focused upon the "discoveries" of youth (the word "discovers" or "discovering" occurs three times in the eight lines), and how each discovery, mundane or exotic, alters our sensibilities. They follow hard upon one another and culminate in the "discovery" of death, the ultimate disillusionment of wonder, and the spondee that concludes the fourth stanza, "déad hánd," drops into the poem like a heavy weight, bringing the romance of youth, and the music of the poem itself, to a full stop:

> The Arabs took us. We knew
> The dead horses. We were discovering coffee,
> How it is to be drunk hot, with bare feet
> In Canada. And the immortal music of Chopin
>
> Which we had been discovering for several months
> Since we were fourteen years old. And coffee grounds,
> And the wonder of hands, and the wonder of the day
> When the child discovers her first dead hand.

At this point in the poem, the echoes of Eliot should be apparent. The evocation of youth from the perspective of age or maturity has indeed a "dying fall" beneath the "immortal music of Chopin," and we are witnessing a life being measured out in coffee grounds, if not spoons. And surely the final two lines here allude to the famous lines in "The Love Song of J. Alfred Prufrock" which come to us from Ecclesiastes and Hesiod via Eliot:

> There will be time to murder and create,
> And time for all the works and days of hands
> That lift and drop a question on your plate.

The "dead hand" does indeed drop several questions into the poem, and these occupy the whole of the fifth stanza, which is also Eliotic in its nervous staccato rhythms that recall the confused and tense monologue of the aristocratic woman ("My nerves are bad tonight. Yes, bad. Stay with me / Speak to me. Why do you never speak? Speak. / What are you thinking of? What thinking? What? / I never know what you are thinking. Think") in the "Game of Chess" section of *The Waste Land*. And as in Eliot's passage, the questions here are answered in the succeeding lines by the flat statement of a sobering and disillusioning reality:

> Do you know it? Hasn't she
> Observed you too? Haven't you been observed to her?
> My, haven't the flowers been? Is the evil
> In't? What window? What did you say there?
>
> Heh? Eh? Our youth is dead.
> From the minute we discover it with eyes closed
> Advancing into mountain light.
> Ouch... You will never have that young boy.

The poem proceeds with a Wordsworthian evocation of the child as father of the man, but in modernist-Freudian guise, the image of the "dead" child merging with the image of the dead father in a flickering montage of the subconscious in dreams. There is a confusion of personal identity here, a mingling of life and death, boy and man, decay and permanence, a return from dream vision to trivial observation ("I see / That my clothes are dry") and concluding with a flat statement of an extraordinary occurrence:

> That boy with the monocle
> Could have been your father
> He is passing by, No, that other one,
> Upstairs. He is the one who wanted to see you.
>
> He is dead. Green and yellow handkerchiefs cover him.
> Perhaps he will never rot, I see
> That my clothes are dry. I will go.
> The naked girl crosses the street.

The simple statement "He is dead" should serve to remind us of the continuing presence of death in this poem about "our youth," in much the same way that the continuing references to time in Dylan Thomas's "Fern Hill" (a poem also evoking youth) culminate in the lines "Time held me green and dying / Though I sang in my chains like the sea." In Ashbery's poem we have had to this point "dead puppies," "dead horses," a "dead hand," and the two unequivocal statements "Our youth is dead" and "He is dead." The "Green and yellow handker-chiefs" covering the corpse in the last stanza I quoted may disguise the presence of death (like the "children green and golden" in Thomas's poem), but they are as unreal as a magician's illusion. The horny feet will protrude.

The penultimate stanza is an "explosion" of color, shape, image—youth viewed through the kaleidoscope of age—and the final paradoxical lines of the stanza reinforce the earlier realization that "Our youth is dead. / From the minute we discover it":

> Blue hampers ... Explosions,
> Ice ... The ridiculous
> Vases of porphyry. All that our youth
> Can't use, that it was created for.

The poem concludes with an evocation of age as the unavoidable destiny of all youth, and a return to reality from dream vision. Once again, Prufrockian images linger behind Ashbery's allusions—"the smoke that rises from the pipes / Of lonely men in shirt-sleeves, leaning out of windows?" of "The Love Song" recalls the "old people" and the faces "filled with smoke" of Ashbery's poem, and the escape "Down the cloud ladder" in Ashbery's poem reminds us of the "human voices" that "wake us" at the end of Eliot's poem and transform the mermaids' singing into the din and clamor of the real world. The excursion into "Our Youth" has been an excursion into romantic potential, wonder, delight, emotional purity. We emerge from it as we emerge from a dream, confronting the reality of our own mortality:

> It's true we have not avoided our destiny
> By weeding out the old people.
> Our faces have filled with smoke. We escape
> Down the cloud ladder, but the problem has not been solved.

The "problem" of aging, death, human mortality has indeed not been solved as we return "down the cloud ladder" from the invigorating world of an imaginative reality created by language itself to the exigencies of our pulsing selves.

Speaking of Roussel, Ashbery writes: "It is true that there is hidden in Roussel something so strong, so ominous and so pregnant with the darkness of the 'infinite spaces' that frightened Pascal, that one feels the need for some sort of protective equipment when one reads him" (*Art News Annual*, p. 91). The same immense strength is evident in Ashbery's own poetry, and for both Roussel and Ashbery wordplay and linguistic invention are the foundation for philosophical speculation that takes us to the very brink of our being—the "lonesomeness of words" leading us to a precipice that forces us to cling to the words themselves as a repository for the only "meaning" we can know.

7/

Vision in the Form of a Task:
The Double Dream of Spring

CHARLES BERGER

By now John Ashbery has become a firm pattern in the contemporary mind and ear. We know the feel of his poems, the
figures they cut, although we may be less certain about what
they mean. This circumstance is partly due, I think, to a reluc-
tance on the part of even his greatest admirers to read Ashbery
as they would, say, Stevens. He is so radical and experimental a
voice that one wishes to suspend the normal procedures of interpretation in his presence. After a while, however, the interpretive faculty cries out for its own assuagement and we yield to
that impulse. We then respond to Ashbery with our full in-
tellect, having first been convinced through the ear that the
quest for meaning will be rewarded.

Our contemporaries come to us poem by poem, volume by
volume, as a series of shocks. This sequence is a great blessing,
for we are free to deal with each poem on its own terms and not
as preparation for what comes next. Yet as the oeuvre builds we
can hardly ignore its internal coherence. We need to be alive
both to the individual poem and to the poet's larger shaping
will: that impulse to give his career a form, an emblematic outline. And, especially with poets of our moment, we cannot fail
to see how intensely self-allusive the career often becomes.
James Merrill is a case in point. With Ashbery the poems (and
prose pieces) come tumbling out at us, at least four rich volumes
in the last decade. A future Collected Poems (depressing
thought!) very likely will erode the boundaries between volumes
altogether and simply render the poems chronologically. Such

an edition would certainly help readers discern the relations between poems, but at the cost of losing a sense of where the crossings came, those moments in which the poet's meta-will stood out most clearly.

No volume of Ashbery's is more crucially transitional than *The Double Dream of Spring* (1970). There are some poems in *Rivers and Mountains* (1966) that could have found a place in the later book: "These Lacustrine Cities" and "A Blessing in Disguise," to name two. But *The Double Dream of Spring* as a whole inaugurates a style, a mode of discourse—meditative, less harshly elliptical—that sets it off from the earlier volumes and creates a rhetoric for the subsequent poems to continue, but also to violate. (The poems of *Houseboat Days* [1977] seem to indicate an intention on Ashbery's part to complicate the style in the direction of a return to the elliptical mode.) More important, *The Double Dream of Spring* assumes a stance that Ashbery's later books have not repudiated—that of the poet of high imagination, the visionary. The stance is crossed with obliquity, no doubt: but its presence is undeniable and still astonishing to witness. We can say that in the densely charged lyrics of *The Double Dream*, and especially in its magnificent long poem "Fragment," Ashbery comes into his own and into his inheritance. My scrutiny of this volume attempts to establish the precise terms of this stance, another way of saying that I hope to bring out the full coherence of Ashbery's poetic grammar. Holding hard to the orders of this crucial volume will bring added revelations about Ashbery's whole career to date.

The opening lyrics of Ashbery's books tend to share a common approach to the volumes they inaugurate. Each of these remarkably crystalline lyrics truly *opens* space for the other poems to inhabit: they come first by necessity. Ashbery likes to open his books with prophetic and proleptic lyrics, brief but encompassing. "The Task," at the head of *The Double Dream of Spring* (p. 13), is perhaps the most overtly inaugural poem

Ashbery has written. It is close in spirit to a traditional beginning piece such as Frost's "The Pasture" or Whitman's "By
Paths Untrodden" in its deliberate gesture of placing the poet in
space—Ashbery shrinks the spot to "here"—and in its ironically
understated way of characterizing the poet's enterprise: "I plan
to stay here a little while / For these are moments only, moments
of insight."

The reduced scope of such a plan is attractive in its very insouciance: we think of Whitman lounging, inviting the reader to
come along with him. After all, the poet will make no great
demands; his poems are "moments only." This casual, indeed
deprecating, pose is wholly American. No sooner has Ashbery
done with this bit of masquerade than he begins to describe the
ensuing volume as a journey, the goal of which turns out to be a
possible cure for angst. This is the other side of the American
poet's stance toward his works, a view in which art is a substitute for religion and other forms of psychic healing: "there are
reaches to be attained, / A last level of anxiety that melts / In
becoming, like miles under the pilgrim's feet."

Much of the difficulty readers have with Ashbery stems from
problems in gauging his tone. The difficulty intensifies when it
becomes a question of determining whether or not he is parody-
ing a traditional literary *topos*. This way of posing the reader's
alternatives sets up the question in a misleading way, although I
think that many readers do pose these terms in oppositional
fashion. I think that seasoned readers of Ashbery learn not to
demand of his poems that they move in a univocal direction: he
can both parody and mean "seriously" at the same time, he both
sees and revises simultaneously. At times he appears to war
against the very idea of received tradition, even while acknowledging, by his refusal to give them up, that the old tropes
embody a storehouse of poetic wisdom still alive for us today.

This problem bears upon the opening of "The Task." On the
one hand, there is Ashbery's explicit refusal to use the first-
person pronoun here at the beginning. "They are preparing to

begin again"; whether "they" refers to the Muses or whatever force seems to sponsor and survive the individual singer, the process is started outside the self. *They* pull the strings, initiating the new claim to attention. Although the new romance is a predicated one, even "they" recognize the need for new beginnings, opening outward and away from the origin of things. "Fragment," the last poem in *The Double Dream*, opens with a line that translates this opening and repeats its dialectic of endings and beginnings: "The last block is closed in April."

Once the necessity of a new start is realized, the quester is sent out on his mission, at which point Ashbery breaks into an uneasy, hyperbolic rhetoric that both inflates "the task" and blanks out the voyager. He becomes an Everyman, a too-programmatic fulfillment of the shibboleth that the lyric poet never speaks in propria persona but always *im*personally. This Everyman moves westward as all the great questers do, in search, like Aeneas, of the fugitive lands. There may be hidden autobiographical irony in this, if we consider that *The Double Dream* is composed of poems written after Ashbery returned to America from his self-imposed "exile" abroad. So the exile, or fugitive, is really moving *back* toward home and "that time / In whose corrosive mass he first discovered how to breathe." "First" should be stressed here, since it tends to confirm the drift of the lines back to an origin. Learning "how to breathe" is a striking trope for discovering poetry, here imaged as a *breathing* exercise.

Just as "The Task" enacts a move westward, or homeward again after exile, so it moves from impersonal pronouns toward the discovery of an "I," withheld until the last six lines. We have explored the shifting strategy of self-representation in these lines but have not discussed the mysterious transitional moment that opens the final stanza: "Just look at the filth you've made, / See what you've done." Part of the mystery here is due to Ashbery's fruitfully imprecise use of the second-person pronoun. Are these words meant to be spoken by one part of the self to another part, or do they come from "outside"? If the latter, who speaks them? The entrance of children into the poem just after these words, coupled with their tone of rebuke, leads us naturally to the mother; exactly why she is upbraiding the poet-child is the reader's surmise. The words are harsh and abrupt, as they doubtless were to the child, and yet they do not really interrupt the round of supper, play, and "promise of the pillow... to come." Ashbery sees the parental injunction in perspective, just as he will view all later moments of possible guilt and shame with a kind of steady tolerance and self-forgiveness. Even the moment of transgression has its part in the whole cycle: the mother wounds by day, heals by night.

The reprimand might also issue directly from the poet as an evaluation of his works and days, in the same spirit as Whitman at ebb-point surveying his shattered corpus. The poet's own judgment upon himself would then be an echoing, a repetition of the parental judgment. The seamlessness of "The Task" inclines one to choose all options for interpretation, uniting them to reveal an extraordinary instance of Ashbery touching upon a source, a seemingly random event that goes on meaning, especially when repeated by the adult poet. It is at this level that Ashbery's autobiographical tendencies should be discussed: autobiography is a most complex structure for him, involving little in the way of direct personal reminiscence. It is worth paying close attention to the carefully modulated "descent" of "The Task," in order to discover the place of the "personal" I. The poem slowly drops downward in a countersublime, descendental gesture: from the sun and Everyman as wandering Jew, we drop to the children playing after supper, while the poem ends with a pilgrim touching earth yet intent on the "reaches."

"The Task," then, presents us with a voice that threatens to disrupt, or at least to interrupt. But the poem incorporates that voice by revealing it to be as much an inner as an outer thing. Ashbery's sense of inclusiveness pervades *The Double Dream of Spring* and is sometimes mistaken for homogeneity of tone, as though his poems were not sufficiently differentiated. Metrically speaking, this is surely not true. Ashbery works in a remarkable variety of line lengths, and he is committed to a continual alternation of stanza patternings. *We*, as readers, sometimes tend to homogenize all poets, contemporary or traditional: the great name is invoked as though it meant one thing, one way of writing, one occasion for the birth of the poem.

Prosodic variation is the most obvious way of marking the differences in a poet's repertoire of voices. Within each Ashbery poem, the reader must always be on guard to catch the subtle shifts of perspective, the putting on of different inflections, in order to gather the full range of voice. Before *The Double Dream of Spring*, Ashbery indulged more openly in outrageous ellipses, sharp transitions from one mode of discourse to another. All this is toned down somewhat in *The Double Dream*, making the reader's task even more challenging, for it becomes more difficult to locate crucial moments of vocal scene-changing. Ashbery has never been what we would call a dramatic poet, and the voices he draws into his poems, no matter how far-fetched, are always versions of an elusive but central speaker. With the poems of *The Double Dream*, these competing voices become more strongly perceived as possible modes of self-presentation, within a range extending from the sublime to more natural, perhaps even colloquial measures. And the outrageous poem has hardly disappeared from the volume: "Farm Implements and Rutabagas in a Landscape" may be Ashbery's wildest parody.

"Spring Day," the second poem in *The Double Dream of Spring* (pp. 14–15), reveals Ashbery at his most cunning. The poem crosses internal boundary marks incessantly, and yet the flow of the whole, like "a river breaking through a dam," seems barely to pause as the different streams emerge and dissolve. "Spring Day" is precisely located in time: it is set at the moment of awakening, the lyric time of *aubade*—only here we find the self engaged in monologue. (The more one reads Ashbery the clearer his poetic time frames become.) The situation of the early riser experiencing the freshness of dawn as "cold hope," where cold is a trope of power, is similar to that in Stevens's "The Latest Freed Man." The first two stanzas of "Spring Day" engage cyclicity, the raising and deflating of immense hope, but the tone is not one of exhaustion. After all, night is over and the mind has achieved respite, fending off nightmares. Here I must disagree with David Kalstone even while admiring his eloquence. Kalstone describes the opening stanzas of "Spring Day" in the following way: "Fresh hopes verge into nightmares in the long suspended sentence at the opening of 'Spring Day.' . . . In this supple maze of syntax things seem over, exhausted, before they begin; 'immense hope' turns into 'cold hope' in the 'air that was yesterday.'"[1] Were this true, I do not see how the poem could achieve the cadence of its magnificent close. My disagreement centers on the value of "cold hope"; I read this, again, as a sign of power, to be compared with Stevens's "refreshment of cold air."[2] Kalstone's reading nevertheless exerts a powerful counterpull on more optimistic interpretations of the poem.

Any characterization of "Spring Day" must take its *two* speakers into account. The poem cannot be said to oppose voices so much as blend them, though it acknowledges a different strain of voice by enclosing one of its speeches in quotation marks. Who speaks here: " 'They were long in coming' "? We *are* told that: "The giant body relaxed as though beside a stream / Wakens to the force of it and has to recognize / The secret sweetness before it turns into life." This giant, introduced by the poem's other voice, may be seen as the sleeping Albion within us all, ear attuned to the stream of primordial desire for freedom and release, a river that speaks only at the first breaking of day and then goes underground, like Arnold's buried stream. The giant's speech upon these barely repressed heights deserves to be called sublime. Ashbery concurs by marking off the speaking mountain's sermon for the day, much as Emerson distinguished his radical chant of freedom in *Nature* by inserting quotation marks and assigning the sublime speech to a certain "Orphic Poet."[3] Ashbery's Orphic self begins by declaring that we must break through the shell of custom and tradition:

> "They were long in coming,
> Those others, and mattered so little that it slowed them
> To almost nothing. They were presumed dead,
> Their names honorably grafted on the landscape
> To be a memory to men. Until today
> We have been living in their shell.
> Now we break forth like a river breaking through a dam,
> Pausing over the puzzled, frightened plain,
>
> And our further progress shall be terrible,
> Turning fresh knives in the wounds
> In that gulf of recreation, that bare canvas
> As matter-of-fact as the traffic and the day's noise."

Some of these lines are written in the mode of self-conscious epic simile: the puzzled, frightened plain is a wonderful imitation, not a parody, of Vergilian style. Yet this epic speaker, this giant of the self caught " 'twixt wake and sleep," also acknowledges the need to hold tight to the commonplaces. It is a program both sweet and terrible, as the sublime should be, modulating at the close, while day nears, into an appreciation of the reality principle.

"The mountain stopped shaking"; its Vesuvian speech, as Dickinson would put it, is over, and the poem moves toward the accents of day and inevitable "contradiction." But first there is a last glimpse of the stars, at the moment of fade-out:

> far from us lights were put out, memories of boys and girls
> Who walked here before the great change,
>
> Before the air mirrored us,
> Taking the opposite shape of our effort,

Its inseparable comment and corollary
But casting us further and further out.

The constellations are viewed here as the surviving fragments of
the mythopoeic imagination, from a time before the turn toward
self-consciousness and its attendant dualisms. The trace that
man left in the sky, as sign of his myth-making faculty, was not
a mark of difference but grew rather out of the sense that man
and nature were united. The human image was seen within
nature, not apart from it. But then a "great change" came about
(itself, of course, a heuristic myth): an age of reflection rather
than vision took over, and man saw his image everywhere, but
at the cost of losing his ability to see anything else. When he
now looked into nature, he saw only himself, distorted. Nature
became a commentary upon our traces; while we thought we
were attracting the world to us, we were actually alienating
ourselves in the service of a remorseless consciousness of self.

There is a touch of play here, for this whole dialectic has
grown so familiar that even to repeat it requires somewhere a
saving touch of irony. Ashbery achieves it with the reference to
the starry images of lost heroes and heroines as "boys and
girls," a playfully reductive touch that helps us put the whole
argument in perspective. (Stevens startles us at a similar moment in "Notes toward a Supreme Fiction" when he declares
that "Adam / In Eden was the father of Descartes.")[4] And we
should also remember that Ashbery's Orphic speaker actually
strikes out against the myth of unity and its avatars with their
"names grafted on the landscape" (of the sky?), urging instead a
kind of violence against nature in order to achieve desire.

We are, then, confronted with a double dream upon the
dawning of this spring day. One is the remoter dream of lost
unity, of a time before the fall into the "great change." There is
also the giant's dream, half-slumbering Albion's vision of breaking the chains, even the chains of past myths of freedom. In this

sense Ashbery, at his most visionary, does not look backward as Blake does to "ancient times" as a paradigm for restoration. Both these dreams begin to fade at the moment when the sun and the natural self rise from sleep. Ashbery shows this native self rubbing its eyes, so to speak, and gazing around him: "Wha—what happened?" Has the sun ever been less ceremoniously greeted? The rebound is quick, however, and a truly uncanny voice now emerges as day takes over, but a day now informed by the dream of early morning (those dreams Dante calls the truest). The self that now appears also wants to be healed, but not through any violation of nature. Rather, innocence and beauty are to be attained by becoming at one with "The orange tree," emblem of all that is vital and earthly:

> You are with
> The orange tree, so that its summer produce
> Can go back to where we got it wrong, then drip gently
> Into history, if it wants to.

History is not abjured but becomes an option for the embowered self; it will be engaged on the gentlest of terms. Some readers may find retreat in this, preferring the more strenuous and violent vision of the Orphic speaker. The compensation for such cultivation of the inner forest is the flowering of a tone of remarkable civility and ceremony at the poem's close. One thinks of "A Prayer for My Daughter" when listening to the end of "Spring Day," and yet Ashbery's pastoral precinct shows no trace of social conservatism. There is, rather, an abiding respect for the "growing thing" and an implicit abhorrence of violence—even in the service of vision—that Yeats, alas, did not share:

> No use charging the barriers of that other:
> It no longer exists. But you,
> Gracious and growing thing, with those leaves like stars,
> We shall soon give all our attention to you.

No rhetorical figure could better have described the locus of Ashbery's concern than his phrase "leaves like stars." The sky-bound or sublime constellations and their vestiges of mythic union have disappeared, to be replaced by earthly coordinates, the aim of the natural quester. It is a deeply moving emblem upon which to end a poem: we are entreated to care for the earth's own sublimity.

The threshold moment of sunrise is one that Ashbery faces throughout *The Double Dream of Spring*. "Sunrise in Suburbia," despite its title (which may refer to an inner sense of being stranded outside the city proper) faces "the coming of strength out of night: unfeared" on urban ground (*DD*, p. 49). The poem calls itself a "woven city lament," an elegy either for the city as it now is, or for the self at bay in such a metropolis. Courage *is* certainly what is needed to face the coming day, as Ashbery conceives it in this poem, for the advent of sunrise creates a "morning holocaust, one vast furnace, engaging all tears." Holocaust and furnace are potential opposites here, one standing for destruction by fire, the other for a creative welding of elements. "Tears," a trope for lament, are somehow *engaged* by this early morning fire; the expression moves us away from the threat of being *consumed*. Yet no explanation can fully deflect the poet's strenuous and violent conception of lethal powers arrayed against him. "How quick the sunrise would kill me," Ashbery says along with Whitman—and though both poets send bolts out of themselves as a defense, the danger remains real. The final vision of "Sunrise in Suburbia" can be tempered only by another poem of the threshold moment and its combative harnessing of such energy: "Evening in the Country."

That poem is also oddly titled, unless its speaker proleptically addresses the "sign of being / In me that is to close late, long." However this may be, the poem is surely situated at dawn, ending at the instant of sunrise, monumentally represented. "Evening in the Country" closes with a vision of the sun as an "unblinking chariot," a rhetorical figure that captures both the sun's power (it is a great engine) and its "knowledge" (its eye never shuts, like the world it illumines it is a "vast open"). What is the speaker's stance with regard to this great force?

> We may perhaps remain here, cautious yet free
> On the edge, as it rolls its unblinking chariot
> Into the vast open, the incredible violence and yielding
> Turmoil that is to be our route.

[*DD*, p. 34]

Lines such as these point to a kind of timidity found elsewhere in *The Double Dream:* "It is probably on one of the inside pages / That the history of his timidity will be written." The quotation comes from "French Poems," a sequence in which Ashbery appears to accuse himself of essential cowardice. But we should be wary of taking this pose as the whole truth. "On the edge" is a loaded phrase, filled with traces of the center/periphery dialectic found so often in American poetry. To declare oneself "marginal" may only be another way of saying that the center shifts to where the poetic self happens to be. There is no center except where the central speaker takes up his or her stance. Whitman, in the opening poem of *Calamus,* seems to exile himself to the margin only to then evolve a new version of centrality. We must also remember that the sun is both center and periphery at once. Ashbery's path will become the same as the sun's, for by the end of the poem he is able to call its arc "our route." He does not, it is true, make the logical next connection—that he is at the reins of the sun chariot—but he does not really need to, having summoned all that power into his poem, performed his ritual magic on the sun's own rising.

"We may perhaps remain here" is an equally gnomic phrase, pointing both to exile and to centrality. If we search within the poem for a strongly contrasting "there," we find it in the vision of the city "back there," presumably abandoned by the poet in his retreat:

But if breath could kill, then there would not be
Such an easy time of it, with men locked back there
In the smokestacks and corruption of the city.

[*DD*, p. 33]

"Here" becomes, by contrast, a provincial center away from the lethal *urbs*. The fatal breath Ashbery evokes is more than simple industrial pollution; "breath," as we have seen in "The Task," can stand as a trope for poetry, though we should not forget that it can also refer to "fallen" speech. In either case, breath is threatening, whether it carries the serious rivalry of poetic competition or the malice of common defamation. This sense of the mysterious *other* as a backdrop against which Ashbery plays out his own liberation, yet toward which he experiences ambivalence and guilt, is given full treatment in "Soonest Mended" and "Clouds."

"Here" can also be a gesture indicating the ground upon which the lyric poem always takes its stand—so it was used in "The Task." That ground is always central, the poet hopes, however physically "exiled" it might be. All the community necessary for the poet in this form of exile is provided by versions of his own being: this is one reason why "Evening in the Country" plays with a variety of personal pronouns. A related question concerns where the self begins and ends, especially in its relation to the things of nature:

Now as my questioning but admiring gaze expands
To magnificent outposts, I am not so much at home
With these memorabilia of vision as on a tour
Of my remotest properties.

[*DD*, p. 33]

The pose is reminiscent of an earlier parody of exile, in the Oriental mode, found in the latter sections of "The Skaters." But "Evening in the Country" complicates the question by also treat-

175

ing avatars of the self as remote, first, then as *propre*. We are never quite sure what "I" stands for: Does it indicate a unified or a fragmentary self? Does the ability to say "I" necessarily exclude other states of being? The poem's opening line seems to imply this sort of reductive stability: "I am still completely happy." This static opening should have halted the poem right there, the statement's self-sufficiency reinforced by its containment within one line, the only such "whole" sentence in the poem. The self as still center—it is hard not to supply a comma after "still"—prevails and moves off center only to the extent of indulging in "motionless explorations."

But this stillness belongs only to the moment of threshold. As the sun begins to stir, so does a more active, larger being within, a *second* person requiring, quite naturally, the second-person pronoun:

> Have you begun to be in the context you feel
> Now that the danger has been removed?
>   . . . has the motion started
> That is to quiver your head, send anxious beams
> Into the dusty corners of the rooms
> Eventually shoot out over the landscape
> In stars and bursts? For other than this we know nothing
> And space is a coffin and the sky will put out the light.
> I see you eager in your wishing it the way
> We may join it, if it passes close enough.
>
>   [DD, p. 34]

The two versions, I and you, blend into "we." "I see you," despite its touch of hide-and-seek, has great force at this point, presaging a greater inward visibility as the sun begins its climb. The anxious "I" who has survived a night of threat by drawing in his defenses can now respond as a central man would, tracing his own orbit and drawing the circle as he goes.

I would not want to leave "Evening in the Country" without paying homage to its tone, a mixture of rapture and urbanity, self-composure and ecstasy. The volumes after *The Double*

Dream of Spring have only deepened Ashbery's commitment to this tone and the stance it conveys. His urbanity, like Shelley's, somehow furthers the intensity generated by moments of high imaginative "kindling," a favorite word of Shelley's and one that Ashbery invokes at the center of the companion piece to "Evening in the Country," the more severe lyric "Parergon" (*DD*, pp. 55–56).

Once again we find an opening gambit of achieved self-contentment: "We are happy in our way of life." "Parergon," however, immediately displays a sense of restlessness; it is from the beginning a more troubled poem than "Evening in the Country," more haunted by the urge to reach out to the "others" and communicate one's Orphic wisdom. It is tempting to regard this poem as picking up where "Evening in the Country" left off, a night piece to the other's hymn of the sun, a Penseroso dream-vision to set beside the less searing visions of day. Three lines from its end we are told that the lesson of the poem "eddied far into the night," and throughout there is a sense of heightened dream. The opening pronoun only furthers the temptation to link the two poems: "*We* are happy" seems to pitch us into a space where the disparate selves, having come together as one, now discover the urge to break the stasis of achieved satisfaction. Yet there is no direct movement toward "the others"; rather, the stasis deepens, as "our entity pivots on a self-induced trance / Like sleep." This pivot, or center, gradually discloses itself as a deep desire to speak prophetically to these unreachable others, to be a *vox clamantes*. Ashbery seems to require distance between himself and this desire, a distance attained, first, by confining the straying prophetic voice to the purlieus of dream and then encasing the cry in quotation marks. The effect of the latter has already been seen in "Spring Day." It is open to each reader's judgment to decide how effective is this distancing (I would not call it parody or irony). And how are we to read what follows the address, the passage beginning, "As one who moves forward from a dream"? Have we awakened, or have we simply moved from dream to dream, in a deeper piercing of the darkness?

" 'O woebegone people!' " the voice begins, contrasting its own crying with that in the streets:

> "O woebegone people! Why so much crying,
> Such desolation in the streets?
> Is it the present of flesh, that each of you
> At your jagged casement window should handle,
> Nervous unto thirst and ultimate death?
> Meanwhile the true way is sleeping."

[DD, p. 55]

The last line can be read two ways: more simply, the true way is obscured; but the line might also imply that the true way exists within the sleep of this Orphic dreamer and visionary preacher, who assures us that "it is always time for a change." Ashbery as preacher? We might recall that one of the poems in *Rivers and Mountains* was entitled "The Ecclesiast"; there are many moments in his poetry when he becomes a Stevensian orator who "chants in the dark / A text that is an answer, although obscure."[5] Besides, beneath the surface esprit, some of the poems in *The Double Dream* are unabashedly didactic: "Sortes Vergilianae" and "Some Words" immediately come to mind. The Orphic crier ends on a note of deep irony, however, when he declares, from the vantage of sleep, " 'We need the tether / Of entering each other's lives, eyes wide apart, crying.' " Only in dream can we do so, and will the people listen to our savage cry of assaugement.

The fantasy deepens and we pass from the oracle to the god proper. These terms may seem hyperbolic, but Ashbery casts off restraint as he sends his quester forward into the visionary night. "Parergon" approaches that sacred circle of apotheosis staked out in "Kubla Khan":

> As one who moves forward from a dream
> The stranger left the house on hastening feet

Leaving behind the woman with the face shaped like an
    arrowhead,
And all who gazed upon him wondered at
The strange activity around him.
How fast the faces kindled as he passed!

[*DD*, pp. 55–56]

What is especially remarkable in this final movement is not only
the breakthrough or admission of prophetic fantasy but the context in which we find it. For the "strange activity," or spectacle
of the self draws its inevitable spectators, one of whom may be
the poet's ordinary consciousness standing off to one side and
observing the "stranger." "Weave a circle round him thrice,"
Coleridge cautioned the onlookers in "Kubla Khan." Ashbery's
dangerous stranger reposes, for a moment, in "the enclosure
of some court," some common space now sanctified by his presence. The worshipers are necessary, if only to pay homage to the
difficulty of the quest, and to the fact that only one figure can
bear it:

Yet each knew he saw only aspects,
That the continuity was fierce beyond all dream of enduring,
And turned his head away.

[*DD*, p. 56]

The glow is too bright. Certainly the closing movement is
hyperbolic, but its rhetoric of poetic elevation is one that great
poets have not shied away from. The sense of "continuity," as
Ashbery uses it, involves a kind of apostolic succession of seers.
The dream of poetic divinity, of undying joyousness, extracts a
harsh price from the poet who bears it—he is "caught in that
trap," as the poem's last words tell us, surrounded by the "others."

For too long Ashbery has seemed to readers—especially professional readers—a poet more often casual than relentless
about establishing meaning. His mask of insouciance has man-

aged to remain intact, despite the writing of poem after difficult poem, and the evidence is that each new effort has been aimed hard at getting his subject right—not fixing it forever, but bringing the moment's wisdom and the moment's ephemerality together. Too often, critics have stressed the latter and ignored the former. A myth grew up around Ashbery: he had somehow discovered new dimensions to the poetic act, or a new kind of writing machine, capable of generating poems in the absence of the usual anxieties about subject—more remarkably, poems free from worry about the traditional criteria of greatness. Ashbery has contributed to this myth in subtle ways, but supporters and critics have gone even further, sometimes suggesting that Ashbery had willed himself to be a minor poet, inhabitor of a necessarily diminished sphere. They seize on lines such as the following: "To step free at last, miniscule on the gigantic plateau— / This was our ambition: to be small and clear and free" (*DD*, p. 17).

These lines come from "Soonest Mended," one of Ashbery's most popular poems. It is a poem written firmly in the middle voice and one which seems to erect an aesthetic credo out of holding to the middle range in all things: "a kind of fence-sitting / Raised to the level of an aesthetic ideal." The poem needs to be quizzed on this advocacy, however, if it does not indeed already question itself. One reason "Soonest Mended" is so well liked, aside from its wrought gracefulness and measured tone of loss, is that it gives an image of the poet many readers would like Ashbery to be: casual, urbane, resigned to "an occasional dream, a vision."

Now the poems we have been considering—"The Task," "Spring Day," "Evening in the Country," "Parergon"—are hardly what we would call conversational, although "Evening in the Country" comes closest perhaps to "Soonest Mended" in its use of the long line as a way of achieving flexibility of voice. Yet the conversational measure tightens toward the close of "Evening in the Country," and even though Ashbery keeps to an urbane pitch he manages to ascend the chariot of poetic deity. Readers are probably coming to realize that Ashbery has almost unobtrusively mastered the long line—the line of more than ten syllables—and now uses it as powerfully as anyone before him in the twentieth century. From *Double Dream* to *Houseboat Days* his power over this measure has only grown. The long line is also the visionary line, the mode of Whitman and Blake, and Ashbery has not been reluctant to use it in this task. The lengthened line, however, can trail away from the poet, as it does in "As I Ebb'd with the Ocean of Life," creating an effect of dispersed power and draining strength. Or the line can seem to hover in a kind of fruitful suspension, a creative sense of drift and repose. This feeling steals over one at times in reading Keats's odes, where the lines seem to grow longer than ten syllables as the Keatsian patience spreads its wings. "Soonest Mended" fulfills this last use of the long line almost perfectly, but it is worth noting that the poem is sui generis and not "vintage" Ashbery. More often, Ashbery will begin with a sense of drift but then gather toward some point of vision. The first poem in *Houseboat Days* is a perfect illustration. "Street Musicians" sees rising signs of drift but looks beyond them to what it perceives as a possible source, an "anchor": "Our question of a place of origin hangs / Like smoke."

"Barely tolerated, living on the margin," is something between a boast and a lament. The margin, once again, does not necessarily lead to marginality: it may be the true center. Yet "Soonest Mended" is less sure than other Ashbery poems of the poet's power to be the center wherever he falls out, on the "brink" or what not. I would still argue that even as the poem's seemingly limpid lines crystallize with time and repeated readings, so its sense of marginality inches toward the center. Indeed, the movement is already there in the poem however one interprets it, for the margin of the poem's opening line becomes a "mooring" at the end. The precarious present yields to a sense of origins: the self is where it is as a result of an original event or choice. Our exile to the margin is self-willed. We started out from the margin-as-mooring; we are always placing ourselves by necessity at the brink of a new beginning, a making ready. Only when we lose the trace of the tether back to this site do we regard ourselves as weakly marginal. So the poem will move back through personal memory to an event *in illo tempore*, or sacred time, when the poet's true chronology began.

"Soonest Mended" remains striking within the Ashbery oeuvre not so much for its return at the end to a sense of origination—other poems certainly enact this course—as for its planned, haphazard course *to* that end. David Kalstone has written beautifully of this trajectory. He speaks of the poem's "brave carelessness" and points out, rightly, that "the tone is partly elegiac."[6] Ashbery's suppression of mimesis only partly obscures the clear fact that "Soonest Mended" is, as Harold Bloom calls it, a lament for "Ashbery's generation."[7] Writing at the level he does throughout *The Double Dream of Spring* inevitably means that Ashbery will feel deep ambivalence toward this comically helpless "generation" and toward his own early self. But I must disagree with Kalstone when he says that " 'mooring' sounds as much like death as a new life."[8] He tends to be more concerned with how the poem "shifts quickly from one historical hazard to another," while "the energetic lines breathe the *desire* to assert ego and vitality."[9] As a stylistic description of the poem this cannot be surpassed.

"Historical hazard" is something Ashbery does not often open his poems to; the randomness of the ordinary is not quite the same thing. Such randomness can be organized and redeemed by the solitary eye; but history, or life within the community, can become far more oppressive to the poet. Ashbery's detractors would argue that he closes himself off to what he cannot organize, despite an appearance of the erratic within his poems, and this is hard to dispute. "Soonest Mended" gives us a somewhat coded account of community and offers reasons why this poet must find it dissatisfying. Another poem in the volume, "Clouds," will deal more severely with the need to break away, artistically speaking, from even the most nourishing community. "Soonest Mended" does not quite enact such a break, turning its gentler scrutiny on the poignant inability of any enclave whatsoever to satisfy the desire for true speech. This pathos comes through in a key passage where Ashbery sets the sign of disillusionment against the undeniably sweet faces of the others:

> This is what you wanted to hear, so why
> Did you think of listening to something else? We are all talkers
> It is true, but underneath the talk lies
> The moving and not wanting to be moved, the loose
> Meaning, untidy and simple like a threshing floor.
>
> [*DD*, p. 18]

The powerful enjambment at the end of the third line in this quotation expresses all of Ashbery's ambivalence. "Underneath the talk lies"—so he might wish to leave it, until a softening sets in and he admits that beneath the deceit of social "talk" there hides the shifting forms of desire. The last line in this passage echoes the muse/mother's reprimand in "The Task"—"Just look at the filth you've made"—and here, too, the scatterings wait to be gathered into meaning. This vision of the others, the desired but not "extinct" community, will never fully betray or renounce the spirit of that time and place. It is enough to point, once, to the inevitable wounds that arise when we give and take in mere "talk." About this (least said), soonest mended.

Beyond conversation and beneath the colloquial texture of the poem lies the deep meaning of poetic language:

> Night after night this message returns, repeated
> In the flickering bulbs of the sky, raised past us, taken away
>   from us,

> Yet ours over and over until the end that is past truth,
> The being of our sentences, in the climate that fostered them,
> Not ours to own, like a book, but to be with, and sometimes
> To be without, alone and desperate.
>
> [*DD*, p. 18]

This is the credo that holds the haphazard aesthetic course together, and it is a credo Ashbery is willing to share. He does not astonish the others as he did in "Parergon." In fact, "Soonest Mended" ends with several attempts to register halting progress, so unlike the streaming movement at the close of "Parergon," as though Ashbery were trying to blend defeat with triumph. Does this, in the context of the poem, amount to a version of survivor guilt? Thus, the visionary moment becomes a "hard dole," "action" turns to uncertainty, preparation is "careless." And yet no degree of restraint can fully quell the sense of triumph and power attendant upon recovering the spot of origin at the poem's close. "That day so long ago," the day of poetic inauguration, does not belong to the time frame of memory. It belongs to a greater sequence. To understand the resonances of such a "day" it would help to look at the preceding poem in *The Double Dream*, "Plainness in Diversity" (p. 16). This lesser-known poem abbreviates the course traveled by "Soonest Mended" but moves in a remarkably similar direction. Once again it is the emptiness of "talk" that brings the truth home to the poetic quester; his place is elsewhere:

> Silly girls your heads full of boys
> There is a last sample of talk on the outer side
> Your stand at last lifts to dumb evening
> It is reflected in the steep blue sides of the crater,
> So much water shall wash over these our breaths
> Yet shall remain unwashed at the end. The fine
> Branches of the fir tree catch at it, ebbing.
> Not on our planet is the destiny
> That can make you one.

> To be placed on the side of some mountain
> Is the truer story.
>
> [*DD*, p. 16]

The second stanza continues to construct an outline of the journey myth, as it uses "the sagas" to discover a fitting point of origin and a worthy end to the quest:

> There is so much they must say, and it is important
> About all the swimming motions, and the way the hands
> Came up out of the ocean with original fronds,
> The famous arrow, the girls who came at dawn
> To pay a visit to the young child, and how, when he grew up
>   to be a man
> The same restive ceremony replaced the limited years
>   between,
> Only now he was old, and forced to begin the journey to the
>   stars.
>
> ——— [*DD*, p. 16]

"Plainness in Diversity" locates us in myth more firmly than "Soonest Mended" chooses to do; but the gesture of starting out with which the latter concludes is also, surely, a version of heroism.

Another account of this truer—that is to say, more severe—poetic autobiography comes in the mysterious poem "Clouds" (*DD*, pp. 67–69), a terse lyric of bounded quatrains, gnomic and revealing at the same time. The poem tells something of the same story as "Soonest Mended," but its voice is wholly different. "Clouds"—the title becomes clear only in the last line—has none of the evasive charm of "Soonest Mended." It judges the generation out of which Ashbery emerged with harsher accuracy and claims expansive, indeed Dionysian, powers for its own speaker. (Semele, upon whom the poem devolves at the close, was the mother of Dionysus.) The opening quatrain can hardly be matched elsewhere in Ashbery's writing for its uncanny mixture of power and prophecy, on the one hand, tranquillity and reverie on the other:

> All this time he had only been waiting,
> Not even thinking, as many had supposed.
> Now sleep wound down to him its promise of dazzling peace
> And he stood up to assume that imagination.
>
> [*DD*, p. 67]

These lines might stand as epigraph to *The Double Dream of Spring*, the volume in which Ashbery first truly stands up to assume the task of poethood. What distinguishes "Clouds" from other such moments of declaration is its preoccupation with what came before. Both "Parergon" and "Evening in the Country" showed glimpses of the *others*, the dark background against which Ashbery measures the intensity of his own flare. Here the poet broods more penetratingly on the character of these others—the poets, let us say, with whom Ashbery started out. The names of this generation are well known. Ashbery schematizes the setting in "Clouds" and leaves us with a strong, if intentionally vague, impression only of an avant-garde enclave worrying problems of continuity and rupture. Ashbery turns to judge them, sounding like an abstract version of Yeats assessing the poets of the nineties:

> There were others in the forest as close as he
> To caring about the silent outcome, but they had gotten lost
> In the shadows of dreams so that the external look
> Of the nearby world had become confused with the cobwebs
>   inside.
>
> [*DD*, p. 67]

"They had gotten lost": *he*, on the other hand, has been found. "Clouds" gives itself over to declaring this difference, which amounts to declaring its speaker greater than the others—"He shoots forward like a malignant star," as the poem later puts it—while at the same time holding him true to the poetic program of this early coterie. "Clouds" emblematizes the conflict in Ashbery's crossing from the early phase of *Some Trees* and *The Tennis Court Oath* to *Rivers and Mountains* and *The Double Dream of Spring*. We might choose to see the promise of this early phase as fulfilled in the poems of *The Double Dream*—yet how can one fulfill the experimental, the tentative? And how can one establish continuity with a phase that was itself committed to personal and historical discontinuity?

> How can we outsmart the sense of continuity
> That eludes our steps as it prepares us
> For ultimate wishful thinking once the mind has ended
> Since this last thought both confines and uplifts us?
>
> [*DD*, p. 68]

This stanza, the ninth of fourteen, marks the point of transition in the poem. The preceding stanzas turned over the question of continuity, of resisting what the poem calls "joining," even while acknowledging the need to forge "separate blocks of achievement and opinion." "Clouds" scatters penetrating kernel descriptions of avant-gardism, none of which is more striking than the following:

> And the small enclave
> Of worried continuing began again, putting forth antennae
> into the night.
>
> How do we explain the harm, feeling
> We are always the effortless discoverers of our career,
> With each day digging the grave of tomorrow and at the same
> time
> Preparing its own redemption, constantly living and dying?
>
> [*DD*, p. 68]

The poem's "sestet," its final five or six stanzas, grants that we can never "outsmart the sense of continuity," but it does not take this as a sign of defeat. Rather, Ashbery drops any note of elegiac helplessness and strikes out, in a remarkable evocation of animal vitality. No more worried continuing, no more sleek antennae:

> He was like a lion tracking its prey
> Through days and nights, forgetful
> In the delirium of arrangements.
>
> [*DD*, p. 68]

The conceit is striking and outrageous. We hunt down "continuity," even devour it at moments, but we cannot extinguish the concept or the species itself: we are tied to our prey. The circle of tracking and destruction is obsessive, a "delirium of arrangements." We waste the present in this *quest for* a present uncontaminated by the past. We locate ourselves on the outer rim of this devastation, pushing farther into the brake:

> The birds fly up out of the underbrush,
>
> The evening swoons out of contaminated dawns,
> And now whatever goes farther must be
> Alien and healthy, for death is here and knowable.
> Out of touch with the basic unhappiness
>
> He shoots forward like a malignant star.
> The edges of the journey are ragged.
> Only the face of night begins to grow distinct
> As the fainter stars call to each other and are lost.
>
> Day re-creates his image like a snapshot. . . .
>
> [*DD*, p. 68]

The glory and the sorrow of the avant-garde are acted out here, in the flight outward and the inevitable return to habitual nature: our image rendered by someone or something else.

"Clouds" is a powerfully condensed poem, ascetically framed and argued. Vision is not deflected as it is in "Soonest Mended"; there is no pretence of lassitude, no effort to mask the true desires of the poetic self. In fact the poem is so clear about how it places its speaker that we, as readers, perhaps search for evasions that simply are not there. This is one of the more curious reactions Ashbery inspires in his audience. But even if we pay homage to the obliquity of presentation in "Clouds," we cannot fail to recognize the poem's true prey as it emerges with the abrupt invocation of Semele, the mother of Dionysus. If the god is about to be born at the end of the poem, he is about to be born again, into poetry, at the poem's opening. The shock of these terms is itself instructive: it cautions us against reading Ashbery too casually.

On the way toward "Fragment" and away from these charged lyrics, we might think about some poems in *The Double Dream of Spring* that seem to exist for the sheer sake of performance. Intended to elude interpretation, these poems never become nonsensical. Instead, they end as parodies where, more often than not, the matter of parody can be located in the "serious" poems of the volume. The place of texts such as "Variations, Calypso and Fugue on a Theme of Ella Wheeler Wilcox," "Farm Implements and Rutabagas in a Landscape," "Some Words," "Sortes Vergilianae," is crucial: nearly every line, every moment from these variously wild poems can be "related" to more coherent structures of meaning elsewhere in *The Double Dream*. These poems mock interpretation on their own ground—they mean, but mean elsewhere, anywhere else but within their own boundaries. A residual trace of guilt can be found in Ashbery toward the whole enterprise of false coherence, and this is why he makes his readers collaborate so strenuously in the hermeneutic process of coming upon meaning. He seems at times deliberately to mar his poems, although I would argue that this occurs more often in *Houseboat Days* than in *The Double Dream of Spring*. His bad conscience at approximating the "traditional" poem with its criteria of lucidity and comprehensibility is somewhat appeased by the overtly experimental poems in his volumes: these disperse meaning as much as other poems concentrate it. It is not that the experimental poem in *The Double Dream*, for instance, is formless; on the contrary, this kind of poem is overdetermined by form. Meaning goes along for the ride. What these experimental poems do best is to exaggerate and hypostatize thematic concerns and prosodic patterns that exist everywhere in *The Double Dream*. The volume is extraordinarily well-knit and, in a sense, it is these willful, seemingly unbounded pieces that most remind us of this fact. Such experimentation is *vitally* parasitic; it is alive in itself but also needs the preexistence of texts found elsewhere: a bit of doggerel from Ella Wheeler Wilcox, the "Popeye" cartoon, a French text by Arthur Cravan, the notion of a privileged "sacred" text that exists as pure anteriority (Vergil). For a poem that stands alone we must turn to the deeper experimentalism of a true masterpiece: "Fragment."

The title at first leads us to expect jaggedness in the poem's lines—frequent and sharp transitions—certainly not the overt symmetry of fifty ten-line stanzas, parodically reminiscent of stately Renaissance pageantry. Yet, if we look closer, is there not a sense of completion in the title's emphasis on the singular: "Fragment," not "Fragments"? (Suppose Pound had called his epic *Canto*?) So, even if the poem stands in synecdochic relation to some external whole, it completely embodies its own partiality. It is a whole fragment. There are, not surprisingly, many tag lines, emblematic moments in the poem, that help us to parse the title: "The stance to you / Is a fiction, to me a whole" (*DD*, p. 78) is one such moment in which Ashbery flatters his song. A later passage turns against this self-flattery and broods about the poem's possible incompleteness:

> the externals of present
> Continuing—incomplete, good-natured pictures that
> Flatter us even when forgotten with dwarf speculations

About the insane, invigorating whole they don't represent.
[*DD*, p. 93]

Insane, invigorating: Is the whole worth capturing? Deciding this is as difficult as trying to locate the poem's transitions, which are everywhere and nowhere. We are tricked by the title and by an earlier mélange like "The Skaters" into readying ourselves for a tour de force of ellipsis. Yet the poem flows and flows, somehow running over its points of switchover, eliding its own elisions in a credible portrait of continuity. The lines, however seemingly discontinuous, are held together by a metrical or rhythmic hum, a buzzing undertone of similitude and relationship.

Whether it opens on a note of closure or aperture, "Fragment" clearly *does* begin with a marked point of departure. It is also worth noting that the poem's last stanza seems to be a clear end-sign. This is a good reminder to the reader not to ignore sequence entirely, even at moments of exasperation (or release), when the thread of continuity appears most strained. Invoking April as it does, "Fragment" pays homage to the hallowed starting ground for the long poem in English, from Chaucer to Eliot. And indeed, the poem's first six lines are among the most densely and richly allusive Ashbery has yet written. The poem opens by seeming to deny the possibility of further openings: "The last block is closed in April." Whatever "block" may mean, from building metaphor to cell block, the overt sense in the line moves toward grim, monosyllabic finality. Yet the force of "April" as a point of origin or place of aperture overrides any terminus, impelling the line as a whole to say: "The last block is closed in aperture"; we move toward a new opening even as we shut down or shut out the past (the last).

The focus on "her face" in the poem's second line introduces a series of concentric circles of reference, where "she" comes to stand for the beloved in all her avatars: lover, mother, muse, earth itself. Ashbery's cynosure is about as readily identifiable as

Keats's Moneta or Stevens's female imago figures. And, indeed, the powerful apostrophe in stanza two—"your face, the only real beginning, / Beyond the grey of overcoat"—links Ashbery to these two, especially on that mysterious and crucial ground where the origins of Eros and the lyric are intertwined. Ashbery's overt strategy of invocation by repetition and difference does not end here, however; we need to confront the shade of Eliot as well, summoned by the proximity of "memory" to "April," and by the figural substitution for the missing word in the Eliotic triad: April, memory . . . *desire*. Desire, indeed, is the key to the whole of the poem's magnificent opening. It is the "intrusion" that "Clouds over" the beloved's countenance; it is the dream of "older / Permissiveness," as the stanza goes on to call it, a shrewd way of troping upon the erotic storehouse of childhood and adolescence. And desire helps us to understand why the budding forsythia extend a present sympathy to us, in opposition to the "recondite" or buried past, return to which can only involve a lethal falling backward:

> You
> See the intrusions clouding over her face
> As in the memory given you of older
> Permissiveness which dies in the
> Falling back toward recondite ends,
> The sympathy of yellow flowers.
>
> [*DD*, p. 78]

(I do not read "The sympathy of yellow flowers" as being in apposition to "recondite ends." I place a mental ellipsis between lines five and six in the opening stanza.) Here Ashbery separates himself from Eliot, who viewed his Waste Land flowers as anything but sympathetic tokens. For Ashbery, however, the forsythia bloom as an emblem of "a moment's commandment," to use the clarion phrase upon which he closes this first "block" of words. They stand as sign of openness, of potential: Who is equal to imagine them? The second half of this dense inaugurat-

ing stanza finds a credo to withstand the intrusion of the past
and releases the stanza as a whole from its brooding density.
The credo centers on "Space not given and yet not withdrawn /
And never yet imagined: a moment's commandment." The rest
of "Fragment" will explore that space in an attempt to merit the
muse/moment's injunction.

"Fragment" is a poem that endlessly emblematizes itself; its
primary point of reference is itself as an ongoing process of
opening out, creating new imaginative routes, new patterns
among the old hieroglyphs. This preoccupation of the poem
with the poem is linked to the dilemma of the ghostly "author"
who can love only himself:

> that this first
> Salutation plummet also to the end of friendship
> With self alone. And in doing so open out
> New passages of being among the correctness
> Of familiar patterns.
>
> [*DD*, p. 78]

An unwary reader might assume that here, in the poem's second stanza, Ashbery freely acknowledges the perils of solipsism, the rigor mortis of self-love, hoping for a release from both
narcissism and "familiar patterns" (with the latent pun on familiar brought to the surface). A reading such as this would make
for good conventional advice: open yourself to others and release the creative force within you, and so forth. Yet the clear
sense of wishing to end "friendship / With self alone" does not
necessarily imply a turn toward a real erotic other. Nor does it
necessarily imply a break with the family romance (to use
Freud's term); note that Ashbery traces his new passage *among*
the correctness (a loaded word) of the familial maze. What we
do feel is an abandonment of one strategy toward the self replaced by another, one that does not acknowledge otherness so
much as it demystifies the prestige of the self. Otherness is
denied by the insistence upon "familiar" patterns as the ground

for erotic salutation of whatever sort, and the sense of the lone self is also rebuked by the recognition that, as Dickinson says, the "perished patterns murmur"[10] in us—the ghostly ancestors constitute the hushed undertone of our deepest longings. Finally, the crucial notion of fictionality is introduced: "The stance to you / Is a fiction, to me a whole." Once again, Ashbery's syntax operates to create an interpretive dilemma. The sentence seems to imply contrast: "the stance to you [on the one hand], to me [on the other]." But I do not think it works this way: instead Ashbery forces the reader, by his device, to decide what the difference is between a fiction and a whole. We desire such a difference and are reluctant to concede that a whole *might be* only a fiction, a stance, but we cannot really justify the desire for such a state except as nostalgia for a lost sense of objective plenitude.

To Ashbery, then, there is no essential paradox in calling a fiction a *whole* (this issue, of course, bears upon the poem's title); it comes down to a question of belief in the fiction, a Stevensian notion. Moreover, the only difference between "you" and "me" involves shades of belief. Both are, indeed, pronouns or substitutions; the second-person substitution grants that the fictional or linguistic self lives among others, is a partial fiction, while the more proximate "me" regards itself and the self it "replaces" as the whole of things. The sense of you and me converging in one compact—a mutual defense treaty—is sung in the poem's fourth stanza: "You exist only in me and on account of me / And my features reflect this proved compactness" (*DD*, p. 79).

The fiction of wholeness, taking wholeness *as* a fiction, is accompanied throughout "Fragment" by a quest for the center both as origin and as present focal point. "Fragment" opens, as we have seen, with a double statement about origin or starting point: what comes before must be repeated and ruptured at the same time. We end in order to begin again; we *continue* to begin.

The sense we gather of the increased tension in Ashbery's verse as it moves from "The Skaters" to "Fragment" very likely results from the severity of his concern with origins, not merely beginnings, with the center and not those wheeling circles upon which "The Skaters" focuses: "The figure 8 is a perfect symbol / Of the freedom to be gained in this kind of activity" (*RM*, p. 47). Now this distinction certainly does not mean that Ashbery ever comes to rest on a point of pivot in "Fragment"; rather, he is preoccupied with establishing a relation to a center, however absent, however shifting and elusive. For the reader of current criticism as well as poetry, one of the most remarkable things about "Fragment" is its plethora of terms for describing both the quest for centered space and the issue of that quest. No present writer, whether poet or philosopher, can offer us such a rich prism of sensuous tropes for the invisible core. Inded, Ashbery's startling alternation of abstract and concrete modes of diction reminds one of Dickinson's sixth sense for apprehending unexpected sights on the verge of the formless, the invisible.

The poem's fifth stanza offers an "opening" emblem of the center—"that stable emptiness"—and deliberately pairs it with a dry and reductive vision of erotic union: "that coming together of masses." The one, we are told, "coincides" with the other, and this is hardly surprising; to valorize the self for its stability (its "warm antiquity," to use a phrase of Stevens's)[11] is to view any union with another as a mere random collision of physical particles. This flat and somewhat sterile opposition is deliberately put forth by Ashbery as a statement of the given, the ordinary predicament of retentive and self-absorbed inwardness. This is Ashbery's condition, though he presents it here, near the beginning of the poem, in a minor key; more triumphant assertions will follow, when stable emptiness gives way to motion and more fertile cavities. A few stanzas later, for example, the emptiness speaks, the stable center becomes a roaring wind tunnel:

> The hollow thus produced
> A kind of cave of the winds; distribution center
> Of subordinate notions to which the stag
> Returns to die: the suppressed lovers.
>
> [*DD*, p. 80]

Cliché, as usual with Ashbery, only partially deflates; to call this Aeolian cavern a "distribution center" somehow glamorizes the stock term. The feel of the line remains powerful, and we can momentarily forget, as Wordsworth does at a similar juncture in *The Prelude* when earth winds also speak to him, that the rush of sound issues from a hollow.[12] "Hollow," indeed, is close enough to "hallow" for us to think of this cavern as a sacred void or grotto. A touch of myth also creeps in with that most emblematic of creatures, the stag, here invoked as a thirsting for primal waters. The unpredictability of Ashbery's style allows him this use of the stag because it has been preceded by the hopelessly worn phrase "subordinate notions"—a term that, having found itself stranded in a poem, looks forward to some saving figure of speech. Both the source and the quester for that source are fictional creations, illusory but necessary. The hollow must seem to produce the desired sound: it must be the very echo of that desire.

Ashbery soon gives the eye its place, too, at the vacant center. The poem's ninth stanza represents the momentarily centered consciousness standing in "the center of some diamond," coordinating sharp images as they move toward him in a kind of crystal dance. The rhythm is slow and stately; the world moves in upon the poet's eye. The stanza should be read as a refinement of the eye that earlier saw only the coming together of crude masses. Here sight is so sharp that only particulars or particles are at first visible, until even they are broken down into their constituent colors. The idea is to sharpen focus so intensely that the customary world is no longer visible. Sight is supreme, and sight annihilates fact:

196

Slowly as from the center of some diamond
You begin to take in the world as it moves
In toward you, part of its own burden of thought, rather
Idle musing, afternoons listing toward some sullen
Unexpected end. Seen from inside all is
Abruptness. As though to get out your eye
Sharpens and sharpens these particulars; no
Longer visible, they breathe in multicolored
Parentheses, the way love in short periods
Puts everything out of focus, coming and going.

[*DD*, pp. 80–81]

The Roethke of "Four for Sir John Davies" would have appreciated the symmetry of this writing. But the real place to go—if go one must—is to the Stevens of "Asides on the Oboe." This stanza of Ashbery's only grows in stature when the Stevens poem is read alongside it. Stevens's crystal man, his diamond globe, is obviously relevant here, but I also think the poem's epigraph is crucial for Ashbery. "Fragment" everywhere endorses this ethos and this rigor:

The prologues are over. It is a question, now.
Of final belief. So, say that final belief
Must be in a fiction. It is time to choose.[13]

There is a deceptively limpid quality to Ashbery's style that readers have mistaken for indecisiveness. Certainly the poet himself at times conspires with some of his readers to create the impression of overly relaxed meditation. "Fragment" may be the most misleading of Ashbery's poems in this regard. Actually, the seeming ease of Ashbery's verse comes from the astonishing rapidity of his thought. He can at times move with a flickering intensity that works to lighten the weight of his lines; Ashbery may prove opaque, but dense he is not. He elongates a thought as molten steel is stretched. The effect can be to attenuate the thread of reference but not really to weaken it. Ashbery knows the heat of his own mind, and so it is natural to find him, in a remarkable stanza of pure lyric energy, declaring that "your only world is an inside one"—and the source of illumination for this inwardness is a blazing candle of artifice:

> Thus your only world is an inside one
> Ironically fashioned out of external phenomena
> Having no rhyme or reason, and yet neither
> An existence independent of foreboding and sly grief.
> Nothing anybody says can make a difference; inversely
> You are a victim of their lack of consequence
> Buffeted by invisible winds, or yet a flame yourself
> Without meaning, yet drawing satisfaction
> From the crevices of that wind, living
> In that flame's idealized shape and duration.
>
> [*DD*, p. 81]

The erotic flame burns by itself, nourishing itself in the absence of meaning. Yet there is a ghost of an Orphic fertility rite in this flaming crevice. If "Fragment" is in some vestigial sense a love poem addressed to a real person, or a poem of consolation over the impossibility of such a relationship, then a stanza such as this offers searing compensation. "Satisfaction" is self-induced. Given that conclusion, the stanza ends on a note of triumph as it discovers "idealized shape and duration." Yet a certain residual ambivalence creeps into a line such as: "inversely / You are a victim of their lack of consequence." Why a victim? How shrewd the phrasing is here: one grieves, Ashbery insists, over others' lack of consequence, one is victimized by it, even while one grows in power as they decline. (It is worth noting that "they" is a sign of remoteness for Ashberry, an indication of reduced filiation.) "Nothing anybody says can make a difference"; yes, but this seems a rueful declaration.

Yet the consequences of contact—indeed, penetration—with the other are more than rueful: they inspire a sense of loss and waste. Perhaps the poem's most startling image serves to verify Yeats's adage: "the tragedy of sexual intercourse lies in the perpetual virginity of the soul." The moment of intercourse should be a passage to the center; but, as if we did not already know the score, Ashbery reminds us and his "lover" that "The volcanic entrance to an antechamber / Was not what either of us meant" (*DD*, p. 83). Elsewhere in the poem physical contact is rendered as a species of violence—the last stanza, for example, speaks of two people who "collide in this dusk"—and beyond or after collision lies the violence of achieved impact. The cruel and perpetual surprise of erotic union, even physiologically considered, is that any sexual orifice can be only an antechamber. We reach it only to feel somehow more exiled than before: "outside within the periphery." Even in the act of intercourse we find ourselves voyeurs; we are sure that beyond this dividing wall lies the secret. This emblematic episode reverberates throughout the poem and has something to do with the pervasive tone of sober realization in "Fragment," found even at its most visionary moments. Brooding on this picture of tantalizing proximity to the source, one thinks ahead to the poem's penultimate stanza, where the self is caught in its essential isolation:

> back to one side of life, not especially
> Immune to it, in the secret of what goes on:
> The words sung in the next room are unavoidable
> But their passionate intelligence will be studied in you.
>
> [*DD*, p. 94]

It is fully characteristic of Ashbery to extend a "gloss" on an important passage to more than three hundred lines. This is only another way of noting the breathtakingly rich tapestry of "Fragment": every swirl of metaphor leads the reader to a related arabesque elsewhere in the poem. This play of tropes may strike us at first as erratic, governed only by chance; but as we stay with the poem "chance" gravitates toward "dance," to use a revealing internal rhyme found late in the poem (*DD*, pp. 93–94) and one that stays in the mind as a perfect description of the asymmetrical symmetry of "Fragment."

The "volcano" stanza startles us with its dead-endedness. How *are* we to recover from the fate of being "outside / Within the periphery"? This is really only another way of asking after the true center, or at least a truer sense of centeredness than is available in the erotic relationship. For Ashbery, as for other American poets, the way to this sense lies in a marriage, however stormy, of flesh with air. This union more often takes the form of an *agon* between two sources of power, two living allegories of natural process. When self and other meet, the "meeting escapes through the dark / Like a well" (*DD*, p. 83). But when the seer confronts nature he can feel "the oozing sap of touchable mortality" (*DD*, p. 82). This line occurs in a sequence just before the passage into the antechamber of failed eros, a sequence in which Ashbery takes on the wholly American and wholly Romantic enterprise of matching the self first against the sun and then against the emblematic blood orange, fruit of natural process. At the close of stanza twelve Ashbery situates himself at the threshold moment and prepares for the event, or the advent, of the sun's rising. Ashbery calls it the "active memorial," a phrase that refers both to the sun and to the poet's chant of welcome. The break between stanzas eleven and twelve elides not only the sunrise but the whole passage of day, passing through this vacancy to another conventional spot of time—sunset. At this point the poet's powers fail him and "convention gapes."

> This time
> You get over the threshold of so much unmeaning, so much
> Being, prepared for its event, the active memorial.
>
> And more swiftly continually in evening, limpid
> Storm winds, commas are dropped, the convention gapes,
> Prostrated before a monument, disappearing into the dark.
> It would not be good to examine these ages
> Except for sun flecks, little on the golden sand
> And coming to reappraisal of the distance.
> The welcoming stuns the heart, iron bells
> Crash through the transparent metal of the sky
> Each day slowing the method of thought a little

Until oozing sap of touchable mortality, time lost and won.
[*DD*, pp. 81–82]

Through the passage of day, the sun has hardened into a monument; but tomorrow will bring an attempted recovery, not in an effort to battle the sun directly—that is Whitman's way—but in a more "reasonable" measuring of sun flecks on the sand. At this point Ashbery will not heave himself at the sublime. He is open, however, to being shattered anew by the magnitude of sunrise. And yet Ashbery does not quite turn away from the challenge, either, although he appears to ground his sublime aspiration in "a touchable mortality," redirecting his gaze from the sun to the golden fruit of the sun: the blood orange.

> Like the blood orange we have a single
> Vocabulary all heart and all skin and can see
> Through the dust of incisions the central perimeter
> Our imagination's orbit.
>
> [*DD*, p. 82]

In this tiny globe, like a good metaphysical poet, Ashbery sees the great globe and his own spherical nature. The discovery leads him to a sense of his imagination's orbit as being one with the sun's path. The crucial phrase in this magnificent stanza describes that route as "the central perimeter / Our imagination's orbit." What a play on the concept of centrality! The stanza shows us an inside lodged within the periphery, *as* the periphery; it speaks of centrality wandered away from the center yet not errant, but moving in a fixed path. Each word in this gnomic phrase redefines and creates space for the others: central opens the way for perimeter, perimeter is redeemed by central. This is the point upon which Ashbery wishes to take up his stance: the central man on the edge, never lulled into believing that the center will hold nor ever quite willing to view all things as falling apart.

The process of centering and decentering the self is Ashbery's major passion in "Fragment"; line after line works toward mak-

201

ing the axis of vision coincident with the axis of things, only to discover that art requires a necessary disjunction or asymmetry. This quest to fix the place of the poetic self in regard to the external world is triggered by the movement toward the poem's ghostly, erotic other, followed by the harsh recognition that the self is necessarily alone. This detachment toward the erotic object is one aspect of the poem's mystery: Ashbery speaks at a distance from the beloved usually encountered only in formal elegy. In fact, "Fragment" often takes on the eerie tonality of epitaph; the title may be read, on one level at least, as an elegiac epitaph to a lost and impossible attempt to center the self in another.

There is a related peril, however, in regarding any one achieved stance, any one moment, as central: this is the danger of self-limitation or resistance to motion and change. Keats, always open to the temptations of permanence but aware of how they "tease us out of thought," stated the dilemma acutely in his famous letter to Shelley: "My imagination is a monastery, and I am its monk."[14] In the Psyche ode, Keats was careful to leave a window in the mind *open*—"To let the warm Love in!" And we remember those magic casements opening on perilous seas. (Is there a connection here to the title of a poem from *Houseboat Days:* "Wet Casements"?) Stevens goes even further toward resisting this temptation to achieve the center. The epigraph to "Notes toward a Supreme Fiction" regards "the central of our being" as a place in which we rest "for a moment." More graphically yet, in a direct allusion to the Keatsian emblem, Stevens's hermit of a poet's metaphors (his first idea) "comes and goes and comes and goes all day."[15]

The to-and-fro movement of this hieratic persona is something Ashbery affirms everywhere in his poetry. To feel centered is, of course, to feel powerful, to be all one thing. To remain in this feeling is to become a monument to oneself, and this is spiritual death. One must open out new passages of being even while recognizing that the passage begins from the center and moves outward to another center, there to begin again. This kind of movement brings freedom as well as power. The freedom of new passages is a fine trope for the whole concept of the *quest*, and so it is no surprise to find Ashbery, at one point in "Fragment," bestowing the regalia of the quester upon himself as he prepares to invade that other "room," the world:

> To persist in the revision of very old
> Studies, as though mounted on a charger,
> With the door to the next room partly open
> To the borrowed density, what keeps happening to
> So much dead surprise, a weight of spring.
>
> [*DD*, p. 87]

"A weight of spring" may also be read as a "spring weight": when the density of self becomes too pronounced we turn to the borrowed density "out there" as a release.

By putting himself on a charger in this fashion, Ashbery risks the countercharge that he is being merely quixotic. But he keeps the figure in mind and returns to it some nine stanzas later:

> Out of this intolerant swarm of freedom as it
> Is called in your press, the future, an open
> Structure, is rising even now, to be invaded by the present
> As the past stands to one side, dark and theoretical
> Yet most important of all, for his midnight interpretation
> Is suddenly clasped to you with the force of a hand
> But a clear moonlight night in which distant
> Masses are traced with parental concern.
> After silent, colored storms the reply quickly
> Wakens, has already begun its life, its past, just whole and
> sunny.
>
> [*DD*, p. 90]

The uncanny alternation of abstract and concrete tropes continues: where we would expect to find a castle, instead we glimpse "an open structure." If anyone objects that I am pushing the chivalric metaphor too far by seeing this invasion as a grand charge, the next line—"As the past stands to one side, dark and theoretical"—should clinch the comparison. Who is this onlooker if not the Lady of Romance? The dark lady turns out to be no lady at all, but a parent, an "ancestor," as the next stanza informs us. Ashbery has never parodied more subtly and never been more serious in his adherence to the parodied stance. His wit is bewildering here; the quest romance survives, although the quester is not quite a solitary. His companion, no longer an erotic ideal, has become something of a magus, a friendly wizard. The turn from the beloved toward the true subject of the poem could not be clearer. Ashbery quests for a kind of visionary wisdom, or *gnosis*, rather than erotic comfort. In fact, this moment of contact with the ancestor is the closest Ashbery comes to another person in the poem.

Who might this Merlin persona be? We could simply call him an anterior poet figure, a great poet who now appears in the guise of a prophet. This line of poet-prophets starts with Vergil, so it is entirely appropriate to find a poem in *The Double Dream* eintiled "Sortes Vergilianae." I would venture a closer guess, however, as to the identity of this ancestor. "Silent, colored storms": these must be the auroras, and whose key signature are they, if not Stevens's?[16] The rendering of Stevens as magus is a shrewd commentary on the stance that poet does indeed take in "The Auroras of Autumn," and an acknowledgment on Ashbery's part that the two share a common sense of apocalyptic threat.

But just as Stevens moved to unmake the malice of the auroras by "a flippant communication under the moon,"[17] so Ashbery, having paid homage to his true theme, even more than his ancestor, now responds with a flippancy of his own:

> Thus reasoned the ancestor, and everything
> Happened as he had foretold, but in a funny kind of way.
> There was no telling whether the thought had unrolled
> Down to the heap of pebbles and golden sand now

Only one step ahead, and itself both a trial and
The possibility of turning aside forever.

[*DD*, p. 90]

Alongside the rhetoric of homage there is the language of dis-
missal: "The possibility of turning aside forever." The dialectic
between the two accounts for poetic strength. What makes this
strength especially hard to come by is that "the fathers," as a
later stanza puts it, also recognized the need to strike out against
the background of a relatively fixed order:

The fathers asked that it be made permanent,
A vessel cleaving the dungeon of the waves.
All the details had been worked out
And the decks were clear for sensations
Of joy and defeat, not so closely worked in
As to demolish the possibility of the game's ever
Becoming dangerous again, or of an eventual meeting.

[*DD*, p. 91]

The ancestors' sanctification of perpetual questing gets in the
way of the new poet, even if the decks remain clear. Better to
banish all such pictures of the heroic—auroras, ships—and turn
to the difficult freedom of the present image:

I can tell you all
About freedom that has turned into a painting;
The other is more difficult, though prompt—in fact
A little too prompt: therein lies the difficulty.

[*DD*, p. 91]

No one moment in "Fragment" can be definitive: here the
banished pictures return. The reader will find Ashbery toying
throughout with the idea of the poem as picture (he is, after all,
a professional art critic). At one point, Ashbery seems to regard
his framed stanzas as "pictures / Of loving and small things"
(*DD*, p. 83). The bit of Spenserian "season pageantry" that fol-

lows this phrase tries for an intentional allegorical stiffness, as if to mock the poem's vigorous spontaneity. So the seasons pass, filled with details that accrue to "an infinity of tiny ways." Having done with the pretence of controlled picture-making, Ashbery turns against this kind of storytelling in the interests of larger brush strokes. The turn is characteristic of Ashbery's procedure in "Fragment" and elsewhere: offer one mode of working toward the subject, then shatter that way with a truer act of imagination:

> The other pictures told in an infinity of tiny ways
>
> Stories of the past: separate incidents
> Recounted in touching detail, or vast histories
> Murmured confusingly, as though the speaker
> Were choked by sighs and tears, and had forgotten
> The reason why he was telling the story.
> It was these finally that made the strongest
> Impression, they shook you like wind
> Roaring through branches with no leaves left on them.
> The vagueness was bigger than life and its apotheosis
> Of shining incidents, colored or dark, vivid or serious.
>
> [DD, pp. 83–84]

This credo prefers apocalypse over apotheosis, the image of imaginative power (here ironically troped as "vagueness") over the "shining incidents" of pictorial mimesis. Such rich "vagueness" does not betray the present to a static image, nor does it freeze (frieze) the past. Even the old studies must be "revised," as we have seen; the past as well as the future is an open structure in constant need of revisionary invasion by the present. Words for this kind of revision fill "Fragment," suggesting that the whole can never be satisfactorily captured, even when the whole is "past": "version" and "interpretation," in particular, stand out from the text in a number of important passages. The poem's fourth stanza confronts the issue directly, conceding that the poem is a version (in the root sense of "translation") of what is the "only real one"—namely, the external event posited not so much as a stable existence in itself, but rather as the uncapturable referent to which interpretation and revision always point, the *idea* of a referent. For if the real event is truly outside, then all relation ceases:

> Not forgetting either the chance that you
> Might want to revise this version of what is
> The only real one, it might be that
> No real relation exists between my wish for you
> To return and the movements of your arms and legs.
> [*DD*, p. 79]

What is important to note here is Ashbery's free acknowledgement that his poem is one version, one possible text among others. At its strongest it can make us forget other texts, just as its author's centered consciousness can make us oblivious of other centers; but there still remains the specter of a sequence of endless translations:

> And as one figure
> Supplants another, and dies, so the postulate of each
> Tires the shuffling floor with slogans, present
> Complements mindful of our absorbing interest.
> [*DD*, p. 94]

We return to the concept of the central perimeter, which may be rephrased here as the notion of a central text continually revising itself and displacing its own center, seeing itself and its world anew: "Then the accounts must be reexamined, / Shifting ropes of figures" (*DD*, p. 88). This "figure" says it all: in "Fragment" we are dealing with columns of *figures*—tropes—to be added up or interpreted. It makes no difference how the figures are placed: the sum will be the same. (Again, I would argue that only the opening and closing stanzas of the poem cannot be shifted at will.) All that is required of the interpreter is agility enough to climb up or down these "shifty" ropes suspended between no discernible termini.

Or *does* "Fragment" aim at a resolution? The final lines of the poem predict only "flat evenings / In the months ahead," but a few stanzas before this Ashbery ventures on what seems like a more optimistic prophecy:

> People were delighted getting up in the morning
> With the density that for once seemed the promise
> Of everything forgotten.
>
> [*DD*, p. 93]

This "lighthearted" density might be a resolution we could achieve: a present peace in the absence of memory. But even before this vision fully takes hold, Ashbery imagines the counterpart within us of such healthiness—the invalid inside us who cannot forget that history means death:

>   and the well-being
> Grew, at the expense of whoever lay dying
> In a small room watched only by the progression
> Of hours in the tight new agreement.
>
> [*DD*, p. 93]

What then would be a good agreement between the various hours? To answer this, I must go outside the bounds of "Fragment" to one of the shorter lyrics in *The Double Dream*, "Years of Indiscretion" (p. 46). All versions of the self as presented in this rich volume of poetry can, I believe, subscribe to the poetic ethic of this poem's closing chant:

> Fables that time invents
> To explain its passing. They entertain
> The very young and the very old, and not
> One's standing up in them to shoulder
> Task and vision, vision in the form of a task
> So that the present seems like yesterday
> And yesterday the place where we left off a little while ago.
>
> [*DD*, p. 46]

8/

Against Monuments:
A Reading of Ashbery's
"These Lacustrine Cities"

DAVID RIGSBEE

A poem either invents or inherits the signals by which we understand it. With style, diction, tone, rhythm, and visual presentation, we are usually in the realm of inheritance; but with subject matter we are under the sway of invention. Obviously, so casual an observation as this contains enough exceptions to prevent its being accorded any more than prima facie agreement. Yet as an initial working distinction it will be useful to us as we begin to examine one of Ashbery's most emblematic poems, "These Lacustrine Cities" (*RM*, p. 9), which opens the poet's seminal collection *Rivers and Mountains*. The key to this poem lies in the tension it generates between the voice and its ostensible subject, for it is very much a poem in which one of the poet's greatest virtues (in this case his voice) is tempted to speak to a subject that, while attractive as subject matter, is alien to the voice and would only serve to subvert it.

The astonishing range and flexibility of Ashbery's voice, indeed, suggests the extent to which this poet is capable of spilling over, so to speak, into areas not congenial to his interests or temperament. In other words, it is quite conceivable that Ashbery might at one time or another find himself in a genuine dilemma, countenancing in subject matter what his style condemns in method. Fortunately, Ashbery is aware of the difficulty, and this poem declares that awareness. Thus it is by closely noting the poet's shifts of voice that we can most conveniently come to appreciate what is one of his main "terms of recurrence" (as the jargon has it). Such terms properly understood, can provide levers long enough for serious readers to use adroitly, readers who might otherwise throw up their hands after a poem or two.

Reading Ashbery thus becomes a matter of our willingness to maintain a particular kind of concentration in the face of disjunctive sequences of imagery, drastic shifts in tone, and all manner of apparent nonsequiturs, all of which constitute roadblocks to our usual avenues of apprehension. To say the least, the going can become difficult as the traditional effects of recognition are obscured. Yet these effects, which we have come to expect as formal virtues as well as poetic signals (congruency, for example), are not so much absent as regarded as secondary virtues. And even as our expectations are foiled here, the poem invents other signals by which we may negotiate its terrain. While the effect of voice is certainly one of the most important of these, others have also come to the attention of sensitive critics. Richard Howard, in an admirable essay on Ashbery's work,[1] notes two: the use of voices in competition and the presence of the emblem. Where both these elements are present, they sometimes coincide in such a way that the emblematic sense belongs to the poem's opposing voice, as distinct from its main voice. When this occurs it becomes convenient to see the poem's true subject matter as an instance of the dialectical movement between these voices, which are generally expressions of self-consciousness and desire.[2]

As we are speaking here of voice, perhaps we would do well to make another brief detour, this time to a point made by the contemporary poet and critic Paul Zweig in his book *The Adventurer*. In his discussion of the nineteenth-century novel,[3] Zweig locates the success of the genre's main line in its ability to offer conversation as a means for the "budding personality" to fit itself into the concerns of the larger social order. As such, we might say that the ability to launch into monologue reveals a talent for the creation of the *person*ality (Beckett's monologues spring readily to mind here). Moreover, far from suggesting complicity with the status quo, the ability to keep up a chatter in a world of diminished verbal quality suggests that we are witnessing the creation of a poetic personality capable of withstanding the subversive pressures of its own eloquence.

The emblem, on the other hand, establishes the scale of the poetic undertaking. We will certainly be better able to understand what follows in *Rivers and Mountains* if we can grasp its scale from the beginning, for it should be noted that all of Ashbery's books to date have been *books*, not collections, and each contains the emblematic material by which the scale is indicated, as well as the direction in which the book's concerns will generally be taken.

In the opening poem of *Rivers and Mountains*, Ashbery is at pains to assert the impoverished status both of monuments and, by implication, of moments of illumination that we hasten to raise, so to speak, into monuments. Both of these effects, as we know, have loomed large for the modern lyric, and one of the tasks of this poem will be to examine the impulse to monumentalize emotions. The judgment that results will strike some people as ambiguous, if not ambivalent, for the poet will maintain that, while this impulse in itself is to be censured, it is nevertheless inescapable, and that the difference between monuments to the imagination and, say, monuments to the emotions may amount to such a simple thing as preference. Further, to suppress so basic an impulse is to realize intuitively that it will reappear ironically in some other form. In the poem, Ashbery arrives at this position by first imagining a case in its extremity. By depicting the existence of a powerful monument, he follows the course of its power to its consequences for human endeavor, including his own. The poem opens in such a way as to suggest that the poem's setting has been very much on his mind: "These lacustrine cities grew out of loathing / Into something forgetful, although angry with history."

A city, as we know, is a monument to commerce, to the worst no less than the best examples of human dependency. This has been so since Homer declared the city's symbolic importance by depicting the destruction of Troy as a piecemeal atrocity. Yet something in these cities is *radically* wrong, for these cities have grown "out of loathing" as though some ancient self-despisal were their true soil. If cities are to grow from so negative a condition as loathing, there must be at least a vestigial sense, a nostalgia, for the independence that has been left behind in order for them to be founded. This sense, which the citizens of the lacustrine cities undoubtedly carry, sets their state of contradiction before us right away. By suppressing desire and electing instead to recognize the priority of need, we find that desire, by simple displacement, crops up anyway, tyrannically, in the symbol de luxe, the tower. As a pithy aside, this remark merely announces the existence of our duplicity. Yet the ancient duel of irreconcilable impulses is the subject of our poem, and we can see this clearly by reversing the terms of Octavio Paz's remark: in turning away from our contradiction we find redundacy rising to meet us in the form of the tower, symbolizing our thwarted desire, and yet attended by our actual desires. Such "redundancy" after all, models our chief means of reflection on the quality and scale of desires. Consequently, when the poet tell us that the citizens are still "angry with history," he merely stresses their dilemma while exposing their collective amnesia as a (necessary) fiction:

> They are the product of an idea: that man is horrible, for
> instance,
> Though this is only one example.
>
> They emerged until a tower
> Controlled the sky, and with artifice dipped back

Into the past for swans and tapering branches,
Burning, until all that hate was transformed into useless love.

Once the tower has established its dominance over the cities they stop emerging, seized, as it were, by their contradiction. That the tower controls the sky reminds us too that it has become a substitute for heaven. With this idea in mind, Ashbery has begun to reveal to us the scale on which the poem, as both prelude and critique, operates. Heidegger, in a discussion of one of Hölderlin's poems, remarks elliptically of the "dimension" between earth and heaven from which man takes the measure of himself: "Taking the measure of the dimension is the element within which human dwelling has its security, by which it securely endures."[4] Yet, in our poem, if this dimension has come under the dominance of the tower, we are left with a scale frozen (by a tower of longing), while in the background, obscured and paralyzed, looms the true dimension. Small wonder then that the tower turns "with artifice" to the past. This local means of measuring looks to its origin to retrieve two forms of ornament and uselessness (i.e., sentimental beauty and symmetry). This maneuver is done "With artifice," not art, because the measure established is not generous enough to admit art. Its scale runs from "all that hate" to "useless love," useless now precisely to the extent that the suppressed desire is wrought "by artifice" into nostalgia raised to the height of a tower. Quite a comparable instance of taking the measure occurs in Stanley Kunitz's stately poem "King of the River":

> If the heart were pure enough,
> but it is not pure,
> you would admit
> that nothing compels you
> anymore, nothing
> at all abides,
> but nostalgia and desire,
> the two-way ladder
> between heaven and hell.[5]

213

Yet the human scale receives an even more melancholy critique here, where both nostalgia and desire figure as incompletion. The heaven of the lacustrine cities is equal only to our paltry imaginings; hell, on the other hand, is always equal to itself. That is, it is equal to the particulars of absence of which it is the sum.

But let us return here to our original discussion of the monument. It seems that what we are faced with in the image of the tower amounts to what we might awkwardly term a "will-to-monument," a "burning" desire ironically frozen in its own uselessness before a backdrop of neglected measure: in short, the very charged image of a contradiction. The connections the tower makes to the past result in paradoxical connections into the poem's present, too. In the absence of useful imagination, we naturally loathe what we cannot get rid of (after all, what—given the situation—can we conceive of replacing it with?). Nonetheless, its mocking presence *is* there; the tower seems to be a kind of Ur-monument. Meanwhile, we learn that the cities have ceased to emerge, and we can infer a causal relationship between this and the tower's emergence. A nagging question occurs at this point: if the cities have ceased to emerge, in what sense can we continue to say they exist?

Indeed, this thought has not failed to occur to the poet either, as the next stanza suggests:

> Then you are left with an idea of yourself
> And the feeling of ascending emptiness of the afternoon
> Which must be charged to the embarrassment of others
> Who fly by you like beacons.

Everything has become less substantial now; the feeling of emptiness rises vertically. This is the same motion (with a proportional gradualness) with which we can imagine that our tower was erected. Just as we learn this, the poem's focus narrows into the second person, and we find by this shift that we have been accorded the dubious status of citizenship in the

214

lacustrine cities. We may, of course—as has often been done elsewhere—write off this predatory extension as just a poet's device for enforcing the immediacy of his meaning. Be that as it may, while we may claim only honorary membership by virtue of our disinterested participation in the poem, this "you" has fallen prey to a gnawing self-consciousness, precisely the kind of self-consciousness we feel at having suddenly become characters in the poem. Each denial, each backing off, we charge to the embarrassment of others in an effort to remain intact against what the poem has become. After all, we might say, this is just a poem. The idea of escape by projection informs the poem further as we notice that these "others" fly by like beacons: they are what we project them to be. Yet simultaneously they coincide with their function, which is to search out. Moreover, so pointedly are they described by their brevity and function that their very existence seems ironically circumscribed by this sense of their own integrity. That they are equally self-conscious is also true, and no doubt the others charge their embarrassment to us too. Meanwhile, as we continue to note these divagations, we must not forget the looming presence of the tower. How could we, when it represents the impossibility of our desire and delimits our heaven? Indeed, the essential aloneness of which each citizen is culpable derives from the fact that the artificial tower exists and controls the scale. This derivation runs parallel to the image of projection; thus the image puns visually on a psychological device. If a feeling of emptiness results in a "charge," we might properly ask where this charge comes from, and the answer once again is the tower. We are accustomed naturally to associate towers with beacons, and so when we charge our embarrassment (self-consciousness) to others, we do so *on behalf* of the tower. They (and we) then become its beacons in search of an answer to the very solipsism of which we are the questions. In other words, the solipsism derives from the monument.

At this point the poet's irony, so far controlled within the topography of his poem, begins to emerge in a voice reminiscent of Auden's witnesses.[6] This voice seeks to distance itself even further from its audience, as though to implicate us yet more deeply in the unfortunate situation the poem depicts. It intends to do so by receding in such a way as to set up more explicitly the emotional and aesthetic battle lines only implicit thus far. At this point, not only does the voice move more emphatically into opposition with its subject, but a strategic regrouping of all the poem's forces takes place as well. The "you," for example, now composed of citizens plus readers, finds itself opposed not only to other members of the second person, but also to the persona, suddenly cloned to "we," like the broom of the sorcerer's apprentice:

> The night is a sentinel.
> Much of your time has been occupied by creative games
> Until now, but we have all-inclusive plans for you.
> We had thought, for instance, of sending you to the middle of
>   the desert,
>
> To a violent sea, or of having the closeness of the others be air
> To you, pressing you back into a startled dream
> As sea-breezes greet a child's face.
> But the past is already here, and you are nursing some private
>   project.

The ominous bias of this "we" represents a crest in the poem's ironic tone when we realize that, despite its preposterous plans, it voices true concerns for the commonweal of the lacustrine cities. The poet's plans, on behalf of these others, amount to a kind of poetic shock treatment: the remedies are extreme to the same extent that the problem is grave. The tone, despite its irony, combines compassion with sternness, as if also aware of the enormous attraction implicit in an encounter between voice and adversary.

But, before we experience the effect of this shift in tone, we are told that "the night is a sentinel." We might ask what it purports to guard, since it is customary to consider sentinels as on the lookout for encroaching enemy forces. In this case the citizens of the lacustrine cities compose a force inimical to light (how lightless the first three stanzas are, for example, despite the afternoon). As in Dante, they are furtive selves flickering by the light of their own thwarted ingenuity; they are equally beings for whom the coming of sunlight implies the existence of a scale of being that must not be acknowledged. With the notation of this (we may presume) voiceless sentinel, the poet has prepared us, by way of his Audenesque assumption of the "we," for the fact that the voice is now to be distanced, ironic, and (in that guise) answering to the lightlessness. We may even hypothesize the distance across which the two are situated: it is the valley where the "will-to-monument," the most jejune priority of the cities' life, must face the unpleasant challenge issued to them by the poem's new voice. Looked at this way, the challenge brings to mind Keats's "vale of soulmaking," which stresses the virtues of process over polarization, of dialectic movement over an adherence to categories. The emphasis here is similar, for otherwise (had the poem's voice *not* sought the irony that distance convers) we would be faced with a simple-minded sort of Manichaeanism. Further, because the emphasis implies the virtue of process, it enables the poet to skip the immediate effects of the confrontation (rather in the same way that murder mysteries tend to skip over the sensationalism of the actual deed) and arrive at its consequences.

Having established a scene of confrontation, the poet moves quickly over his controlled geography, dismissing the preoccupations of his adversaries ("Much of your time has been occupied by creative games / Until now"). In doing so, as we can see, the force of irony sharpens into sarcasm, and "creative games" sound suddenly to be nothing more than an effete refinement of the poem's original contradiction. What, for example, could be less generative that a "creative game"? Consequently, the poet's substitute of "all-inclusive plans," in order to break through the citizens' self-imposed deadlock, must first begin with destruction and separation. Accordingly, images of drastic change follow, images that achieve their rhetorical effect by irony and what we presume to be their real effect by surprise.

These images, then, deal first with radical displacement ("We had thought, for instance, of sending you to the middle of the desert, / To a violent sea"). Both removals, though different in kind, seek to accomplish the same effect, that is, they remove the citizens from the metaphorical source of their malaise, and both offer agencies of cleansing. Moreover, each suggests a kind of removal based on poetic justice, for the desert is an extension of the already arid imaginations of the citizens, and the sea extends the lacustrine origins to their conclusion.

Having presented these, the poet employs an alternative image whose quality is not destructive but restorative:

> of having the closeness of the others be air
> To you, pressing you back into a startled dream
> As sea-breezes greet a child's face.

The conditions described here reflect a theoretical reinstatement for the citizens, but not a simple one—it is one that would combine punishment with therapy. We might well question the therapeutic value of the claustrophobia so implicit in this image. Yet it is precisely the reintroduction of this kind of forced intimacy that would begin to wean the citizens from their debilitating attitudes and rejoin them, so to speak, to each other. Should this remedy strike us as violent and intrusive, we would do well to bear in mind that the proposed restorative procedures occur in only two conditional modes: they are metaphorical, and they represent discarded wishes ("We had thought... "). Thus they constitute an exponential literary function by raising the stakes and ramifying what is already a highly literary circumstance (though from the poet's point of view they are real enough). He makes the "literariness" of these rejected considerations clear, in this last of three images, by making a metaphor of a metaphor ("pressing you back into a startled dream / As sea-breezes greet a child's face"). In doing this, he seeks metaphorically to turn back time to a point from which the citizens' elected mistake would not occur. The poet acknowledges that such action amounts to wishful thinking, and with that acknowledgment he withers again to the first person singular, as though the "we" on whose behalf he had been speaking no longer conferred the authority necessary to carry out a real confrontation. Additionally, the action's conditional quality at this point is raised exponentially in precisely the same manner as the metaphors used to describe it. This parallel development, which may seem obvious because metaphors are vehicles parallel to subject matter, is actually a subtle instance of a different kind of parallelism. Not only does he suggest an action that will not take place, but he places the final act in the context of a backward-moving dream, "As sea-breezes greet a child's face." Clearly, time will not be reversed in such a casual manner, and that is the point. The poet's intention in bringing the matter up is simply to suggest that rescue is impossible, even (or perhaps especially) for true dreamers. We might also pause here to note one of the obvious anxieties of any ambitious poet, of which this poem is an expression: precisely when he is a poet, he cannot simultaneously undertake the actions of which he dreams through all the resources of his language. He is a poet, not a man of action, and the impossibility of his "all-inclusive plans" seems to suggest that the two incarnations needed to complete the poet's wishes (expression and action) are mutually exclusive. If we understand this, then we begin to understand why the shifting voice in the poem seems so disembodied: it is only a voice. No wonder then, that he begins a motion toward closure at this point or that the language becomes terse in this stanza's final line: "But the past is already here, and you are nursing some private project."

The private project is of course the monument, whose image looms large in the final two stanzas. Having conceded his own inadequacy as a Keatsian physician, the poet retreats to a simpler level at which he reiterates, this time by way of a cleared vision, the citizens' circumstance and in so doing contents himself with an implied prognosis:

> The worst is not over, yet I know
> You will be happy here. Because of the logic
> Of your situation, which is something no climate can
>   outsmart.
> Tender and insouciant by turns, you see
>
> You have built a mountain of something,
> Thoughtfully pouring all your energy into this single
>   monument,
> Whose wind is desire starching a petal,
> Whose disappointment broke into a rainbow of tears.

The prognosis begins with the observation that the condition ("The worst") from which he has returned will continue, nor is there now reason to believe it will ever be otherwise. Solipsism, as a psychological consequence of misdirected desires, confers only an ignorant and malignant self-sufficiency. Thus we fail in our efforts to break through its shell to the extent that we believe our own alternative ideals. These in fact merely footnote the stages to failure that result from our manipulative beliefs.

A final irony ensues here that speaks directly to Ashbery's method as to the particulars of this poem. If we accept the failure of our most well-imagined devices against a situation "grown out of loathing," then we must withdraw credit for our good intentions too and recognize the integrity of the opponent, as intolerable as that might seem at first. It follows, then, that principles, ideals, and such are not necessarily the handiest things to be found among a poet's paraphernalia if he expects to encounter such an intractable, self-indulgent foe as we have here. Where do we go, then, after we have divested ourselves of our principles? If we examine this situation closely, it appears

that the adversity of living death against which we oppose ourselves existed before the formation of our poetic principles and
idealistic inclinations. Consequently, our principles have been
erected in terms of the poetic adversary and are not independent
of it. They are rather a defense and speak, in effect, the language
of the adversary only because they are formed in response to it.
If this is truly so, then we have arrived at a crossroads at which
we must decide whether poetry formulated thus defensively,
which has been deprived of the status of creative endeavor, can
hope to offer us anything but the spectacle of its constant conflict against all subjects, in which the only monuments that result are the records of its impossible encounters.

Ashbery's answer in this emblematic poem is that there is still
possibility, and the last two stanzas hint at what it is: it lies
finally with the voice itself (as Beckett and Zweig would agree).
At once censorial and descriptive, the voice that figures in these
concluding stanzas emblems the chief means Ashbery will use
in this book (and later) to thread his way out from his own
solipsism (so amply demonstrated in *The Tennis Court Oath*) toward complex encounters with his world.

In these stanzas the poet bids farewell to his own ostensible
subject matter, only to end as description, as naming. By aban-
doning subject matter as symptomatic of the uselessness of
abstractions derived from real dilemmas—as these pages of
commentary must surely give additional credence—the poet
knows he must return to the aboriginal Orphic function of
poetry, which is to give the true name to things. Poetry thus
becomes not a literary game for "solving" problems but a map-
ping of the world as it presents itself to the psyche and later by
extension, so to speak, to the body. In this function the poet is
able truly to discover the scale of living congenial to himself and
to possibility. We recall that this scale (dimension) was exactly
what the lacustrine cities possessed only in caricature. Thus the
poet's attitudes can no more restore their citizens to health than

a serious artist can bring a cartoon character to life. The only remaining treatment is ironic description, and the only possible movement after naming is a brisk exit from the poem.

But before we bring our discussion here to so abrupt a close, let us consider closely the manner in which Ashbery concludes his poem and his involvement with his subject. Obviously he is quite right when he says, in what seems a tart and understated observation, supported by a wonderfully skewed logic:

> Yet I know
> You will be happy here. Because of the logic
> Of your situation, which is something no climate can
> outsmart.

Changes in climate were precisely the agencies by which the poet had earlier fancied he could wean the lacustrine cities from their mistake, but climate, he admits, is no match for a self-perpetuating contradiction ("the logic of your situation"). Thus, having recognized the absurdity and impossibility of his task, he devises an ending commensurate not with his original undertaking, but with the subject, one that returns straight to the poem's predominant symbol, the tower:

> Tender and insouciant by turns, you see
>
> You have built a mountain out of something,
> Thoughtfully pouring all your energy into that single
> monument.

Although this appears merely to sum up much of what has gone before, it goes the previous sections one better by at last specifically naming the tower for what it is. Moreover, by identifying the monument as having already been built, the poet hints at the original contradiction it metaphorically embodies. He ends in a final, masterly trope of irony that accomplishes his new purpose by seeming to contradict his original position against monuments—precisely by composing the last two lines in the language of an epitaph (everyone's monument):

> Whose wind is desire starching a petal,
> Whose disappointment broke into a rainbow of tears.

With a poet so frequently urbane and droll as Ashbery, we can easily overlook the sheer integrity he has maintained in pursuit of his art. The charges of obscurantism and self-indulgence that have steadily accompanied his career have all too often failed to take into account the simple fact that to follow one's nose is always a difficult business. To be sure, his poetry has occasionally led him through some egregious patches of dissonance and nasal singing, and these forays into difficulty have stood out all the more against the sine wave of much contemporary poetry. Yet this poetry has been a continuous meditation not only on the relationship between clarity and complexity, but on its original discriminating uses as well. This, finally, is what the poem, in miniature, has tried to show us.

The Brushstroke's Integrity:
The Poetry of John Ashbery
and the Art of Painting

LESLIE WOLF

> To reproduce beloved objects and little corners of nature is just
> like a thief being enraptured by his legs in irons.
>   Kazimir Malevich

That John Ashbery has been interested in painting, that he
has chosen to look carefully at paintings and commit his as-
sessments of their achievement to paper, is obvious to anyone
familiar with even the barest facts of his biography. During the
decade he lived in Paris (1955–1965), he wrote art criticism for
the *Herald Tribune*; after his return to New York, he was an
editor of *Art News* until 1972; currently, he is art critic for the
weekly magazine *New York*. It is easy, too, to notice the presence
of painting as "subject matter" in Ashbery's poetry, and four of
his seven collections of poetry (I include the forthcoming *As We
Know*) share their titles with paintings. Moreover, any consideration of the relationship between his poetry and the art of painting must note his strategy of using specific paintings "as points
of departure for poems that discover themselves by meditating
on *objets d'art*, and thus displacing them," as David Lehman has
written. But, as we shall see, to have painting as a "subject" is
no guarantee that a poem is *painterly* (as defined by Clement
Greenberg): "loose, rapid handling, or the look of it; masses that
blot and fuse, instead of shapes that stay distinct; large, conspicuous rhythms; broken color; uneven saturations or densities

of paint; exhibited brush, knife, finger or rag marks—in short, a constellation of physical features like those defined by Wolfflin when he extracted his notion of the *Malerische* from Baroque art."[1]

The sestina entitled "The Painter"—the earliest poem collected in Ashbery's first book, *Some Trees*—provides an example worth examining. It is a narrative, rather prosaic poem, even for a sestina, whose end words are "buildings," "portrait," "subject," "canvas," "brush," and "prayer." Fred Moramarco, in his useful essay "The Painterly Poets," has discussed how the stanzas of this poem unfold a parable of modern painting. The painter in the poem is "Sitting between the sea and the buildings," and though we are told that "he enjoyed painting the sea's portrait," he is frustrated by a disinclination to lift his brush and paint a realistic picture, as though "he expected his subject / To rush up the sand, and, seizing a brush, / Plaster its own portrait on the canvas." Following the advice of "the people who lived in the buildings,"

> He chose his wife for a new subject,
> Making her vast, like ruined buildings,
> As if, forgetting itself, the portrait
> Had expressed itself without a brush.

> [*ST*, p. 54]

"Slightly encouraged" by this expressionistic exercise, he takes a casual but radical step: dipping his brush into the sea and painting seawater directly onto the canvas. "He had gone back to the sea for his subject," in the poem's ironic double diction. The response is immediate, as in a dream: "malicious mirth" from "some artists leaning from the buildings," who are provoked to comment:

> "We haven't a prayer
> Now, of putting ourselves on canvas,
> Or getting the sea to sit for a portrait!"

> [*ST*, p. 55]

225

The crisis is neatly evoked, however veiled: neither the self nor the world will anymore sit still and be the artist's subject. And though "Others declared it a self-portrait," the issue surfaces as the seawater dries:

> Finally all indications of a subject
> Began to fade, leaving the canvas
> Perfectly white.
>
> [*ST*, p. 55]

The dilemma has come home to stay; the problematic nature of the subject of our art has entrenched itself *as* its subject, or at least as its persistent theme. Finally, in the poem's envoy, the nature of this new "subject" finds a wonderful articulation:

> They tossed him, the portrait, from the tallest of buildings;
> And the sea devoured the canvas and the brush
> As though his subject had decided to remain a prayer.
>
> [*ST*, p. 55]

"As though his subject had decided to remain a prayer." The teleuton "prayer," fortunately, is one rich enough to suggest all the forms of the modern artist's struggles.

This may be a parable of modern painting, but painterly poetry? No. The language of Ashbery's sestina, however ingenious and suggestive, is primarily denotative—"utilitarian," in Valéry's sense. It has the suppleness only of good prose, aided considerably by felicitous lining. But, as I shall suggest below, the poet's development after the volume in which "The Painter" appeared reveals freedoms, darings, and a willingness to confront the authentic "difficulty" of the medium that are only crudely suggested in *Some Trees*. Never again, with the brilliant exception of "Self-Portrait in a Convex Mirror," will an issue, a "motif"—as Cézanne preferred to call his subject—pose long enough to have its picture taken. As our ostensible subject "dissolves," and with it any direct relationship between art and sensible reality, "the mimetic function of art is limited to an imitation of the artist's immediate sensibility—not an external or objective scene or series of events."[2] A new and complicated freedom emerges as the fulcrum of the dialectic between the artist and the world shifts inward. This has happened literally before our eyes in the painting of the past hundred years; it has also happened, less obviously, in the verbal arts, and especially in poetry.

Leaving the author of "The Painter," for the moment, floundering in "the high interiors of the sea" (Melville's phrase) which have fascinated many of this country's most vital imaginations, let us look more closely at the arts of poetry and painting with an eye toward discovering their unity and differences. Wallace Stevens suggested their essential unity in an address entitled, "The Relations between Poetry and Painting," when he cited Baudelaire's idea of an "unascertained and fundamental aesthetic" of which "poetry and painting are related but dissimilar manifestations." No poet, Stevens noted, "can have failed to recognize how often a detail . . . or remark in respect to painting applies also to poetry. All these, to the extent that they have meaning for poets as well as painters, are specific instances of relations between poetry and painting." These statements suggest an approach that they regrettably do not pursue, for Stevens declines, later in the same address, to discuss relations between "this poet and that painter, this school and that school," claiming this would entail little more than "much tinkling of familiar cymbals." He is content to stress that in an era "in which disbelief is so profoundly prevalent, or, if not disbelief, indifference to questions of belief, poetry and painting, and the arts in general, are . . . a compensation for what has been lost. Men feel imagination is the next greatest power to faith."[3]

It is unfortunate that Stevens did not see fit to descend from this general plateau to a more specific examination of his subject, especially since at the time of these remarks, 1951, the painting that has come to be known as abstract expressionism was being recognized and installed as the central paradigm of the creative process of the midcentury. In its radical assumptions, rooted firmly in an awareness of the achievements of the past and in a recognition of "the crisis" in painting that cried out for a new focus and orientation, abstract expressionism not only represented a breakthrough in the realm of painting but issued into the neighboring precincts of literature and music, shock waves whose reverberations are still very much alive today, three decades later. It would be interesting to hear Stevens address himself to the challenges of this new movement, the obvious backdrop for John Ashbery's development as a poet; but in the absence of any such commentary it becomes necessary to look ourselves for a firmer basis on which to elucidate the "specific instances" Stevens invoked.

In considering Ashbery's relationship to painting, I think we must resist the temptation to proceed by attending to those specific paintings on which some of his poems are based. It is perhaps part of his wisdom that he chooses to address certain maverick painters of the past (Parmigianino, Ingres, de Chirico)—men with whom he feels a spiritual kinship—rather than those contemporary or recent artists whose work his own most closely parallels. It will first be necessary to look briefly at how painting weaned itself from the burden of representation; at the role the cubist "explosion" played in this process in the early decades of this century; and at how the abstract expressionist movement in the years after World War II addressed the impasse bequeathed by cubism to carry painting to a new understanding of its own mission, creating in the process a new relationship between the artist and his medium. If we can trace in these evolutions a gradual relinquishing of "the object" and see how it reentered painting with a changed status in the "anatomical" landscapes, "impossible" transitions, and thoroughly ambiguous space of Gorky, Pollock, and de Kooning, we will be in a position to examine how the world denoted by referential language departed poetry—a process begun self-consciously by Baudelaire, Mallarmé and Valéry—and re-emerged, with a new status, in the loosened matrix of Ashbery's idiom. For in much the same way that painters such as de Kooning broke out of the cubist framework created by Picasso and Braque, Ashbery has left behind the relatively static "prisms" of even such a sophisticated poet as Stevens to develop a mobile semantic that depends upon a continuous dialogue between the artist and his own work—a dialogue in which the artist's experience of the world, including his experience of making the poem, becomes, to an unprecedented degree, the subject of the work.

> When I kiss D____, I keep my eyes open and her face close-up is doubled.—Picasso

The history of modern painting, as it is taught in the universities, commonly takes as its starting point the Impressionist movement which emerged from the naturalism that prevailed before. Many historians begin with Claude Monet, seeing in his conception of vision as a blending and interpreting of light the first strong "awareness of process" that increasingly characterizes later painters. The Impressionist theory of color, evolved by Monet and Renoir, was based on the perception that "all the colors on the canvas influence each other": the colors of the apples in the still life were now echoed by the greens, violets, and browns modeling the "white" tablecloth, and black gave up its dominant role in shadow to make room for the systematic tempering of colors by admixtures and close juxtapositions of their complementaries. This technique tied the surface of the canvas together and gave it an autonomy it had lacked while subject to such academic techniques as chiaroscuro. The plane of chromatic relations constructed by the Impressionists resulted in a kind of atmospheric screen—one way, as modern nonobjective painters say, of "refusing the object." But the evolution of Impressionist painting must be ultimately seen as a variety of experimental techniques in the service of "realism." It is in the late work of Paul Cézanne that a more problematic "refusal" surfaces.

The Impressionists, in their announced aim of "painting light," had looked at the world "subjectively"—but it was the world, nevertheless, that they had looked at and tried to render. Cézanne wanted to break through this "subjectivism" and penetrate to "the structure of things." His mature ("Postimpressionist") work stressed horizontals, verticals, and geometric forms in an architectural way, even as his intense focus on different parts of the canvas loosened and bent perspective, showing us different objects or sections of landscape from different points of view. It is ironic that this attempted "greater realism" should have laid bare the tension between illusionism and the structure of the paint on the canvas's surface that had been concealed by the techniques of painters since the Renaissance. But it was precisely this explicit tension—a "difficulty" that inheres in the process of presenting three-dimensional space on a two-dimensional plane—that made Cézanne's art such a decisive turning point. "Cézanne's anxiety," said Picasso, "that is what interests us."

The cubists may have misunderstood Cézanne's paintings—or at least his intentions—but it is widely recognized that it was this "misunderstanding" that led them to take his problem to a different level. We can see, in the resolving lens of subsequent developments, that his late canvases propose a new dimension of self-awareness in the act of painting, "an awareness of dialectical problems in the very process of art which could only be solved by a revolutionary transformation of its cognitive status . . . . The old language of art was no longer adequate for human consciousness."[4] Cubism proposed a new language, declaring itself an art of conception from the start. It was born of a new focus on the picture plane itself, recasting "representational" elements into a new dialectic of not only visual, but conceptual ambiguity. If the cubists "assassinated the object," as was charged, "so much the worse for objects," Picasso said. But it was not really true that the cubists got rid of the object (there were more abstract artists—Kandinsky, Mondrian, Malevich—of whom this could be said); they took it apart and reconstructed it in a multiplicity of relationships. Picasso emphasized that one always started in the real world, with something, "then one can remove traces of actuality." Still, as Herbert Read has pointed out,

This was the moment of liberation.... Once it was accepted that the plastic imagination has at its command, not the fixities of a perspectival point of view (with the consequent necessity of organizing visual images with objective coherency), but the free association of any visual elements... then the way is open to an activity which has little correspondence with the plastic arts of the past.... The vital difference consists in whether the artist in order to agitate the human sensibility proceeds from perception to representation; or whether he proceeds from perception to imagination, breaking down perceptual images in order to recombine them in a nonrepresentational structure. [His] conceptual structure must still appeal to human sensibility, but the assumption is that it does this more directly, more intensely and more profoundly in this new way than if burdened with an irrelevant representational function.[5]

Cubism, then, opened the field and may rightly be considered this century's first great consolidated style. But, as one historian has suggested, an "authentic style" "is a maturation that is out-dated almost at the instant it appears: it is contemporary for only a brief span; then it becomes a convention."[6] The great burst of creativity with which the century began lasted roughly twenty-five years. The surrealist movement of the twenties, with its conspicuous interest in the unconscious, extended further the range of painting by bringing both new and traditional techniques of figuration to bear on new kinds and organizations of content. What was new, in painters like Ernst and Miró, was their emphasis on spontaneous and intuitive methods for creating pictorial sensations. But though many great painters (Matisse, Klee, and that enigmatic colossus Picasso, to name three) continued to work independently and fruitfully for years afterward, by 1930 the "Masters of Paris," in the words of Thomas Hess, "were filling out the images of their art to the limits. The crisis of modern art rapidly was defined in terms of: 'What Is There Left To Do?' "[7] The period preceding World War II was thus a time of consolidation and digestion of the innovations achieved earlier. It was the years during and after the war—which we shall examine shortly—that saw the second important creative upheaval of our time as one painter after another, energized by the methodology of the surrealists, abandoned the strictures of cubism to forge a new kind of painting that was both abstract and painterly at the same time. What is most important for our purposes is to recognize the degree to which painting had become conscious of its own freedoms and limitations as it addressed the imagination. In this light, we can agree with Harold Rosenberg and Thomas Hess when they reject the statement that the history of modern painting is one of "a growing rejection of the third dimension."[8] This development is really just one aspect of what Hess has called "an increasing revelation of the artist's means, both technical and conceptual... a progressive stripping away of technical disguises and masks for content"[9] until art became, as Stevens said of poetry, "the process of the personality of the poet."

Baudelaire had articulated this awareness reached in painting nearly a hundred years earlier when he wrote: "The whole visible universe is but a storehouse of images and signs to which the imagination will give a relative place and value; it is a sort of pasture which the imagination must digest and transform."[10] The history of this attitude in poetry, from Baudelaire and Rimbaud through Mallarmé and Valéry and the moderns, has included a growing recognition that in order to create an instrument that works on the imagination, the poet must divert his materials—the words of his language—from their habitual usage. And if the Symbolism of Mallarmé and Valéry never produced an art equal to the majesty of its theories, it nevertheless delineated clearly the orientation that Pound, Eliot, Crane, and Stevens brought to the task of writing poems during the first half of the twentieth century. While painters were dissecting the "process" of vision to construct an art that challenged the mind's ability to assimilate and synthesize forms, these poets were transforming their medium into a catalyst of the imagination ("the poem of the mind in the act of finding / What will suffice"—Stevens), recognizing that they were addressing a new and accelerating hunger ("it has not always had to find"). Stevens, who called the imagination "the only genius"—"It is intrepid and eager and the extreme of its achievement lies in its abstraction"[11]—said the poet must "somehow create a 'nongeography' in the mind, for the imagination must be a violence from within that protects us from a violence without."[12] He was careful to emphasize, however, that while the poet is to be measured "by his power to abstract himself," he must "withdraw with him, into his abstraction, the reality on which lovers of truth insist." How does the poet "abstract reality"? Stevens is crystal clear: "by placing it in his imagination."

Let us consider what different forms a "reality placed in the imagination" may take in poetry and painting. I have suggested earlier that Ashbery's poetry, after *Some Trees*, is *analogous* to "action painting" (a term not entirely appropriate, as we shall see, but adequate here). But what does it mean to say a visual art is "analogous" to a verbal or symbolic one? There is an essential difference between a medium whose basic element is *nonsignificant* and one whose element is inherently denotative. The painter has an immediate freedom to depart from "representation" that is limited only slightly by the historically conditioned associations that attach to the colors he applies to his canvas. To reach this state of freedom in a verbal art, the poet must use the signifying quality of his medium *against itself*. Poets have always

233

done this to a greater or lesser extent in their attempt to create the "tension" that elevates their language from a merely referential function. Valéry in particular has written eloquently of the poet's need to work through language by working *on* language, a process that requires that he become a "maker of deviations." Not all deviations are permitted to him, Valéry notes, "but it is precisely his business and his ambition to find the deviations" that create meaning in novel and beautiful ways. The poet is advised to employ whatever means he can devise— "rhymes, inversion, elaborated figures, symmetries and images"—to retard the reader's progress through the language of the poem, to alert him to the possibilities of alternate and incompletely formed coherencies. Indeed, the New Critics, following Pound and Eliot, brought to a new height the awareness of the ways tension and dissonance can be fused into a poetic idiom, looking to the example of the Metaphysical school of Donne for its development of an agile "language of paradox." Here we can usefully borrow from Ernst Gombrich's analysis of cubism in order to appreciate how twentieth-century poetry has taken this lesson to heart: "If illusion is due to the interaction of clues and the absence of contradictory evidence, the only way to fight its transforming influence is to make the clues contradict each other and to prevent a coherent image of reality from destroying the pattern in the plane."[13] As one critic has written of this statement, "A Cubist painting resists all our attempts to apply 'the test of consistency.' ... By intentionally scrambling representational clues, the Cubist painter thus forces us to 'accept the flat surface with all its tensions.' The ambiguity cannot, in other words, be resolved."[14]

Notice in Gombrich's statement that the aim is to fight the "transforming influence" of "illusion"; for illusion is what allows us to be unconscious of the medium through which we are apprehending reality. Poets like Crane and Stevens—and Ashbery— will not allow us this unconsciousness. One need only consider Crane's arresting adjective-noun combinations—

"improved infancy," "immaculate venom," "petalled word"—
or his use of negating prefixes and suffixes—"and your head
unrocking to a pulse"—to see one form the poem's "resistance"
may assume. Stevens's strategy is outwardly quieter, if no less
insistent. One thinks of the subtle sliding weights moving beneath his strategic repetition of words, transforming them into
semantic merry-go-rounds, or the bold contradiction of some of
his gestures ("If all the green of Spring was blue, and it is"—
"Connoisseur of Chaos"). Entangled in a medium whose primary burden in ordinary usage is to refer to external reality, the
poet must arrange the "brushstrokes" of his tableau in such a
way that they yield contradictory clues. To do this the poet
must, as Stevens directed, approach language abstractly—that
is, transport reality into his imagination. That way he can "use"
reality without committing himself to any particular reality. The
language must inevitably employ some species of "deviation"—
syntactic dislocation, dissonant diction, variations within repetition—if the poet is to wrest his words from an easy, habitual
assimilation.

Moreover, the poet knows "that the communication of a poetic state that involves the whole feeling organism is a different
thing from the communication of an idea," as Valéry put it. Here
Ashbery's idiosyncratic use of voice adds something vital to the
array of techniques in the poet's repertoire; his uncanny ability
to wring from a group of words an inflection that makes it into
an emblem of attitude allows him much greater mobility than
any poet I know of before him. It is this tactic, finally, that
enables him to "speak so deeply into our unprepared knowledge / Of ourselves, the talking engines of our day" (*AW*, p.
88). Ashbery knows it is the medium that enacts the "process
of the personality of the poet," and that this detached relationship to language grants him a new freedom to orchestrate voice.
The poet is not to be identified with any of the inflections he
evokes; rather, he is the arena in which they meet and argue and
coexist:

> There are those who do care for that
> Kind of outline, distant, yes, but warm,
> Full of the traceable meaning that never
> Gets adopted. Well, isn't that truth?
>
> ["The Picnic Grounds," *AW*, p. 98]

> All right. Let's see—
> How about "The outlook wasn't brilliant
> For the Mudville nine that day"? No,
> That kind of stuff is too old-hat. Today
> More than ever readers are looking for
> Something upbeat, to sweep them off their feet.
> Something candid but also sophisticated
> With an unusual slant. A class act
> That doesn't *look* like a class act
>
> ["Litany," *AW*, p.35]

> We are all talkers
> It is true, but underneath the talk lies
> The moving and not wanting to be moved, the loose
> Meaning, untidy and simple like a threshing floor.
>
> ["Soonest Mended," *DD*, p. 18]

Ashbery would hold with Stevens that the poem dwells "in the contention, the flux / between the thing as idea / and the idea as thing," but the poetry from which the three excerpts above were taken has expanded Stevens's willingness to occupy this "dual" world in a way that allows it to harbor many more contexts and conflicts than does Stevens's work. One hears the echo of Stevens behind this gesture:

> the carnivorous
> Way of these lines is to devour their own nature, leaving
> Nothing but a bitter impression of absence, which as we know
> involves presence, but still. . . .
>
> ["The Skaters," *RM*, p. 39]

But how different a presence it is! The colloquialism of even this "abstract" discussion permits it to be entered into far more immediately than any utterance of Stevens's monolithic persona. Ashbery takes for granted that his audience "has / Already witnessed the events of which you write, / Tellingly, in your log" (*HD*, p. 20) and knows that this audience attends not to information, but to the excitement and eccentricity of the *shape* of the information ("How to receive this latest piece of information. / *Was* it information?" ("Soonest Mended," *DD*, p. 17). The more unusual its elements, the more novel the relationships between those elements, the more gratifying it is that the gesture creates a movement that is felt to be true. However complex the intellectual issues his poems address themselves to, Ashbery understands that his intellectuality needs sensuous objectification. He wants to tell us "something about time / That only a clock can tell you: how it feels, not what it means" (*HD*, p. 29).

> Hamlet: Do you see yonder cloud that's almost
> in shape of a camel?
> Polonius: By the mass, and 'tis like a camel, indeed.
> Hamlet: Me thinks it is like a weasel.
> Polonius: It is backed like a weasel.
> Hamlet: Or like a whale?
> Polonius: Very like a whale.　　　　　*—Hamlet*

We left our discussion of painting at that moment when a small group of artists in New York were about to create the new painting that has come to be known as "abstract expressionism" (though many other names—tachism, neoplasticism, abstract surrealism—have also been used). Ashbery has said, "I have perhaps been more influenced by modern painting and music than by poetry"; to see how this is true, let us look at the emergence, in the decade before the publication of *Some Trees*, of this new painterly aesthetic, with particular attention to Willem de Kooning, a friend of Ashberry's and the painter who most brilliantly demonstrates the radical freedoms and ambitions of the new movement. De Kooning was not the first abstract expressionist—this distinction probably belongs to Arshile Gorky, or even to the German-born painter Hans Hofmann, whose art school in New York had an immeasurable influence, beginning in the thirties, on the younger painters (Gorky, Pollock, de Kooning, and others) who were to overshadow him. I choose de Kooning not only because he is, to my mind, the greatest painter of the modern age, but also because, in the development of his career, we can see the kind of growing mastery that allows us to trace those qualities that have come to define abstract expressionism for more and more people.

I have referred to the "impasse" that had come about as cubism exhausted its methods and began to be felt as a constraint by the American painters of the forties. The response to this situation of the "first generation" painters of the New York School, as they have been called, took two main directions. The "gestural abstractions" of the first group—Gorky, Pollock, and de Kooning—are more obviously connected to painters as various as Picasso, Miró, Matisse, and early Kandinsky. The work of the second group, including painters like Rothko, Newman, Still, and Ad Reinhardt, is based on large expanses of color, in some instances "hard edge" and geometric, with an almost total lack of figuration, and recalls the explorations of Mondrian, early Malevich, and Josef Albers. The first group is far more relevant to a consideration of Ashbery: their emphasis on the brushstroke and even on figurative "drawing" set against or blended into a looser, more ambiguous space suggests freer and more spontaneous activity on the part of the painter. The artists of this group are tied together more by a common attitude than by any similarities in their finished paintings. They embraced the notion that the *act* of creating, in the words of curator Edward Henning, "is 'open' and involves the artist in a complex evolution consisting of a search for solutions to multiple, interacting and flexible problems. The solutions at which he arrives, and even more, the problems that he selects, reveal the nature and the intensity of the artist's experience of the world."[15]

These painters, in other words, regarded the canvas as "an arena in which to act—rather than as a space in which to reproduce, redesign, analyze or 'express' an object, actual or imagined."[16] The importance of this shift is that the painter becomes an actor, and the spectator must approach the canvas with assumptions different even from those that equipped him to look at a cubist painting. As Harold Rosenberg, an early champion of this art and originator of the term "action painting," defines it: "What gives the canvas its meaning is... the way the artist organizes his emotional and intellectual energy as if he were in a living situation.... Since the painter has become an actor, the spectator has to think in a vocabulary of action: its inception, duration, direction—psychic state, concentration and relaxation of the will, passivity, alert waiting. He must become a connoisseur of the gradations among the automatic, the spontaneous, the evoked."[17] The painter becomes an active force inside the canvas, beginning, usually, with only a general notion of where he is headed. This recalls Valéry's statement that "drawing is a way of thinking." But the artist is not merely representing "abstract relations," nor is he working under conditions of total freedom—for, as de Kooning has said of his own work, "abstract shapes" must have "likeness." This is why de Kooning's painting, despite its devotion to the conspicuous freedoms for which "action painting" is known, retains strong ties to the figuration present in all classicism. His gestures carry hints of representation even as they embody these hints in a fluid and "paradoxical" matrix; they evoke objects and suggest perspective even as they deny them. Only in the presence of this kind of dialectic can "each stroke... be a decision," in Rosenberg's phrase, that is "answered by a new question."

It is in the creation of this tension that de Kooning connects with Ashbery. The latter's poetry is a mode of discourse that proceeds by assertions, reflections, digressions, and reversals in which are embedded vividly etched moments of *concrete* apprehension. One need only read a sentence like

> This stubble field
> Of witnessings and silent lowering of the lids
> On angry screen-door moment rushing back
> To the edge of woods was always alive with its own
> Rigid binary system of inducing truths
> From starved knowledge of them.
>
> ["No Way of Knowing," *SP*, p. 567]

to see that the sharply felt moment in the third line, its rapid and schematized vividness, is subsumed into an elegant abstract gesture; a moment may go by before it becomes, at the same time, a "description" of the human head. This instance points to the way Ashbery's poetry has moved beyond the presentational mode of Stevens into an aesthetic of *enactment*. To be sure, images will always remain the poet's primary tool, but only by undercutting their denotative solidity can the poem usher us into an "increasingly convincing darkness" where "the words become palpable, like a fruit / That is too beautiful to eat" (*HD*, p. 15). If it sounds as though we are caught between worlds, Ashbery spells it out for us in unmistakable terms:

> Only then did you glance up from your book,
> Unable to comprehend what had been taking place
> Or say what you had been reading.
>
> ["The Other Tradition," *HD*, p. 2]

We stand half-in, half-out—or, rather, we enter fully into an imaginary world, but we have taken with us, "into our abstraction," that "reality on which lovers of truth insist" which allows us to *experience* our knowledge more fully than we could through reading any merely abstract idiom. Stevens had the same designs on us, but, as Perloff has pointed out: "Ashbery turns the Stevens mode on its head by cutting off the referential dimension. Obscure as Stevens' poems so often are, they do convey particular meanings. . . . Ashbery, on the other hand, subverts signification as fully as possible."[18] This statement is not exactly true (though *The Tennis Court Oath* tries hard to redeem it—see below). The evolution we see in some painters' work, Mondrian's, for example, of painting without depiction of any kind will not find a true analogy in poetic art. The movement away from "signification" is not entirely possible in language, as we have noted. And Ashbery, despite his ironic comments ("Are we never to make a statement?"), builds his poetry out of what Auden called (in his introduction to *Some Trees*) "calculated oddities" that do nevertheless make gestures of meaning. But these gestures so often collide and contradict each other that the *final* meaning of Ashbery's idiom consists in the enactment of paradox, the insistence that any unequivocal statement is unfaithful to the prismatic nature of reality, the "reality at cross-purposes with itself that first caused you to grow restless," as he wrote in "The System."

From this point of view, Stevens—Ashbery's favorite poet—is a kind of poetic "cubist" out of whom has sprung Ashbery's de Kooning: Stevens contradicts the object but retains it as "motif" in much the way Picasso did; but Ashbery, like de Kooning, "dares to remove the object further before reconstructing it."[19] Pound's notion of the image as "that which presents an intellectual and emotional complex in an instant of time" has not lost all its relevance, but Ashbery is writing after that "watershed," articulated by Charles Olson, when "the discrete [isn't] any longer a good enough base for discourse," when "the sentence itself has become an exchange of force," not "a completed thought."[20] In his attempt to make consciousness itself his model, to enact "the false starts and unknown destinations of the embattled imagination . . . its struggle for escape and transcendence,"[21] Ashbery has launched a veritable river of paradoxical argument in which swim casual axioms, ironic self-commentaries, and disembodied fragments of voice as well as

Pound's images, all swept along by a resilient and cunningly engineered syntax that both rushes us forward and slows us down, stretching out the moment of perception, harboring us in its "difficulty." The result is sentences, to quote a recent advertisement for this season's swimsuits, that "look fast even while standing still."

The poem has become an arena of impulses, and Ashbery's characteristic methods of generating and sustaining them constitute a poetic equivalent of the improvisational strategies painters like de Kooning devised to loosen and animate the cubist framework they inherited. Both Ashbery's poetry and de Kooning's painting mean to challenge our thresholds of assimilation through a deft art of suggestion and metamorphosis. When we talk about the idiom succeeding, in either case, we are talking about an idiom that is attractive and graceful, but that resists immediate assimilation. Perhaps we are reminded of Donald Barthelme's "Paraguay"—"not the Paraguay that exists on our maps"—where "such is the smoothness of surfaces . . . that anything not smooth is valuable."[22] To participate in the life that takes place there, we must first make peace with its protean ambiguity. But ultimately, to borrow Eliot's words, "the only method is to be very intelligent." Then, perhaps, we can understand, with "The Ecclesiast" of *Rivers and Mountains*, how "the shoe pinches, even though it fits perfectly."

> From a confusion of shapes, the spirit is quickened to new inventions.—Leonardo da Vinci

In one of the poems in *Some Trees*, Ashbery announced that

> All beauty, resonance, integrity
> Exist by deprivation or logic
> Of strange position.
>
> [*ST*, p. 74]

And this "logic of strange position" found no more extreme incarnation than in the poet's next collection, *The Tennis Court Oath*. Many readers, confronting its pages of grammatical chunks and non sequiturs, would agree with Harold Bloom's remark: "The Ashbery of *The Tennis Court Oath* may have been moved by de Kooning and Kline, Webern and Cage, but he was not moved to the writing of poetry."[23] There are striking poems in the book with long, relatively coherent passages (e.g., "How Much Longer Will I Be Able to Inhabit the Divine Sepulcher . . . "), but on the whole this poetry fails to sustain energy. "Yet though we knew the course *was* hazards and nothing else," as Ashbery later wrote (*DD*, p. 18), we miss here the ballast that gives the hazards their ultimate significance; that continuity of feeling which sets in relief the poems' arrests and shifts is absent. Critics have compared "The Tennis Court Oath," "Leaving the Atocha Station," "The New Realism," and the sprawling numbered sequence "Europe" to the collages of visual artists as diverse as Max Ernst, Joseph Cornell, and Robert Rauschenberg.[24] I think, though, that collage is not so easily achieved with words. Let us remind ourselves that any verbal art unfolds over a period of time, not in an instantaneous gestalt or even a rapid scanning process. A poem exploits our expectation that language address itself, even for short intervals, to a sustained concern or feeling, if not always to a subject, and the logic that guides visual collage must undergo some transformation to create poetry that draws the reader through its movement. The poet must weld his fragmentary perceptions or events into an idiom that *seems* to adhere to the procedures of his medium even while subverting or contradicting them. Ultimately, in creating such verbal machinery, Ashbery's poetry, from *Rivers and Mountains* onward, resembles collage only in the way de Kooning's painting does—the poet building his tableau through the orchestration of words, the painter through the orchestration of pigment (not wire, straw, glass, or photographs). Ashbery's poetry during the past ten years has developed into an increasingly long-lined and acrobatic mode of gesturing that permits the line to bear more kinds of weight and generate or subtract momentum ever more subtly. In this mode, he has won through to a kind of freedom very few poets ever enjoy. The surface of his poetry, like that of the abstract expressionist painting we have been considering, is striking for its freshness and unpredictability; its lack of "finish" allows it to breathe. In the same way de Kooning invents "shapes that will switch meaning and position, jump the tracks of formalistic composition to act as background and foreground, positive and negative... hill and thumb, letter and mouth,"[25] Ashbery's serpentine sentences, eclectic diction, and numerous "blurring" devices (indefinite or ambiguous pronouns, shifting tenses, eccentric subordination, etc.) permit him to move gracefully between gestures woven of images and commentary on the very process in which he is involved. Richard Howard has written of Ashbery's impulse "to break out of the legalities of a compositional system and to address the reader directly."[26] Howard compares these moments of direct address to the practice in heraldry of embedding a smaller blazon (a "blazon *en abyme*") within the primary one as a kind of commentary on the latter. The notion of these blazons *en abyme* provides a good index of the increasing agility and density of Ashbery's idiom: as he has evolved a longer "stroke," he has become more able to integrate these commentaries or emblems of self-awareness into the primary surface of the poem, so that in the later books we find the commentary fusing with the poem's suggestive descriptions into a seamless idiom that rarely displays a "break" as overt as "Yes, friends, these clouds pulled along on invisible ropes / Are, as you have guessed, merely stage machinery" (*HD*, p. 50). Instead, the poem addresses its ostensible subject at the same time as it proposes a self-reflexive awareness. This constitutes a fascinating poetic version of the abstract expressionists' "dialogue" with the canvas. The question is not one of illusionism versus nonillusionism; rather, it is one of a shifting and self-conscious illusionism. Just as de Kooning changes his relationship to the gestural abstractions with which he is filling his painting, Ashbery's voice is constantly modulating its relationship to both its images and its propositions. In *As We Know*, for example, the poet manages to be inside and outside at once:

> So that the roundness
> Was all around to be appreciated, yet somehow flat
> As well, and could never be trusted
> Even though the rushes slanted all one way
> In the autumn wind, and the leaves
> And branches tried to slant with them
> In a poem of harmonious dejection, but it was
> Only picture-making. Under
> The intimate light of the lantern
> One really felt rather than saw
> The thin, terrifying edges between things. . . .
>
> ["Litany," *AW*, pp. 15–16]

Indeed, the prismatic quality of the poet's stance is carried to a new extreme in the poem from which these lines are taken, a sixty-page meditation composed in two adjacent columns that offer themselves simultaneously. Opposite the excerpt just quoted is an equally beguiling "limbo":

> Furthermore, there was nothing like
> Shadows of oranges
> In the new game, nothing fanciful
> And abstract one step away from foggy
> Reality. The series were all sisters
> Back in the fifties when more of this
> Sort of thing was allowed. Two could
> Go on at once with special permission
> And the dreams were responsible to no base
> Of authority but could wander on for
> Short distances into the amazing nearness
> That the world seemed to be.
>
> ["Litany," *AW*, pp. 15–16]

The phrase "a poem of harmonious dejection" recalls Picasso's definition of a picture as "a horde of destructions" or Harold Rosenberg's comment about "action painting": "To maintain the force to refrain from settling anything, [the artist] must exercise in himself a constant No."[27] The painter, in other words, exerts a great effort to keep things ambiguous. In this light the "painterly" handling of words consists not in extensive use of colors, objects, or figures, or in the sketching of clear pictures, but in detaching language from any *consistent* referential process so that it can do more than one thing in the fertile ground of the imagination. "Parts are neutralized," wrote Brian O'Doherty of de Kooning's paintings, "in a way that enables them to bear multiple functions."[28] De Kooning has said that "everything must be made abstract" before he can use it.[29] The result is that "When a subject (for example, a woman) appears in a de Kooning, it appears like an abstraction embedded in the real subject—the process. . . . The artist becomes 'the idea, the center and the vanishing point himself—and all at the same time.' (—de Kooning) He is an organizing principle who disappears, leaving system upon system of cross-reference attempting to define itself."[30]

A look at a canvas from the mid-1950s (when de Kooning entered his fifties—Ashbery's age at the time of *Self-Portrait*, *Houseboat Days*, and *As We Know*) will give body to this description. Let us choose the magnificent *Gotham News*, which I think we can consider a form of self-portrait (the artist, when asked if it were impossible now "to paint a face," replied, "It is impossible not to"). The picture presents the viewer with an explosion of intersecting and contradictory planes, a kind of cubist grid in the process of collapsing. Behind the paint and visible around its edges are columns of reversed newsprint that were transferred to the canvas before the artist began. From this chaos emerges a "face"—one eye frontally seen, hollow, outlined in burgundy with a satin sheen on the upper lid, the other eye defined by a triangular yellow green brushstroke and positioned obliquely,

246

with a spot of sky blue at the innermost corner. The "chin" of this figure consists of a subtly modeled elbow and biceps with an eerie red ribbon running through the ivory white muscle. The curve of the head is deformed by a black, boot-shaped anvil that seems to have slammed into the face at the place where the nose should be, as though the momentum from the cocked arm/chin had issued not in a fist but in this incongruously "objectified" force. At the center of the canvas, where the boot is kicking in the face, the strong suggestion of a third "eye" stares at the impending object. Where is the nose? It's on the floor: beautifully painted striations of pink, magenta, and purple that have been "packaged" in an unmistakably Picassoid outline. The "arm" responsible for this violence is locked into place by a reinforced stirrup or brace that lends a deliberateness and firmness to the tableau.

The real majesty of this painting derives only partly from the disciplined freedom of the brushstrokes and the virtuosity of the palette. It comes as much from the majesty of the conception: the statuesque angles of the mismatched eyes suggest the beautiful pose of a doomed narcissism, being rammed by its own instrument, an arm that is also a chin. This face that has lost its nose, its balance, its keel, is a vision of "the stoic pose" Ashbery referred to in "The System," "tinged with irony and self-mockery."

But that cubist nose on the floor is not merely an instance of dissociation. It has a positive aesthetic function as well, and serves to demonstrate how de Kooning has succeeded "in violating that space in such a way as / to leave it intact" (*HD*, p. 67). The magic-marker line defining the nose contrasts sharply with the handling of paint everywhere else on the canvas and works, I think, like one of those blazons *en abyme* we see in Ashbery's poems. It is a form of "direct speech" or commentary, in this case on the fate of the cubist aesthetic as it tries to grapple with the tensions and incompatible forms of energy alive in contemporary consciousness. The nose detaches itself from the rest of

247

the canvas even as it is integrated into it on the surface, revaluing the weight of the other parts, imbuing the entire painting with a new dimension of self-consciousness. This art, wrote Brian O'Doherty,

> doesn't turn tradition upside down, but rather inside out. A part becomes a whole. The Velázquez is a whole filled with parts. But we have invented the converse: a part filled with wholes. . . . This seems to me a description of de Kooning's paintings of the mid-fifties, the period in which his art most clearly declared its ambitions. *Police Gazette* and *Saturday Night* are parts containing a distracted congress of wholes.[31]

My examination of this painting is undertaken with the belief that being disassembled by the slapped, voluptuous colors of a de Kooning painting and getting lost in the serpentine gestures and "impossible" transitions of an Ashbery poem are more than remotely analogous. Both artists have moved beyond "an anxiety about making formal sense—that is, relationships—between parts [to] an interest in deepening discontinuities so that we can see them better."[32]

Faced with the "savage" brushwork of de Kooning, or the "explosive" dripped lines of Pollock, critics have charged that their art is too "accidental." Yet one critic and friend of Pollock's has noted that "Pollock painting—one of the most radical visions in the history of art—is, to my mind, a very calm sight. It lacks that frenzy so dear to the public's melodrama of the creative process. Pollock's intelligence is what comes through most clearly."[33] And Thomas Hess, a long-time friend of de Kooning's, has pointed out that the "expressionism" many see in the artist's paintings is deceptive, just as "Renoir's and Matisse's women looked Expressionist when they were new. . . . De Kooning looks at his environment as coolly as Cézanne."[34]

Witnesses of Ashbery's acrobatic mode may be tempted to find it equally random or formless. It is not that Ashbery's poems do not have their measure of randomness; rather, as

Ashbery has said, "I am attempting to keep meaningfulness up to the pace of randomness.... I really think that meaningfulness can't get along without randomness and that they somehow have to be brought together."[35] A close look at even the *sounds* of some of his lines belies the charge that the poet is not exercising control: "To step free at last, miniscule on the gigantic plateau" ("Soonest Mended," *DD*, p. 17)—note the way "miniscule" closes the mouth and "plateau" opens it up again. In the line that comes next—"This was our ambition: to be small and clear and free"—as we mentally pronounce the three final adjectives, we find our lips receding into the hint of a smile. At the end of "Hop o' My Thumb"—

> There are still other made-up countries
> Where we can hide forever,
> Wasted with eternal desire and sadness,
> Sucking the sherberts, crooning the tunes, naming the names
> [*SP*, p. 33]

—the three pairs of words in the last line move from consonance to rhyme to literal identity, enacting a subliminal form of convergence. These lines may have been composed rapidly, but we cannot help but see how wedded to the poem's ambitions are its technical resources.

Let us finally consider one of Ashbery's most challenging poems, one that engages his entire methodology, to see how we are taken to a place "both there / And not there," where the freedom to inhabit images and ideas is not hampered by formal considerations or "plausibility." Clement Greenberg has found, in paintings like *Gotham News*, a "plastic and descriptive painterliness that is applied to abstract ends but continues to suggest representational ones."[36] He calls this "homeless representation," and I think in the late poem "Daffy Duck in Hollywood" (*HD*, pp. 31–34)—a self-portrait, again—we can discover a verbal equivalent. Ashbery here is at the height of his powers as a "self that sustains itself on speech" (Stevens). The poem is a kind of biography of the impulse toward self-definition in an era when

> the consciousness of history has transformed itself from a libera-
> tion, an opening of doors... into an almost insupportable bur-
> den.... It's scarcely possible for the artist to write a word (or
> render an image or make a gesture) that doesn't remind him of
> something already achieved.[37]

But the voice Ashbery launches in this poem does support the burden of self-consciousness; it proceeds by incorporating whatever scraps lie at hand, including colloquial epigrams ("It's not the incomplete importunes, but the spookiness / Of the finished product"), shards of the poetic past (*Hamlet* and *Paradise Lost*), incongruous archaisms ("Therefore bivouac we / On this great, blond highway"), shorthand codes ("Grab sex things"), borrowings from architecture ("by New Brutalism standards"), comic-book characters ("Daffy Duck," "the Fudds' garage"), Hollywood street names ("the 2300 block of Highland / Fling Terrace"), operas, *cartes du Tendre* and even "a mint-condition can of Rumford's Baking Powder." This poem, as clearly as any Ashbery has written, takes into account that consciousness today is hungry and complicated enough to want an experience that both presents and reviews itself at once. The sheer length and number of directions taken by some of his sentences are an embodiment of the difficulty with which the mind mired in "consciousness of history" finds its way. Indeed, Ashbery sometimes seems to have the same aspirations for a single statement that poets like Donne brought to whole poems. What is exhilarating and new in this is the way the network of voices in the poem is used to animate and propel the almost impossibly eclectic and allusive diction. This poetry asks readers to hear inflections not only in the briefest fragments but also in the image-choked busyness of complex sentences. For only then are the attitudes summoned that make the poem's arguments and reversals into emblems of a complicated response to experience.

"Something strange is creeping across me," the poem announces itself, and a catalog of items immediately comes "clattering through the rainbow trellis / Where Pistachio Avenue rams the 2300 block of Highland / Fling Terrace." Another shift: "He promised he'd get me out of this one, / That mean old cartoonist, but just look what he's / Done to me now!" Soon, predictably enough, "everything is getting choked to the point of / Silence" and after a "magnetic storm" over "the Fudds' garage,"

> Suddenly all is
> Loathing. I don't want to go back inside anymore. You meet
> Enough vague people on this emerald traffic-island—no,

—hanging on that break, the reader wonders what aspect of the statement the poet will amend. The answer is the least expected:

> —no,
> Not people, comings and goings, more: mutterings,
>   splatterings. . . .

Two lines later begins one of Ashbery's most labyrinthine gestures, an eleven-line potpourri that moves from "That geranium glow over Anaheim" to the France of "the Princesse de Clèves." These references are not, as one critic has noted, examples of cheap satire, but playful evocations of "magic places with a peculiar momentum and zest all their own."[38] "Wait!" cries a voice, "I have an announcement!" and we are grateful for what the poet elsewhere calls "the imaginary pause." Soon, though, "The allegory comes unsnarled," and what follows is a poignant reminder of the conditions of our communication. This "emblazoned" commentary on the poem's progress is one of Ashbery's most athletic moments:

That this is a fabulation, and that those "other times"
Are in fact the silences of the soul, picked out in
Diamonds on stygian velvet, matters less than it should.
Prodigies of timing may be arranged to convince them
We live in one dimension, they in ours. While I
Abroad through all the coasts of dark destruction seek
Deliverance for us all, think in that language: its
Grammar, though tortured, offers pavilions
At each new parting of the ways.

[*HD*, pp. 32–33]

The last two lines, following three Milton gave Lucifer in
Paradise Lost, constitute a virtual anthem of Ashbery's aesthetic,
an approach which, "though tortured, offers pavilions" at the
moments of fracture and shift. After this thoughtful chord, the
lengthy "reviews" of the poem's style that Ashbery places in the
mouth of "Aglavaine" are welcome comedy:

"If his
Achievement is only to end up less boring than the others,
What's keeping us here? Why not leave at once?"

[*HD*, p. 33]

Ashbery's confidence that we will not leave rests on his belief,
articulated elsewhere, that "the eye / Extracts a progress from
almost anything"—the same belief that fuels de Kooning's her-
culean disruptions and flirtations with chaos. As Aglavaine's
speech concludes, "The storm finished brewing" (i.e., began),
and the poet returns to reason with us outside the protective
quotation marks:

Since all
By definition is completeness . . . why not
Accept it as it pleases to reveal itself?

[*HD*, p. 34]

And, shortly, the crisis of "parts and wholes" we saw enacted in
Gotham News is directly confronted:

252

> No one really knows
> Or cares whether this is the whole of which parts
> Were vouchsafed—once—but to be ambling on's
> The tradition more than the safekeeping of it.
>
> [*HD*, p. 34]

Taking heart from this credo of mobility, the poet verbalizes that form of egolessness almost indistinguishable from passivity that has run like a current through the poem:

> This mulch for
> Play keeps them interested and busy while the big,
> Vaguer stuff can decide what it wants—what maps, what
> Model cities, how much waste space. Life, our
> Life anyway, is between... ,
>
> [*HD*, p. 34]

in that "no-environment" de Kooning has said he tries to create in his paintings. The poem's last lines invite us to live with the poet in the clear lens of his "voice," so that we may

> have our earnest where it chances on us,
> Disingenuous, intrigued, inviting more,
> Always invoking the echo, a summer's day.
>
> [*HD*, p. 34]

This poem, like de Kooning's paintings of the fifties and like his even more fluid masterpieces of the mid-seventies, appropriates the world and transports it into the imagination where we can move with a freedom impossible in any representational art. Ashbery involves us in sentences whose machinery makes us feel *how*, not *what*, they mean, and after we have become sensitive to the moves that serve his "desperate quest masked as an ease with things" (Bloom), we become ourselves the medium for their operation. This poetry creates in us a palpable current of feeling that is held like some plastic entity, to be shaped, twisted, expanded, and diffused, that blossoms from within itself and is replaced by new blossoming. In wielding the reader's "state of attentiveness," which Ashbery has said is all the reader must bring to the poem, in molding the energy the reader donates to the enterprise that is the poem, the poet is handling a substance that, despite all the work of scholars, remains as mysterious as electricity was to scientists a hundred years ago, when it was known as "the imponderable fluid." He seeks to conduct us to an "elsewhere," as Julien Levy wrote of his friend Arshile Gorky, "which cannot be described or analyzed by critics, but only recognized by affection."[39]

10

"Syringa": John Ashbery and Elliott Carter

LAWRENCE KRAMER

Every so often, poems that faithfully mirror the intricacy of our inner lives take on a strange clarity when the right composer sets them to music. The mixing of incoherent feelings in much of Heine, for instance, becomes a luminous ambivalence in Schumann's *Dichterliebe*; and the suppressed edginess in much of Stefan George sounds most clearly in Schoenberg's *George-Lieder*. In cases like these, the music takes on cognitive as well as emotional weight. It becomes a kind of meditation, which "speaks" through the interplay of musical and poetic structures and which works to disclose a shared esthetic—perhaps even a shared vision. Recently a major American composer, Elliott Carter, has written such meditations on the poetry of two of his contemporaries, Elizabeth Bishop and John Ashbery. Carter's setting of Ashbery's "Syringa," the poem about Orpheus that appears in *Houseboat Days*, had its premiere at Carter's seventieth-birthday concert in December 1978. The audience on that occasion heard a piece intensely characteristic of its composer, something unmistakably his; yet it also heard something in the music that is unmistakably Ashbery's, as if there were only one way to sing an Ashbery poem, and this was the way. Carter's "Syringa" echoes Ashbery's concern with "the way time feels as it passes";[1] it reflects Ashbery's revaluation of poetry as a mimesis of the mind's private life; it even illuminates Ashbery's difficulty, which continues to trouble some readers. At the same time Carter's music discloses, by mirroring, what might be called an aesthetic of simultaneity, something close to the center of both men's achievements.

Before turning to Carter's "Syringa," and its illumination of Ashbery's, it is necessary to say a few words about Carter and his music. Since his *First String Quartet* of 1951, Carter has been exploring the possibility of making music by combining instrumental lines or groupings that are entirely independent of each other. In a way, this is simply an imaginative extension of the basic musical principle of the independence of parts: the principle that melody, bass, and inner voices must develop in such a way that they retain their individual identities as they blend together. Carter's parts, however, are so independent that they may be playing at different tempos, in different meters, and with different thematic material. Carter's *Third Quartet*, for instance, is composed out of two duos: one for violin and cello, and one for violin and viola. The two groups are even asked to sit separately on the concert stage. The result of this arrangement is to draw attention away from the music's linear dimension, its forward movement in time, and to emphasize its vertical dimension, the texture created by simultaneous sounds, which in traditional music constitutes harmony. One listens hardest to the shifting vertical relationships between the differentiated groups as they couple and uncouple, mock and echo, respect and ignore each other.

In Carter's "Syringa," the form taken by this simultaneous presentation of individual voices—"polyvocality" for short—is determined by Ashbery's text and becomes a gloss on it. To see just how this happens, one has to begin where the music does, with a sense of the poem. Ashbery's "Syringa" is a series of reflections on the Orpheus myth. Its burden, as so often in Ashbery's work, is loss, a loss that makes three demands: first, that it must be represented poetically; second, that it must be represented with reticence; and third, that it must be represented without evasion. Many of Ashbery's poems can be understood as solutions to the problem of reconciling these obviously antagonistic demands, and "Syringa" is one of them. Its solution is to use Orpheus's loss of Eurydice as a deliberately unsubtle metaphor for a personal loss of the speaker's, at the same time as it declines ever to identify the speaker's loss or even to allude to it until the poem ends, at which point the personal loss is "no longer / Material for a poem." The effect of this is slightly dizzying. Someone who meditates on Orpheus's loss to escape the burden of his own loss is actually just pretending to meditate on Orpheus. The speaker in Ashbery's poem, however, is *not* pretending that: he is only *pretending* to pretend it. The personal loss is an open secret; the tale of Orpheus that hides its identity is also an exposure of its presence. As a result, the speaker's refusal to refer to his own loss does not seem evasive; it seems ascetic, as if he were constructing an elegy while refusing himself the implicit consolations of personal pathos—praise, memory, understanding. At the same time, Orpheus's loss becomes a topic of authentic concern in the poem, not just a pretext. The poem is, in effect, polyvocal. It has a meditative voice that engages in a tranquil, resigned consideration of the problem of loss as presented by Orpheus, and it has an elegiac voice, full of lament and desire, that uses the Orpheus myth to utter "hidden syllables" of personal sorrow.

These two voices are always moving in opposite directions. The elegiac voice, which is to some degree the voice of Orpheus himself, is always retrospective, always "coming back / To the mooring of starting out" ("Soonest Mended," *DD*, p. 19), the lost past. Against this, the meditative voice poses a refusal to overinvest the self in the "stalled moment" of remembered happiness. Whereas the elegiac voice resists the passing of time, the meditative voice seeks to consent to time's every motion, to ask for nothing more than the "flowing" and "fleeting." Against an Orphean time, it sets a Heraclitean one. Despite this divergence, however, the two voices of the poem are tightly woven together. In fact, there is no moment in "Syringa" when either voice sounds apart from the other; both are simultaneously present throughout. The conventional way to put this would be to say that throughout the poem the speaker is ambivalent; but that is precisely how I would prefer not to put it. Ambivalence implies conflict; the poem discloses none. Its feeling tone is a unity, a singularity; but it is polyvocal. Its two voices compose only one utterance, just as, say, Carter's *Third Quartet* is itself not a pair of duos but music polyvocally *composed* of two duos.

The details of how Ashbery accomplishes his polyvocal form will emerge gradually. For the moment, its projection in Carter's "Syringa" can be described. "Syringa" is composed for mezzo-soprano, bass, and chamber ensemble. The mezzo takes on the role of the poem's meditative voice, and it is she who sings the text of Ashbery's "Syringa." Her music is simple, graceful, and generally quiet. Articulating each word of text with great clarity, it evokes a mood of lucidity and contemplation. At the same time, passing through the text without repetition or embellishment, the mezzo line embodies the consent to the passing of time that is the poem's central meditative attitude. The mezzo's polyvocal partner is, of course, the bass. Singing simultaneously with the mezzo and independent of her, the bass provides the poem's Orphean voice, filling in what Carter describes as the "subliminal background that might be evoked in the mind of a reader" of Ashbery's text.[2] The bass sings, in ancient Greek, an agitated, complex, mournful part, one that sometimes suggests archaic, melismatic vocal styles. With his passionate chanting, lingering over the dead in a dead language—the dead's language?—the bass suggests the will to lament, the exaltation of regret, that characterizes Orpheus in the poem and that constitutes, in the meditative voice's view, his "mistake."

In traditional music, these two voices might be opposed to each other through contrastive statements and developments, just as in traditional poetry (Tennyson's "The Two Voices," for example) they would enter into an antiphonal argument. Overlapped, or "layered," as they are in the two "Syringa" texts, the voices are not *opposed* to each other at all, but *posed against* each other. Each remains perfectly distinct; yet the two together form a singularity, a kind of third voice, that is the integral voice of "Syringa"—the voice one hears in how the music sounds, how the poem reads. Carter underscores the radical oneness of this voice by bringing its constituent voices together at crucial moments by means of bilingual puns, several of which Andrew Porter points out in his *New Yorker* notice of the premiere of "Syringa."[3] The most important of these comes at the end of the piece, where the mezzo intones the poem's last word, "summer," while the bass sings *"soma, sema"* (body, tomb). This rapprochement of the voices is particularly poignant because it occurs as, simultaneously, the meditative voice approaches lament at last and the Orphean voice surrenders lament in exhaustion. Each voice, in other words, takes on the other's role as a way of falling silent, of finding relief from "the evil burthen of the words" (*HD*, p. 71). In the poem, the same thing happens when the meditative voice at last acknowledges that its own loss constitutes a reanimation of the Orpheus myth, "In whose tale are hidden syllables / Of what happened . . . / In some small town, one indifferent summer" (*HD*, p. 71). Here, in its one act of personal memory, the meditative voice accepts the identity with Orpheus that it has so far left to its polyvocal partner. Yet at the same time it forecloses all further lament by stopping the poem.

So far, the relationship between the voices in both "Syringa" texts has appeared mainly as a form of antirelationship, a pure copresence, but there is more to it than that. Ashbery's poem gives the impression that its meditative voice is at once both haunted by the figure of Orpheus and far remote from him, a condition that could be described as intimate detachment. Orpheus is a recurrent but fluctuating presence in the meditative movement of the poem, which is always drawing near him and then pulling away:

> The seasons are no longer what they once were,
> But it is in the nature of things to be seen only once,

> As they happen along, bumping into other things, getting
>   along
> Somehow. That's where Orpheus made his mistake.
>
> [*HD*, p. 69]

One odd image even mocks Orpheus as a sentimentality, a cloud with a silver lining, at the same time as it revives him in immediate nature:

> But how late to be regretting all this, even
> Bearing in mind that regrets are always too late, too late!
> To which Orpheus, a bluish cloud with white contours,
> Replies. . . .
>
> [*HD*, p. 71]

In Carter's setting one gets the similar impression that the bass is half-trying to "reach" the mezzo, who is deaf to his music, a suggestion reinforced by the positioning of the singers at opposite ends of the stage. Carter embodies this relationship of unachieved dialogue in his treatment of the music's instrumental ensemble. With momentary exceptions, the instrumental music of "Syringa" aligns itself with the bass, not with the mezzo. This music is generally complex, densely textured, and restless, a perfect background for the bass's dark musings and lamentations. Even the timbre of the ensemble is slanted toward the bass. "Syringa" is written for guitar, violin, viola, cello, double bass, alto flute, bass clarinet, English horn, piano, and percussion. The piece's predominant colors are accordingly dark, and its predominant tessitura is low. This disposition of forces tends to isolate the mezzo in her serenity and detachment against a troubled, sometimes violently agitated background. In part this is a background that she transcends, hovers above; in part it is the aural landscape that contains her and prompts her song.

Carter's instrumental texture also reflects the source of this intimate detachment: the poem's internal questioning of poetry itself. By isolating the mezzo as he does, Carter underscores both the simplicity of her part and its clarity as declamation, thus creating the impression that what she is doing is closer to recitative—the musical equivalent of speech—than it is to song. Similarly, part of the asceticism of the poem's meditative voice is its sense that song, and thus by the oldest of tropes, poetry, is limited, that "it isn't enough / To just go on singing" (*HD*, p. 70). The meditative voice does not want to sing, because song is the instrument of regret, even of wild grief. It is Orpheus' lament that "rends rocks into fissures" and makes the sky shudder; it is the power of lament that sets the poet against nature in a futile attempt to treasure the stalled moment. The meditative voice, in consequence, tries to write a poem, "Syringa," that is divested of poetry's intrinsic power to exalt the trauma of grief. This antagonism to the poem—a poem that in some sense demands to come into being because "love stays on the brain" (*HD*, p. 69)—is what prompts the meditative voice to pretend that its loss is too painful to acknowledge. In fact, the self does not need to be protected from the loss at all; rather, the loss has to be protected from the poem. A loss that changes everything, like Orpheus's, is too important and too fragile a thing to be entrusted to the elegaic fury that goes "streak[ing] by, its tail afire, a bad / Comet" (*HD*, p. 71), recalling the "wandering mass of shapeless flame," the "pathless comet" that haunts another Orphean mourner, Byron's Manfred. If there must be a song, and it seems there must, then it has to be a song that is content with "the way music passes," that is willing to "participate in the action" of passing time. It must be a song isolated from the "something, those people, / Those other ones, call life" (*HD*, p. 69) because it consents to be "flowing, fleeting." Such a song casts out remorse, not for the Yeatsian reward of suddenly finding that everything we look upon is blessed, but for the simple ability "to utter an intelligent / Comment on the most thought-provoking element" presented by history as it "flashes past" (*HD*, p. 69). Carter, perhaps, does not follow Ashbery's irony quite that far, but this ascetic song is still what his mezzo—musically isolated, almost reciting—sings.

But why does the mezzo's song coincide with the text of the

poem? Carter's answer is that the bass voice in his piece is "sub-liminal," and the poem, in its own terms, endorses his choice to make it so. Ashbery's "Syringa" has two voices but only one speaker, and its speaker is identified with the meditative voice. To that extent, Ashbery "gives" the poem's text to the more soft-spoken of the voices, just as Carter does. The poem's Orphean voice is more elusive, something heard in or under the speaker's speech; its place is "the back of the mind, where we live now" ("Saying It to Keep It from Happening," *HD*, p. 30). Sometimes, as Carter perceives, the Orphean voice comes from the back of the reader's mind. That happens whenever one re-calls that the speaker is thinking of Orpheus only because he *is* the Orpheus of "a totally different incident with a similar name" (*HD*, p. 71), so that everything he says is a covert lament. Else-where, the Orphean voice lives in the back of the speaker's own mind and appears when the speaker lingers over images too poignant or appealing to be confined by the meaning intended for them. When, for example, we hear that to ask for more than the fleeting of time is to "become the tossing reeds of that slow, / Powerful stream, the trailing grasses playfully tugged at," we hear, too, under the negation, an Orphean song of unity, power, and even of eros.

Even more powerful is the similar polyvocality of the poem's most intense passage:

> Singing accurately
> So that the notes mount straight up out of the well of
> Dim noon and rival the tiny, sparkling yellow flowers
> Growing around the brink of the quarry, encapsulizes
> The different weights of the things.
>
> [*HD*, pp. 69–70]

The poem's title authorizes us to surmise that the "sparkling yellow flowers" are syringa, which is a form of saxifrage. As its name suggests, saxifrage is a flower that breaks rocks, which it does here at the brink of the quarry. But Orpheus's lament breaks rocks too; and the connection invests the lament with a sense of fecundity. The flower breaks rocks with its beauty, affirming life on a desolate terrain, which is the traditional burden of elegaic song.[4] When song rivals the flowers, it turns the "fissure" of the quarry into a generative source, "the well of dim noon." The poem presses the point by another play on "syringa," which is derived from "syrinx," the Greek word for panpipe. True, the meditative voice may make this generous acknowledgment of the power of song only in order to get beyond it, to say that "it isn't enough / To just go on singing." But that voice says so, precisely, as it does go on singing, making a poem, "Syringa," that is named for the rock-breaking flower and prompted by loss.

Like its counterpart in Carter's music, the Orphean voice in Ashbery's poem in part assumes its "subliminal" quality by carrying suggestive overtones of earlier "songs." This allusiveness seems to belong to the Orphean voice alone, as a reflection of its impulse to fix on the past—a quality that Carter's bass reflects by its fluent passage through texts by Sappho, Ibycus, Plato, Aeschylus, "Orpheus," and others. Allusion, except as cliché ("'The end crowns all'"), tends to resonate with the elegaic strain in "Syringa," which is the price paid by the meditative voice for its ascetic immersion in the flowering present. This happens with the yellow flowers, which recall the traditional flowers of pastoral elegy among their other associations, and it happens, too, with the "bad comet" that suggests Manfred. Manfred is a cautionary instance to the meditative voice, but he is also an Orphean figure who sees his Eurydice after her death, then sees her vanish, and later dies in what he thinks of as triumph, without "mind[ing] so much about his reward being in heaven" (*HD*, p. 70).

This thinning of the meditative texture in favor of elegaic implication—an effect mirrored, as we have seen, by Carter's treatment of instrumental line and color—underlies the seemingly incongruous section of the poem in which some horses reflect on an electrical storm. For the meditative voice, the horses provide another instance of the Orphean "mistake," in this case a belief in the power of music to heal the gaps in nature:

> The horses
> Have each seen a share of the truth, though each thinks,
> "I'm a maverick. Nothing of this is happening to me,
> Though I can understand the language of birds, and
> The itinerary of the lights caught in the storm is fully apparent
>   to me.
> Their jousting ends in music much
> As trees move more easily in the wind after a summer storm
> As is happening in the lacy shadows of the shore-trees, now,
>   day after day."
>
> [HD, pp. 70–71]

From the meditator's viewpoint, the horses naively mythify the way things "happen along" in time, "bumping into other things" and finally vanishing, their nature being "to be seen only once." What's more, by refusing to acknowledge that the storm is happening to *them*, the horses, again naively, deny the burden of their own mortality. And of course the meditator is right, as his talking (anyway, thinking) horses clownishly show with their overtones of children's stories and animated cartoons. On the other hand, the horses do outsing him, with their lyrical vision of trees in the wind. And talking horses are not always clownish. The horses most relevant in a classical context are the ones that speak to another Orphean hero, another man doomed by loss. In the *Iliad*, Achilles' horses speak to him after "the light from [his] fair elaborate shield [shoots] into the high air."[5] What the horses say to Achilles acknowledges both the true nature of temporality and the limits mortality puts on life and beauty; their poetry is elegiac, Orphean:

> But for us, we two could run with the blast of the west wind
> Which they say is the lightest of all things; yet still for you
> There is destiny to be killed in force by a god and a mortal.

Ashbery's horses also say something worth hearing. They speak for the conciliatory power of elegy, and their image of the wind, like that of their Homeric doubles, suggests something set beyond destiny in either of its traditional meanings, transcendent freedom or poetic inspiration. The horses' Orpheism may be naive, but that compromises them just so far; after all, they're only horses.

Ashbery's use of the horses might remind us that a horse, since 1922 at any rate, has been sacred to Orpheus:

> But what shall I dedicate to you, master, say,
> who taught the creatures their ear?—
> My memory of a day in Spring,
> in evening, in Russia—, a horse....
>
> (*Sonnets to Orpheus*, 1:20)[6]

In a sense, "Syringa" finds in its polyvocality a way to fulfill the demand of that other Orphean poet, Rilke, who asked of the god himself that he live always in two realms, one of being and one of not-being. Much of the burden of the *Sonnets to Orpheus* is the recognition that this dual existence is both terribly difficult and terribly necessary. Ashbery's poem reflects both the difficulty and the necessity, but it tries to do more than aspire to a dual existence; it tries to achieve one. The nature of that achievement is, I hope, now clear, but to feel its full resonance it is necessary to look at it from a new perspective. For Ashbery's polyvocality raises some important questions, both ontological and esthetic, about the issue most central to it: time.

One of the reasons that the union of Carter's music with Ashbery's poetry seems so right and inevitable is that, in varying degrees, both men handle time in a way that both broadens the boundaries of temporality in the arts they practice and constitutes a critique of previous temporal forms. Earlier I pointed out that Carter's polyvocal style diverts emphasis from the linear progression of his music to its vertical presence. One way to develop this observation is to say that in its stress on the vertical, Carter's music resembles the prolongation and transformation of a single enormous chord, and in particular of the textured duration—built from elements of melody, harmony, rhythm, color, spacing, and so on—that a chord creates. The process of the music coincides with a kind of pulsation or turbulence within the duration; from a linear point of view, nothing really "happens." Carter redoubles this effect by constantly changing the metrical pulse of his music, and by writing polyrhythmically as well as polyvocally—that is, writing in different meters simultaneously or subdividing the same meter in asynchronous ways. This makes the linear flow of the music impossible for a listener to measure, and so merges each moment of the music seamlessly with the moments around it. Not that Carter tries to negate the linear dimension, as do composers like Steve Reich or Philip Glass. Carter *is* concerned with the projection of his music through time; but he explicitly defines the role of linearity in his work as supplementary or contextual:

> In a piece that deals primarily with the poetry of change, transformation, reorientation of feelings and thoughts, and gradual shifts of emphasis, as do most of my works ... the matter of succession of material becomes very important, since how the ideas are formed and how they are related and connected gives expression to the poetry they evoke. Thus, the individual instant, the characterized sound or brief passage, like trees in a storm, gain an added meaning by their contexts.[7]

What Carter suggests by this passage is, among other things, the same doubleness of vision that Ashbery reflects in "Syringa." The flowing and fleeting of time is absolute, and the work of art is so formed that it submits to that flow without trying to wrench it into shape. Change, transformation, and reorientation are paramount. Yet the "poetry" lies in "the individual instant," the brief evocative passage that one is constantly tempted to treasure as it recedes.[8]

Ashbery is perhaps less willing than Carter to preserve the linearity of his work. As Carter's polyvocal forms create a continuous "chord," Ashbery's create a continuous moment of awareness for which there is no convenient name or image, but which might be called a texturing of consciousness. This is a single apprehension almost too full to sustain itself, one in which the eye "sharpens and sharpens" particulars until,

> no
> Longer visible, they breathe in multicolored
> Parentheses, the way love in short periods
> Puts everything out of focus, coming and going.
> ["Fragment," *DD*, p. 81]

I will risk the generalization that, at least in Ashbery's work since *Rivers and Mountains*, this texturing of consciousness is most often polyvocal, and that its voices, like those in "Syringa," are discontinuous: each thrives on what the others leave out, each says what the others leave silent. As in Carter's music, the "vertical" relationship of these voices shifts constantly, but their basic disposition is constant. As a result, nothing can be said to "happen" in an Ashbery poem except a duration. The poetry simply writes itself out on

> the front page
> Of today, looming as white as
> The furthest mountains, and oh, all kinds of things
> Caught in that net and shaken.
> ["Fragment," *DD*, p. 91]

This point comes across clearly in "Syringa," which ends only by reaching the point of origin it has never left, the memory of what happened "in some small town, one indifferent summer." Nothing has changed but the clock; and the poem has been a kind of fable about itself, one of the "Fables that time invents / To explain its passing" ("Years of Indiscretion," *DD*, p. 46).

Ashbery's gift is to transcribe those fables. As a rule, an Ashbery poem does not articulate a process but simply lets a

textured consciousness persist shimmeringly for a given duration, which is presented as something like an *objet trouvé*. Within
that duration, the poem's voices participate in the continuous
flow of the present, without imposing any shape on it or experiencing what Richard Howard calls "the invoked anxiety of
closed form."[9] The nature of this flow is to be quirky, inconsis-
tently coherent, and, contrary to conventional expectation, non-
linear. Time flows, but not in a straight line; it flows every which
way. Ashbery's poems, accordingly, though they have meditative voices to them, are not the meditations they are often called.
They are uncertain reflections in "a randomness, a darkness of
one's own" ("The Ice-Cream Wars," *HD*, p. 61), a darkness in
which the mind "happens along" but does not change, though
its objects do. In their form, these poems suggest a new way of
defining subjective time, in which the mind, as the only constant presence, presides over a continuous recession of objects
into absence—some of which it is reluctant to let go.

One consequence of this is that Ashbery's poetry makes a
radical shift away from the style of subjectivity that has prevailed in most poetry since the nineteenth century. Ashbery, as
a rule, likes to show how the mind goes rather than where it
goes. For most poets after Wordsworth, the mind has "gone" in
a pattern of conflict and resolution, or of crisis and resolution,
prompted by certain difficulties in the relation between the self
and the world.[10] But Ashbery, by leading his poetry into the
kind of temporality I have just described, makes conflict and
crisis impossible and so finds the horizon of calm that prevails in
much of his work, even when it embraces the extremities of loss,
as it does in "Syringa." The poetry thereby transcends the pattern of self-aggrandizement, anxiety, and disappointment that
leads

> To pain,
> And the triumph over pain, still hidden

In those low-lying hills which rob us
Of all privacy, as though one were always about to meet
One's double
                 ["Houseboat Days," *HD*, p. 38]

and so, by the tradition of the doppelgänger, to meet one's death. Such sublime doings may always take part in a poem, may stem from one of its voices, as from the Orphean voice in "Syringa"; but the poem is never determined by them. The cool mezzo always tempers the fiery bass who enriches the sound of her voice.

"What I am writing to say is, the timing, not / The contents, is what matters" ("Fantasia on 'The Nut-Brown Maid,'" *HD*, p. 85). Ashbery's timing, like Elliott Carter's, is a way of ramifying the present which upsets our unacknowledged illusion that time is simple. With Carter this takes the form of continually superimposing different metrical structures, all of which are themselves in constant change. Given so many shapes, polyvocally fused together, time loses the quality by which we customarily identify and measure it—its periodicity. What remains is a kind of eddy, full of complex swells and pulsations. With Ashbery, something quite similar holds true, as the superimposition of different layers of awareness, either concerned with different things or concerned with the same things differently, dissolves the illusion of narrativity by which time is commonly forced to make sense. And this creates an eddy of its own, each surge of which

                          unrolls
Its question mark like a new wave on the shore.
In coming to give, to give up what we had,
We have, we understand, gained or been gained
By what was passing through, bright with the sheen
Of things recently forgotten and revived.
                ["Blue Sonata," *HD*, pp. 66–67]

In this rich collage of a present, coming is going, giving is giving up, having is having had, and vice versa—actions that do not cancel each other, but that coexist in one bright sheen. Even more important, perhaps, to understand in the ramified present is to question, or more accurately it is to think and feel within the curve of a question mark that cannot be followed by an answer, but only by another question mark. Understanding is thus a matter not of knowing, but of being, and in particular of being in, of consenting to, time: "it's time / That counts, and how deeply you have invested in it" ("Saying It to Keep It from Happening," *HD*, p. 29). To understand is to participate.

And perhaps that's it: perhaps that last sentence is not just a reading of Ashbery, but also a prescription for how to read him. If what I have been saying here makes sense, the authenticity of Ashbery's poetry requires that it refuse to interpret the complexities of experience and refuse to make drama out of interior life. It is not that the poems have no meaning, or hide their meanings; it is that they, like Carter's compositions, consist of a plurality of meanings woven into one fabric. Readers in growing numbers are finding the result exhilarating, but it is no secret that others are antagonized by it. Ashbery is not an aggressive poet, and it is somewhat surprising to see what anger his work can generate in those readers who feel he is too attached to "the singular and the original," that "his frequent daring deviations from one theme to another... destroy the continuity and gradual development of his ideas." (It ought to be reassuring that these comments were not made about Ashbery: they were written by Wenzel Thomaschek about Beethoven's *First Piano Concerto*.) Yet the element of opacity in Ashbery, which is really the singularity, the richness of what I have been calling the texturing of consciousness, is not a negativity but a plenitude. Unlike Mallarmé, to whom he has been inappropriately compared,[11] Ashbery does not leave empty spaces in his poetry to suggest a void. Quite the contrary: where spaces would be left empty by the anxious exclusiveness of a single voice, a measured present, a rigorous selfhood, Ashbery fills them. Reading him, accordingly, like listening to Carter, requires a certain readiness to immerse oneself in a fullness one cannot hope to dominate. Perhaps the difficulty of this is the risk it entails to the part of subjectivity we are most anxious about, our sense of our identity:

> no part
> Remains that is surely you. Those voices in the dusk
> Have told you all and still the tale goes on.
> ["Self-Portrait in a Convex Mirror," *SP*, p. 71]

Yet what comes of this is worth the risk: the sense of a consciousness free of rigid boundaries, yet still itself, and true to itself:

> Vibrating to the distant pinch
> And turning out the way I am, turning out to greet you.
> ["The Chateau Hardware," *DD*, p. 73]

Notes

1. DAVID LEHMAN: Introduction

1. Robert Boyers, "A Quest without an Object," *Times Literary Supplement*, September 1, 1978, p. 962.

2. W. H. Auden, Foreword to *Some Trees* (New Haven: Yale University Press, 1956), pp. 11–16.

3. Frank O'Hara, "Rare Modern," *Poetry*, February 1957, p. 312.

4. John Simon, "More Brass than Enduring," *Hudson Review*, autumn 1962, pp. 457–458.

5. Harold Bloom, *Figures of Capable Imagination* (New York: Seabury Press, 1976), p. 174.

6. In *Saturday Review*, August 8, 1970, p. 34.

7. Roger Shattuck, "Poet in the Wings," *New York Review of Books*, March 23, 1978, p. 40.

8. Boyers, "Quest without an Object," p. 963.

9. Charles Molesworth, "'This Leaving-out Business': The Poetry of John Ashbery," *Salmagundi*, summer–fall 1977, pp. 25, 39–41.

10. See "John Ashbery: The Charity of the Hard Moments," in Bloom, *Figures of Capable Imagination*, pp. 169–208.

1. DOUGLAS CRASE: The Prophetic Ashbery

1. Ashbery's dust-jacket description of the society portrayed in *Forgetting Elena*, the novel by Edmund White (New York: Random House, 1973). The description seems appropriate here too, especially after mention of the Hamptons.

2. Ashbery would call the influence slight. One reads at page 72 in David K. Kermani's *John Ashbery: A Comprehensive Bibliography* that "The Picture of Little J. A. in a Prospect of Flowers" owes only its title to Marvell. Still, that's owing quite a bit, and I think we are welcome to our suspicions. The Kermani bibliography is indispensable to the "serious student" and was to me also.

3. This is from the chapter "The Alchemical Ventriloquist" in

Joseph H. Summers, *The Heirs of Donne and Johnson* (New York: Oxford University Press, 1970), p. 143. I am in debt to Professor Summers both for his argument and for the stimulus to begin this essay.

4. Robert Pinsky, *The Situation of Poetry* (Princeton: Princeton University Press, 1976), pp. 79–81.

5. I stick to poetry in these comments because one has only to read the journals in business, the professions, academia, or government to be aware that pleniloquence has not abated in other fields. The inflation of American speech was noted by de Tocqueville, among others. We might wonder that the reaction against this national trait should be most severe in poetry, the very art that is said to preserve and exemplify its national tongue.

6. I stole this phrase from John Shearman, *Mannerism* (Harmondsworth, Middlesex, England: Penguin Books, 1967), where I also found the word *imparmiginare* at p. 64.

7. Wylie Sypher, *Four Stages of Renaissance Style* (Garden City, N.Y.: Doubleday, 1955), p. 119.

8. Rubin's testimony from his book *Growing (Up) at Thirty-seven* is quoted by Christopher Lasch, "The Narcissist Society," *New York Review of Books,* September 30, 1976, p. 5.

9. Arnold Hauser, *The Social History of Art,* vol. 2 (New York: Vintage Books, n.d.), pp. 113–116, 127.

10. The term "grandiose self" was suggested by Heinz Kohut and has been adapted by Otto Kernberg to refer to the structure of the narcissist self. Kernberg, *Borderline Conditions and Pathological Narcissism* (New York: Jason Aronson, 1975), pp. 263 et seq. Quentin Anderson uses the strikingly congruent term "imperial self" to refer to the self invoked by Emerson in American literature. Anderson, *The Imperial Self* (New York: Alfred A. Knopf, 1971). Dr. Kernberg refers to a psychoanalytic construct; Professor Anderson refers to a cultural one. And the sociologists and social historians who now speak of the grandiose self presumably refer to a construct that is socioeconomic. Maybe this is just another instance of all Gaul being eternally divided into three parts, but it would be interesting to see someone try to consolidate what appears, to a layman anyway, to be in reality inseparable.

11. Lasch, "Narcissist Society." Richard Sennett, "Destructive Gemeinschaft," *Partisan Review* 43, no. 3 (1976): 341–361. Sennett, *The Fall of Public Man* (New York: Alfred A. Knopf, 1977), pp. 1–12, 323–336. Hans Morgenthau and Ethel Person, "The Roots of Narcissism," *Partisan Review* 45, no. 3 (1978): 337–347.

12. Emerson, of course, was on principle inconsistent, and in making him the butt of argument I am being unfair to his later pessimisms. But since it is the early, optimistic Emerson who took hold in the national pysche, I think the emphasis here is justifiable.

13. This is the attitude I think David Kalstone is on to when he points to "myths of diminution" in *The Double Dream of Spring*. Professor Kalstone's insight is in his book *Five Temperaments* (New York: Oxford University Press, 1977), p. 191.

2. MARJORIE PERLOFF: "Fragments of a Buried Life"

1. Sue Gangel, "An Interview with John Ashbery," *San Francisco Review of Books* 3, no. 7 (November 1977): 12.

2. John Ashbery, "On Raymond Roussel," *Portfolio and Art News Annual*, vol. 6 (autumn 1962); rpt. in Raymond Roussel, *How I Wrote Certain of My Books*, ed. and trans. Trevor Winkfield (New York: Sun, 1977), p. 55.

3. Robert Boyers, "A Quest without an Object," *Times Literary Supplement*, September 1, 1978, p. 962.

4. John Berryman, *The Dream Songs* (New York: Farrar, Straus and Giroux, 1969), p. 104.

5. See Norman MacKenzie, *Dreams and Dreaming* (New York: Vanguard Press, 1965), p. 217.

6. The OED gives two meanings of "commensal" used as a substantive: (1) One of a company who eat at the same table, a mess-mate, and (2) *Biol.* An animal or plant which lives attached to or as a tenant of another, and shares its food. Both meanings apply here.

7. Ashbery, "On Raymond Roussel," p. 51.

8. John Ashbery, "The Impossible" (review of Gertrude Stein's *Stanzas in Meditation*), *Poetry* 90, no. 4 (July 1957): 241.

9. Roger Cardinal, "Enigma," *20th Century Studies* 12 (December 1974): 45, 56.

10. Gangel, "Interview with John Ashbery," p. 12.

11. M. H. Abrams, "Structure and Style in the Greater Romantic Lyric," in *From Sensibility to Romanticism: Essays Presented to Frederick A. Pottle*, ed. Frederick W. Hilles and Harold Bloom (New York: Oxford, 1965), p. 528. See also Robert Langbaum, *The Poetry of Experience* (New York: Norton, 1957), chap. 1 passim.

12. John Ashbery, "Reverdy en Amérique," *Mercure de France* (Special Issue: Pierre Reverdy), 344 (January/April 1962): 111. Ashbery's phrase is "des phénomènes vivants."

13. Marjorie Perloff, "Symbolism/Anti-Symbolism," *Centrum* 4 (fall 1976): 78–79.

14. Cf. Rimbaud's famous catalog of "anti-art" art works in *Une Saison en enfer:* "J'aimais les peintures idiotes, dessus de portes, décors, toiles de saltimbanques, enseignes, enluminures populaires; la littérature demodée, latin d'église, livres érotiques sans orthographe, romans de nois aïeules, contes de fées, petits livres de l'enfance, opéras vieux, refrains niais, rhythmes naïfs. [I loved absurd paintings, door panels, stage sets, backdrops for acrobats, signboards, popular engravings; literature that is out of fashion, Church Latin, erotic books with bad spelling, novels of our grandmothers, fairy tales, little books of childhood, old operas, silly refrains, artless rhythms.]" See Rimbaud, *Oeuvres,* ed. Suzanne Bernard (Paris: Garnier, 1960), p. 228.

15. John Ashbery, "Paris Letter," *Art International* 6, no. 3 (1962): 59.

3. JOHN KOETHE: The Metaphysical Subject of John Ashbery's Poetry

1. Kenneth Koch is said to have once remarked that the paradigmatic Ashbery line would be "It wants to go to bed with us."

2. David Kalstone, *Five Temperaments* (New York: Oxford University Press, 1977), p. 195.

3. David Hume, *The Treatise of Human Nature,* book 1, part 4, section 6.

4. Immanuel Kant, *Prolegomena to Any Future Metaphysics,* 3d part, section 46.

5. Immanuel Kant, *Critique of Pure Reason,* A350.

6. Arthur Schopenhauer, *The World as Will and Representation,* book 2, section 278.

7. Ludwig Wittgenstein, *Tractatus Logico-Philosophicus,* 5.63–5.641.

8. Kalstone, *Five Temperaments,* p. 187.

9. Kant, *Prolegomena,* 3d part, section 46.

10. Marjorie Perloff, *Frank O'Hara: Poet among Painters* (Braziller, 1977), pp. 135–136.

11. Hume, *Treatise,* book 1, part 4, section 6.

12. "In Memory of My Feelings," *The Collected Poems of Frank O'Hara,* ed. Donald Allen (New York: Knopf, 1971), p. 257.

13. Kalstone, *Five Temperaments,* p. 195.

14. Perloff, *Frank O'Hara,* p. 136.

15. Art column in *New York* 11, no. 35 (August 28, 1978): 104.

16. Ibid.

4. DAVID LEHMAN: The Shield of a Greeting

1. John Ashbery, "The Invisible Avant-Garde," in *Avant-Garde Art,* ed. Thomas B. Hess and John Ashbery (London: Collier-Macmillan, 1968), p. 184.

2. John Ashbery, "Turandot," in *Turandot and Other Poems* (New York: Editions of the Tibor de Nagy Gallery, 1953), n.p.

3. Delmore Schwartz, "The Isolation of Modern Poetry," in *Selected Essays of Delmore Schwartz,* ed. Donald A. Dike and David H. Zucker (Chicago: University of Chicago Press, 1970), p. 10.

4. Interview with David Lehman, October 17, 1977.

5. T. S. Eliot, *The Complete Poems and Plays, 1909–1950* (New York: Harcourt Brace, 1962), p. 128.

6. A similar rationale may be found for Ashbery's decision against using a reproduction of the Parmigianino painting on the cover of *Self-Portrait in a Convex Mirror.* For it was the poem's intention to replace the picture as much as to renew it, to recreate it verbally so as to make visual reference irrelevant. "The painting was, after all, a pretext for the poem, a very discursive one that hops from one thing to another, and it's not to be viewed as an essay on the painting. I wanted to discourage that kind of connection" (interview of October 17, 1977).

7. John Ashbery, "To a Waterfowl," in *Locus Solus* 2 (1961), 7.

8. The phrase is Ashbery's. "Well, that's one of those remarks I once made and can't remember what I meant. I suppose it was a way of saying that I tend to think in a polyphonic way and want my poetry to speak in a choir or cluster of voices" (interview of October 17, 1977).

9. I am indebted to Harry Mathews for drawing my attention to Gertrude Stein's distinction between an accident and a coincidence: "An accident is when a thing happens. A coincidence is when a thing is going to happen and does." The quoted sentences appear in Miss Stein's "portrait" of Henry James, in *Writings and Lectures, 1909–1945,* ed. Patricia Meyerowitz (Penguin, 1974), p. 291.

10. John Ashbery, *Three Plays* (Calais, Vt.: Z Press, 1978), p. 10.

11. John Koethe, "Freely Espoused," *Poetry* 117, no. 1 (October 1970): 58.

12. Ashbery, *Three Plays,* p. 4.

5. KEITH COHEN: Ashbery's Dismantling of Bourgeois Discourse

1. See Julia Kristeva, *La révolution dans le langage poétique* (Paris: Seuil, 1975), for perhaps the most thoroughgoing application of this postulate. She treats the work of Lautréamont, Rimbaud, and Mal-

larmé, poets with whom it could be shown Ashbery has a great deal in common.

2. Roland Barthes, *S/Z* (Paris: Seuil, 1970). Under what Barthes calls the "referential code" are included the clichés, bits of proverbial wisdom, and character stereotypes produced by the bourgeois discourse in France of the 1810s and 1820s.

3. Ancient myth functioned in a somewhat similar manner. Lévi-Strauss has demonstrated that, by telling a story that managed to embrace two contradictory opinions or versions of reality, a myth was able to resolve possible contradictions and thus make the people who told or heard it more at home in their world—or within the framework of power relations of their society.

Extrapolating from Lévi-Strauss's precepts, Barthes argues that the myth of today is a certain type of ideology-filled speech (*Mythologies,* trans. Annette Lavers [New York: Hill and Wang, 1972], pp. 109 ff.). Society reproduces the patterns of power in bits of ideology, whether political slogans or television commercials, so as to ensure general public approbation of those patterns and hence continuity of the society's status quo.

4. The mutual reinforcement of Protestantism and bourgeois ideology has been explicitly or implicitly described in the works of an American literary tradition generally distinct from Ashbery's filiation (which includes mainly Continental sources: the French symbolists, Valéry, the surrealists). While the two lines of development may in part begin together in Whitman, later exposés of the Protestant-bourgeois alliance, in novelists such as Dreiser and Dos Passos, have very little else in common with Ashbery.

5. In "The Skaters" (*RM,* p. 39) and in the opening of "The New Spirit" (*TP,* p. 3).

6. Cited in Marjorie Perloff, *Frank O'Hara: Poet among Painters* (New York: Braziller, 1977), p. 12.

6. FRED MORAMARCO: The Lonesomeness of Words

1. The early reviews of *The Tennis Court Oath* may be found in the following periodicals and newspapers: *Christian Science Monitor* (Sept. 6, 1962), p. 210 (G. D. John); *New York Times Book Review* (July 15, 1962), p. 4 (X. J. Kennedy); *Poetry* 100 (summer 1962): 393 (Mona Van Duyn); *Saturday Review* 45 (May 5, 1962): 24 (James Schevill); *Partisan Review* 473 (spring 1962): 290 (R. W. Flint); *Virginia Quarterly Review* (spring 1962),

p. 324 (Samuel Morse); *Voices* (Sept.–Dec. 1962), p. 42 (Kimball Flaccus); *Hudson Review* (autumn 1962), p. 455 (John Simon); *Spirit* (July 1962), p. 91 (James E. Tobin).

2. Harold Bloom, "John Ashbery: The Charity of the Hard Moments," in his *Figures of Capable Imagination* (New York: Seabury Press, 1976), pp. 169–209. Another excellent discussion of Ashbery's work, which also includes a negative appraisal of *The Tennis Court Oath*, is W. S. Di Piero, "John Ashbery: The Romantic as Problem Solver," *American Poetry Review*, July–August 1973, pp. 39–42.

3. David Shapiro discusses the influence of Roussel upon Ashbery in his "Urgent Masks: An Introduction to John Ashbery's Poetry," *Field*, no. 5 (fall 1971), pp. 32–45. I asked Ashbery specifically about Roussel's influence in *The Tennis Court Oath*, and he responded as follows: "I'm not conscious of any influence of Roussel in *The Tennis Court Oath* poems, although come to think of it, in the title poem, the line about the lettering clearly visible in the margin of *The Times* was probably suggested by an episode in *Locus Solus*, in which it was a question of coded messages in the London *Times*. Although Roussel is one of my greatest admirations, I don't feel that he has directly influenced my work very much, though I could always be mistaken. Aside from a suggestion of his poem 'La Vue' in my poem 'The Instruction Manual,' I think the main lesson for my work that I have drawn from him is his uniqueness. I would like my work to be as unique (but in other ways, of course) as Roussel's, if that were possible."

7. CHARLES BERGER: Vision in the Form of a Task

1. David Kalstone, *Five Temperaments* (New York: Oxford University Press, 1977), p. 190.

2. Wallace Stevens, *Opus Posthumus* (New York: Knopf, 1957), p. 116.

3. See *Nature*, vol. 8, "Prospects."

4. Wallace Stevens, *Collected Poems* (New York: Knopf, 1954), p. 383.

5. Stevens, *Collected Poems*, p. 479.

6. Kalstone, *Five Temperaments*, p. 192.

7. Harold Bloom, *Figures of Capable Imagination* (New York: Seabury Press, 1976), p. 185.

8. Kalstone, *Five Temperaments*, p. 192.

9. Kalstone, *Five Temperaments*, p. 192.

10. See her poem #724.

11. Stevens, *Collected Poems*, p. 139.

12. Wordsworth, *The Prelude*, book 2, 11, 306–310.

13. Stevens, *Collected Poems*, p. 250.

14. See his letter of August 1820.

15. Stevens, *Collected Poems*, p. 381.

16. Cf. Bloom, *Figures*, p. 199.

17. Stevens, *Collected Poems*, p. 418.

8. David Rigsbee: Against Monuments

1. Richard Howard, "John Ashbery," in his *Alone with America: Essays on the Art of Poetry in the United States since 1950* (New York: Atheneum, 1969), pp. 18–37 passim.

2. The expressions with which I distinguish these voices do not derive from my reading of Richard Howard.

3. Paul Zweig, *The Adventurer* (New York: Basic Books, 1974), pp. 9–13 passim.

4. Heidegger, in his cautiously turgid style, goes on to remark in his essay:

> Taking the measure of the dimension is the element within which human dwelling has its security, by which it securely endures. The taking of measure is what is poetic in dwelling. Poetry is a measuring. But what is it to measure? If poetry is to be understood as measuring, then obviously we may not subsume it under just any idea of measuring and measure.
>
> Poetry is presumably a high and special kind of measuring. But there is more. Perhaps we have to pronounce the sentence, "Poetry is a *measuring*," with a different stress. "*Poetry* is a measuring." In poetry there takes place what all measuring is in the ground of its being. Hence it is necessary to pay heed to the basic act of measuring. That consists in man's first of all taking the measure which then is applied in every measuring act. In poetry the taking of measure occurs. To write poetry is measure-taking, understood in the strict sense of the word, by which man first receives the measure for the breadth of his being. Martin Heidegger, ". . . Poetically Man Dwells . . . ," in *Poetry, Language, Thought*, trans. Albert Hofstadter (New York: Harper Colophon Books, 1975), pp. 221, 222]

5. Stanley Kunitz, *The Testing Tree* (New York: Atlantic–Little, Brown, 1971), pp. 16, 17.

6. W. H. Auden, *Collected Shorter Poems, 1927–1957* (New York: Random House, 1964), p. 65. The lines I had in mind were from "The Witnesses" and go as follows:

> We've been watching you over the garden wall
>   For hours:
> The sky is darkening like a stain;
> Something is going to fall like rain,
>   And it won't be flowers.

9. LESLIE WOLF: The Brushstroke's Integrity

1. Clement Greenberg, "After Abstract Expressionism," in *New York Painting and Sculpture: 1940–1970*, ed. Henry Geldzahler (New York: Dutton, 1969), p. 361.

2. Fred Moramarco, "John Ashbery and Frank O'Hara: The Painterly Poets," *Journal of Modern Literature* 5, no. 3 (1976): 443–444. I am indebted to Mr. Moramarco for my analysis of "The Painter."

3. Wallace Stevens, "The Relations between Poetry and Painting," in his *The Necessary Angel: Essays on Reality and the Imagination* (New York: Vintage, 1951), p. 171.

4. Herbert Read, *A Concise History of Modern Painting*, rev. ed. (New York: Praeger, 1968), p. 29.

5. Read, *Concise History*, pp. 96–97.

6. Wylie Sypher, *Rococo to Cubism in Art and Literature* (New York: Vintage, 1960), p. xxiv.

7. Thomas Hess, *Willem de Kooning* (New York: Braziller, 1959), p. 8. This is one of two books by Hess with the same title (see note 8); I will distinguish them by date.

8. Thomas Hess, *Willem de Kooning* (New York: Museum of Modern Art, 1968), p. 23. The phrase is Clement Greenberg's.

9. Hess, *Willem de Kooning* (1968), p. 23.

10. Sypher, *Rococo to Cubism*, p. 125.

11. Stevens, "Imagination as Value," in *Necessary Angel*, p. 139.

12. Sypher, *Rococo to Cubism*, p. 318.

13. Ernst Gombrich, *Art and Illusion: A Study of the Psychology of Pictorial Representation*, the A. W. Mellon Lectures in the Fine Arts, 1956 (New York: Pantheon, Bollingen Series, 34, no. 5, 1960), p. 281.

14. Marjorie Perloff, "'Transparent Selves': The Poetry of John Ashbery and Frank O'Hara," *Yearbook of English Studies* 8 (1978): 171–196.

15. Edward B. Henning, *Fifty Years of Modern Painting: 1916–1966* (Cleveland: Western Reserve University, 1966), p. 98.

16. Harold Rosenberg, "The American Action Painters," in his *The Tradition of the New* (New York: McGraw-Hill, 1965), p. 25.

17. Rosenberg, "American Action Painters," p. 29.

18. Perloff, " 'Transparent Selves,' " p. 14.

19. Sypher, *Rococo to Cubism*, p. 323.

20. Charles Olson, "Equal, That Is, to the Real Itself," quoted by Robert Creeley, "Introduction to *The New Writing in the USA*," the *Poetics of the New American Poetry*, ed. Donald Allen and Warren Tallman (New York: Grove Press, 1973), p. 258.

21. David Lehman, "The Shield of a Greeting: The Function of Irony in John Ashbery's Poetry," Chapter 4 of this volume.

22. Donald Barthelme, "Paraguay," in his *City Life* (New York: Bantam, 1971), p. 28.

23. Harold Bloom, "On John Ashbery," *Salmagundi*, nos. 22–23 (1973), p. 107.

24. In an interview with Fred Moramarco, Ashbery described the affinity he felt for Rauschenberg's collages. "When I came back to New York for two years (1964–65) . . . one of the first things I wrote about was a show of Rauschenberg's . . . . At that time it seemed as though this was the next logical way in which daring in art could express itself . . . . I can see now how those junk collages of Rauschenberg influenced me at that point." Moramarco, "John Ashbery and Frank O'Hara: The Painterly Poets," *JML* 5, no. 3 (1976): 455.

25. Hess, *Willem de Kooning* (1959), pp. 29–30.

26. Richard Howard, "John Ashbery," in his *Alone with America* (New York: Atheneum, 1969), p. 20.

27. Rosenberg, "American Action Painters," p. 32.

28. Brian O'Doherty, "De Kooning: Notes toward a Figure," in his *American Masters* (New York: Random House, 1973), p. 120.

29. Ibid.

30. Ibid.

31. Ibid., p. 119.

32. Ibid., p. 125.

33. Brian O'Doherty, "Jackson Pollock's Myth," in his *American Masters*, pp. 106–107.

34. Hess, *Willem de Kooning* (1968), p. 125.

35. Interview, *The Craft of Poetry: Interviews from the New York Quarterly*, ed. William Packard (Garden City, N.Y.: Doubleday, 1974), p. 121.

36. Greenberg, "After Abstract Expressionism," p. 363.

37. Susan Sontag, "The Aesthetics of Silence," in her *Styles of Radical Will* (New York: Dell, 1970), p. 14.

38. Marjorie Perloff, " 'Tangled Versions of The Truth': Ammons and Ashbery at Fifty," *American Poetry Review* 7, no. 5 (1978): 11.

39. Julien Levy, *Arshile Gorky* (New York: Harry N. Abrams, 1966), p. 36.

10. LAWRENCE KRAMER: "Syringa"

1. Quoted by Richard Kostelanetz, "How to Be a Difficult Poet," *New York Times Magazine*, May 23, 1976, pp. 18–33.

2. Program notes to the premiere of "Syringa," December 11, 1978.

3. "Famous Orpheus," *New Yorker* 54, no. 47 (January 8, 1979): 56–62.

4. For more on Ashbery and elegy, from a different standpoint, see my "The Wodwo Watches the Water-Clock: Language in Postmodern British and American Poetry," *Contemporary Literature* 18, no. 3 (summer 1977): 319–342.

5. This and the following quotation from the *Iliad* are somewhat modified from the Richmond Lattimore translation (Chicago: University of Chicago Press, 1951).

6. Translation by M. D. Herter Norton (New York: Norton Library, 1942).

7. Liner note on the recording of Carter's *Concerto for Orchestra*, Columbia Records M 30112. It should be emphasized that Carter's music is powerfully, even agressively linear at the level of the individual voices. It is when the voices are superimposed to create a totality that they surrender their linear impetus to the vertical resonance of polyvocal time. Much of Schoenberg's work creates a similar surrender of harmonic tension to a totality that subdues it.

8. For a discussion of temporality in modern American music, see Wilfrid Mellors, *Music in a New Found Land* (New York: Hillside Press, 1975), pp. 102–121, 145–168.

9. Review of *The Double Dream of Spring, Poetry* 117 (1970–71): 53.

10. The classic discussion of this pattern remains M. H. Abrams's "Structure and Style in the Greater Romantic Lyric," in *From Sensibility to Romanticism: Essays Presented to Frederick A. Pottle*, ed. Frederick W. Hilles and Harold Bloom (New York: Oxford University Press, 1965), pp. 527–560.

11. By Roger Shattuck, review of *Houseboat Days, New York Review of Books* 25 (March 23, 1978): 38.

Bibliography

Literary Works by John Ashbery

Turandot and Other Poems. New York: Editions of the Tibor de Nagy Gallery, 1953.

Some Trees. New Haven: Yale University Press, 1956; reprinted, New York: Ecco Press, 1978.

The Tennis Court Oath. Middletown: Wesleyan University Press, 1962.

Rivers and Mountains. New York: Holt, Rinehart and Winston, 1966; reprinted, New York: Ecco Press, 1977.

The Double Dream of Spring. New York: Dutton, 1970; reprinted, New York: Ecco Press, 1976.

Three Poems. New York: Viking, 1972.

Self-Portrait in a Convex Mirror. New York: Viking, 1975.

Houseboat Days. New York: Viking, 1977.

As We Know. New York: Viking, 1979.

A Nest of Ninnies. A novel written collaboratively with James Schuyler. New York: Dutton, 1969; reprinted, Calais, Vt.: Z Press, 1975.

The Vermont Notebook. Drawings by Joe Brainard. Los Angeles: Black Sparrow Press, 1975.

Three Plays. Calais, Vt.: Z Press, 1978.

For Ashbery's literary criticism, art criticism, essays, translations, reviews, and uncollected poems, see David K. Kermani's *John Ashbery: A Comprehensive Bibliography*, New York and London: Garland, 1976.

Selected Criticism of John Ashbery's Poetry

For a fuller listing, comprehensive through 1975, consult David K. Kermani's bibliography.

Auden, W. H. "Foreword." In *Some Trees*, by John Ashbery, pp. 11–16. New Haven: Yale University Press, 1956.

Bloom, Harold. "John Ashbery: The Charity of the Hard Moments." In his *Figures of Capable Imagination,* pp. 169–209. New York: Seabury Press, 1976.

Boyers, Robert. "A Quest without an Object." *Times Literary Supplement,* September 1, 1978, pp. 962–963.

Cott, Jonathan. "The New American Poetry." In *The New American Arts,* ed. Richard Kostelanetz, pp. 146–152. New York: Horizon, 1965.

Di Piero, W. S. "John Ashbery: The Romantic as Problem Solver." *American Poetry Review,* July–August 1973, pp. 39–42.

Donadio, Stephen. "Some Younger Poets in America." In *Modern Occasions,* ed. Philip Rahv, pp. 241–243. New York: Farrar, Straus and Giroux, 1966.

Ehrenpreis, Irvin. "Boysenberry Sherbet." *New York Review of Books,* October 16, 1975, pp. 3–4.

Howard, Richard. *Alone with America: Essays on the Art of Poetry in the United States since 1950.* New York: Atheneum, 1969, pp. 18–37.

———. "Sortes Vergilianae." *Poetry,* October 1970, pp. 50–53.

Kalstone, David. *Five Temperaments.* New York: Oxford University Press, 1977, pp. 170–203.

Koch, Stephen. "The New York School of Poets: The Serious at Play." *New York Times Book Review,* February 11, 1968, pp. 4–5.

Kostelanetz, Richard. "How to Be a Difficult Poet." *New York Times Magazine,* May 23, 1976, pp. 18–33.

Lieberman, Lawrence. "Unassigned Frequencies: Whispers out of Time." *American Poetry Review,* March–April 1977, pp. 4–18.

Molesworth, Charles. " 'This Leaving-out Business': The Poetry of John Ashbery." *Salmagundi,* summer–fall 1977, pp. 20–41.

Moramarco, Fred. "John Ashbery and Frank O'Hara: The Painterly Poets." *Journal of Modern Literature* 5, no. 3 (September 1976): 436–462.

O'Hara, Frank. "Rare Modern." *Poetry,* February 1957, pp. 310–313.

Perloff, Marjorie. " 'Transparent Selves': The Poetry of John Ashbery and Frank O'Hara." *Yearbook of English Studies* 8 (1978): 171–196.

Shapiro, David. "Urgent Masks: An Introduction to John Ashbery's Poetry." *Field* (Oberlin, Ohio), no. 5 (fall 1971), pp. 32–45.

Shattuck, Roger. "Poet in the Wings." *New York Review of Books,* March 23, 1978, pp. 38–40.

Notes on Contributors

CHARLES BERGER teaches English at Yale University. He is a contributing editor of *Poetry Miscellany*.

KEITH COHEN is an associate professor of comparative literature at the University of Wisconsin, Madison. Yale University Press is publishing his critical study *Film and Fiction: The Dynamics of Exchange*. A novel, *Natural Settings*, will be published in fall 1980 by Full Court Press.

DOUGLAS CRASE's poems have appeared in *Poetry, American Poetry Review, The New Yorker, Poetry in Motion,* and other magazines. He has taught at the University of Rochester.

JOHN KOETHE is an associate professor of philosophy at the University of Wisconsin, Milwaukee. *Domes,* a collection of poems, won the Frank O'Hara Award in 1972. Koethe has published essays in philosophy, literary criticism, and art criticism in such magazines as *Philosophical Review, Poetry, Parnassus,* and *Art News*.

LAWRENCE KRAMER teaches English and comparative literature at Fordham University, Lincoln Center. His scholarly work includes numerous articles on nineteenth- and twentieth-century poetry and on poetry and music.

DAVID LEHMAN teaches English and creative writing at Hamilton College. His poems and critical essays have appeared in the *Times Literary Supplement, Poetry, Partisan Review,* and the *Paris Review. Day One,* his most recent collection of poems, was published in 1979.

FRED MORAMARCO, professor of English at San Diego State University and formerly the director of the School of Literature there, has published articles in such journals as *Mosaic, American Literature, Journal of Modern Literature, Western Humanities Review,* and *The Nation.*

MARJORIE PERLOFF, Florence R. Scott Professor of English at the University of Southern California, has published widely on poetry and poetics. Her books include *The Poetic Art of Robert Lowell* (1973) and *Frank O'Hara: Poet among Painters* (1977; rpt. 1979). Her *The Other Tradition in Modern Poetry: Rimbaud to the Present* will be published by Princeton University Press in 1981.

DAVID RIGSBEE teaches English at the University of North Carolina, Greensboro. Coeditor of *The Ardis Anthology of New American Poetry,* Rigsbee has published poems and translations from the Russian in the *American Poetry Review,* the *New Yorker,* and elsewhere. *Stamping Ground,* a collection of poems, was published in 1976.

LESLIE WOLF teaches writing at the University of Redlands. His poetry has appeared in *Partisan Review, Seneca Review, Zero,* and *Poetry in Motion.*

Index of Ashbery's Works

Index

General Index

Index

Index

Library of Congress Cataloging in Publication Data

Main entry under title:

Beyond amazement.

Bibliography: p.
Includes index.
1. Ashbery, John—Criticism and interpretation—Addresses, essays, lec-
tures.   I. Lehman, David, 1948–
PS3501.S475Z59   811'.54   79-6850
ISBN 0-8014-1235-8
ISBN 0-8014-9183-5 pbk.